Complete Study Edition

King Lear

Commentary | Complete Text | Glossary

edited by

SIDNEY LAMB

Associate Professor of English,
Sir George Williams University, Montreal

LINCOLN, NEBRASKA   68501

ISBN 0-8220-1422-X

King Lear

SHAKESPEARE WAS NEVER MORE MEANINGFUL—

. . . than when read in Cliff's "Complete Study Edition." The introductory sections give you all of the background information about the author and his work necessary for reading with understanding and appreciation. A descriptive bibliography provides guidance in the selection of works for further study. The inviting three-column arrangement of the complete text offers the maximum in convenience to the reader. Adjacent to the text there is a running commentary that provides clear supplementary discussion of the play as it develops. Obscure words and obsolete usages used by Shakespeare are explained in the glosses directly opposite to the line in which they occur. The numerous allusions are also clarified.

SIDNEY LAMB—

. . . the editor of this Shakespeare "Complete Study Edition," attended Andover Academy and Columbia University, receiving the Prince of Wales Medal for Philosophy and the Moyes Travelling Fellowship. Following graduate studies in Elizabethan literature at King's College, Cambridge, from 1949 to 1952, he became a member of the English Faculty of the University of London's University of the Gold Coast in West Africa. Professor Lamb joined the faculty of Sir George Williams University, Montreal, in 1956.

King Lear

Contents

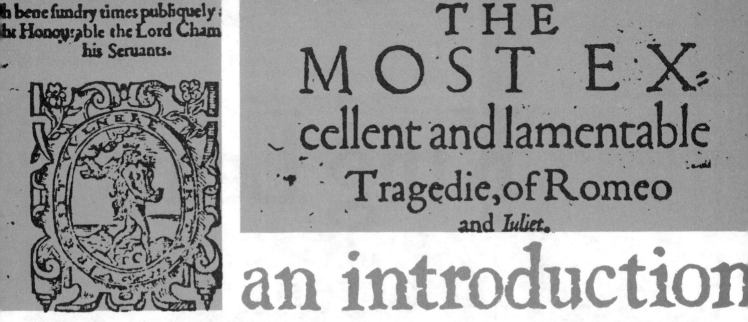

h bene fundry times publiquely :
he Honoyrable the Lord Cham
his Seruants.

THE MOST EX-
cellent and lamentable
Tragedie, of Romeo
and *Iuliet*.

an introduction

THE
Tragicall Historie of
HAMLET,
Prince of Denmarke.

By William Shakespeare.

Newly imprinted and enlarged to almost as much
againe as it was, according to the true and perfect
Coppie.

AT LONDON,
Printed by I. R. for N. L. and are to be fold at his
shoppe vnder Saint Dunstons Church in

Two books are essential to the library of any English-speaking household; one of these is the Bible and the other is the works of William Shakespeare. These books form part of the house furnishings, not as reading material generally, but as the symbols of religion and culture—sort of a twentieth-century counterpart of the ancient Roman household gods. This symbolic status has done a great deal of damage both to religion and to Shakespeare.

Whatever Shakespeare may have been, he was not a deity. He was a writer of popular plays, who made a good living, bought a farm in the country, and retired at the age of about forty-five to enjoy his profits as a gentleman. The difference between Shakespeare and the other popular playwrights of his time was that he wrote better plays —plays that had such strong artistic value that they have been popular ever since. Indeed, even today, if Shakespeare could col-

William to Shakespeare.

lect his royalties, he would be among the most prosperous of playwrights.

During the eighteenth century but mostly in the nineteenth, Shakespeare's works became "immortal classics," and the cult of Shakespeare-worship was inaugurated. The plays were largely removed from their proper place on the stage into the library where they became works of literature rather than drama and were regarded as long poems, attracting all the artistic and psuedo-artistic atmosphere surrounding poetry. In the nineteenth century this attitude was friendly but later, and especially in the early twentieth century, a strange feeling arose in the English-speaking world that poetry was sissy stuff, not for men but for "pansies" and women's clubs. This of course is sheer nonsense.

This outline will present a detailed analysis of the play and background information which will show the play in its proper perspective. This means seeing the play in relation to the other plays, to the history of the times when they were written, and in relation to the theatrical technique required for their successful performance.

G. B. Harrison's book *Introducing Shakespeare*, published by Penguin Books, will be of value for general information about Shakespeare and his plays. For reference material on the Elizabethan Theater, consult E. K. Chambers, *The Elizabethan Theatre* (four volumes). For study of the organization and production methods of this theater see *Henslowe's Diary* edited by W. W. Greg. Again for general reading the student will enjoy Margaret Webster's *Shakespeare Without Tears,* published by Whittlesey House (McGraw-Hill) in 1942.

The remainder of the Introduction will be divided into sections discussing Shakespeare's life, his plays, and his theater.

LIFE OF WILLIAM SHAKESPEARE

From the standpoint of one whose main interest lies with the plays themselves, knowledge of Shakespeare's life is not very important. Inasmuch as it treats of the period between 1592 and 1611, when the plays were being written, knowledge of his life is useful in that it may give some clues as to the topical matters introduced into the plays. For instance, the scene of Hamlet's advice to the players (Act III Scene ii) takes on an added significance when considered along with the fame and bombastic style of Edward Alleyn, the then famous actor-manager of the Lord Admiral's Players (the most powerful rivals of Shakespeare's company).

This biography is pieced together from the surviving public records of the day, from contemporary references in print, and from the London Stationer's Register. It is by no means complete. The skeletal nature of the biographical material available to scholars has led commentators in the past to invent part of the story to fill it out. These parts have frequently been invented by men who were more interested in upholding a private theory than in telling the truth, and this habit of romancing has led to a tradition of inaccurate Shakespearian biography. For this reason this outline may be of use in disposing of bad traditions.

In the heyday of the self-made man, the story developed that Shakespeare was a poor boy from the village, virtually uneducated, who fled from Stratford to London to escape prosecution for poaching on the lands of Sir Thomas Lucy, and there by his talent and a commendable industry raised himself to greatness. This rags-to-riches romance was in the best Horatio Alger tradition but was emphatically not true. The town records of Stratford make it clear that John Shakespeare, father of the playwright, was far from a pauper. He was a wealthy and responsible citizen who held in turn several municipal offices. He married (1557) Mary Arden, the daughter of a distinguished Catholic family. William, their third son, was baptized in the Parish Church in 1564. He had a good grammar school education. Ben Jonson's remark that Shakespeare had "small Latin and less Greek" did not mean the same in those days, when the educated man had a fluent command of

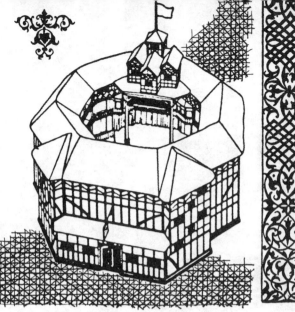

Exterior view of "The Globe"

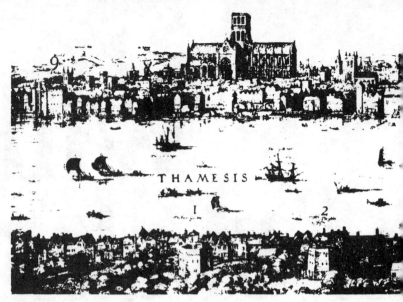

Shakespeare's London

Interior view of "The Globe"

an introduction to Shakespeare

Latin and probably at least a reading knowledge of Greek, as it does now when classical scholars are few. The remark has been construed by the Horatio Alger people as meaning that Shakespeare reached London a semi-literate bumpkin; it is nonsense. It means merely that Shakespeare was not a university man, as most of the writers were, and that the University Wits were taking out their jealousy in snobbery and pointing out that Shakespeare used less purely literary symbolism than they did.

Shakespeare married Ann Hathaway when he was eighteen years old. She was some years older than he and the marriage seems to have been a rather hasty affair. Five months after the marriage, Suzanna, the first child, was born. Two years later, in 1585, twins Hamnet and Judith were baptized.

No one knows when Shakespeare came to London. The first mention of him occurs in the bad-tempered pamphlet which Robert Greene, one of the University Wits and a famous playwright, wrote just before his death. Greene complains of "an upstart crow, beautified with our feathers, that with his tiger's heart wrapped in a player's hide, supposes he is as well able to bombast out a blank verse as the best of you; and being an absolute Yohannes factotum, is in his own conceit the only Shakescene in a country." This was written in 1592 and indicates not only that Shakespeare was in London at the time, but that he was writing plays and beginning to make such a name for himself as to call forth the jealous apprehension of an established writer.

The next year, 1593, was a year of plague, and by order of the Lord Mayor and the Aldermen, the theaters were closed. The players, disorganized by this action, went on tour outside of London. During this year Shakespeare's two long poems, *Venus and Adonis* and *The Rape of Lucrece,* were entered in the Stationer's Register. Both were dedicated to the Earl of Southampton.

The public theaters had not been established very long. The first of these, called the Theatre, was built for James Burbage in 1576. By 1594, there were three such theaters in London, the two new houses being the Curtain and the Rose. By 1594, also, the three most celebrated of the writers, Kyd, Greene, and Marlowe were dead, and Shakespeare had already a considerable reputation. Before this date the theaters had been largely low class entertainment and the plays had been of rather poor quality. Through the revival of classical drama in the schools (comedies) and the Inns of Court (tragedies), an interest had been created in the stage. The noblemen of the time were beginning to attend the public theaters, and their tastes demanded a better class of play.

Against the background of this

increasing status and upper-class popularity of the theaters, Shakespeare's company was formed. After the 1594 productions under Alleyn, this group of actors divided. Alleyn formed a company called the Lord Admiral's Company which played in Henslowe's Rose Theatre. Under the leadership of the Burbages (James was the owner of the Theatre and his son Richard was a young tragic actor of great promise), Will Kemp (the famous comedian), and William Shakespeare, the Lord Chamberlain's Company came into being. This company continued throughout Shakespeare's career. It was renamed in 1603, shortly after Queen Elizabeth's death, becoming the King's Players.

The company played at the Theatre until Burbage's lease on the land ran out. The landlord was not willing to come to satisfactory terms. The company moved across the river and built the new Globe theater. The principal sharers in the new place were Richard and Cuthbert Burbage each with two and a half shares and William Shakespeare, John Heminge, Angustus Phillips, Thomas Pope, and Will Kemp, each with one share.

Burbage had wanted to establish a private theater and had rented the refectory of the old Blackfriars' monastery. Not being allowed to use this building he leased it to a man called Evans who obtained permission to produce plays acted by chil-dren. This venture was so successful as to make keen competition for the existing companies. This vogue of child actors is referred to in *Hamlet,* Act II Scene ii.

The children continued to play at Blackfriars until, in 1608, their license was suspended because of the seditious nature of one of their production. By this time the public attitude towards the theaters had changed, and Burbage's Company, now the King's Players, could move into the Blackfriars theater.

Partners with the Burbages in this enterprise were Shakespeare, Heminge, Condell, Sly, and Evans. This was an indoor theater, whereas the Globe had been outdoors. The stage conditions were thus radically altered. More scenery could be used; lighting effects were possible. Shakespeare's works written for this theater show the influence of change in conditions.

To return to the family affairs of the Shakespeares, records show that in 1596 John Shakespeare was granted a coat of arms and, along with his son, was entitled to call himself "gentleman." In this year also, William Shakespeare's son Hamnet died. In 1597 William Shakespeare bought from William Underwood a sizable estate at Stratford, called New Place.

Shakespeare's father died in 1601, his mother, in 1608. Both of his daughters married, one in 1607, the other in 1616.

During this time, Shakespeare went on acquiring property in Stratford. He retired to New Place probably around 1610 although this date is not definitely established, and his career as a dramatist was practically at an end. *The Tempest,* his last complete play, was written around the year 1611.

The famous will, in which he left his second best bed to his wife, was executed in 1616 and later on in that same year he was buried.

THE PLAYS

Thirty-seven plays are customarily included in the works of William Shakespeare. Scholars have been at great pains to establish the order in which these plays were written. The most important sources of information for this study are the various records of performances which exist, the printed editions which came out during Shakespeare's career, and such unmistakable references to current events as may crop up in the plays. The effect of the information gathered in this way is generally to establish two dates between which a given play must have been written. In *Hamlet* for instance, there is a scene in which Hamlet refers to the severe competition given to the adult actors by the vogue for children's performances. This vogue first became a serious threat to the professional companies in about 1600. In 1603 a very bad edition was published, without authorization, of *The*

Queen Elizabeth

an introduction to Shakespeare

Elizabethan types

Lute, standing cup, stoop

Tragical History of Hamlet, Prince of Denmark by William Shakespeare. These two facts indicate that *Hamlet* was written between the years of 1600 and 1603. This process fixed the order in which most of the plays were written. Those others of which no satisfactory record could be found were inserted in their logical place in the series according to the noticeable development of Shakespeare's style. In these various ways we have arrived at the following chronological listing of the plays.

1591 *Henry VI Part I*
      Henry VI Part II
      Henry VI Part III
      Richard III
      Titus Andronicus
      Love's Labour Lost
      *The Two Gentlemen
        of Verona*
      The Comedy of Errors
      The Taming of the Shrew

1594 *Romeo and Juliet*
      *A Midsummer Night's
        Dream*
      Richard II
      King John
      The Merchant of Venice

1597 *Henry IV Part I*
      Henry IV Part II
      Much Ado About Nothing
      Merry Wives of Windsor
      As You Like It
      Julius Caesar
      Henry V
      Troilus and Cressida

1601 *Hamlet*
      Twelfth Night
      Measure for Measure
      All's Well That Ends Well

      Othello
1606 *King Lear*
      Macbeth
      Timon of Athens
      Antony and Cleopatra
      Coriolanus

1609 *Pericles*

1611 *Cymbeline*
      The Winter's Tale
      The Tempest
      Henry VIII

At this point it is pertinent to review the tradition of dramatic form that had been established before Shakespeare began writing. Drama in England sprang at the outset from the miracle and morality plays of the medieval guilds. These dramatized Bible stories became increasingly less religious as time passed until finally they fell into disrepute. The next development was the writing of so-called *interludes.* These varied in character but often took the form of bawdy farce. As the renaissance gathered force in England, Roman drama began to be revived at the schools and the Inns of Court. Before long English writers were borrowing plots and conventions wholesale from the classic drama. The Italian model was the most fashionable and consequently was largely adopted, but many features of the old *interludes* still persisted, especially in plays written for the public theaters.

With the development among the nobility of a taste for the theater, a higher quality of work became in demand. Very few of

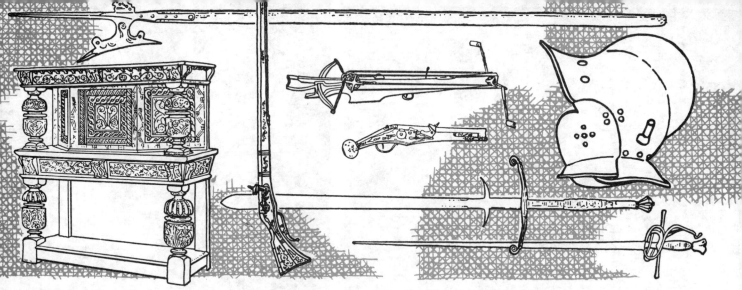

Court cupboard, crossbow, guns, sword, rapier, halberd, burgonet

the very early plays have survived. The reason for this is that the plays were not printed to be read; no one considered them worth the trouble. A play was strung together out of a set of stock characters and situations with frantic haste, often by as many as a dozen different men. These men who worked on plays did not regard their writing activity as of prime importance. They were primarily actors. With the cultivation of taste for better plays came the idea that the work of a playwright was an effort demanding special skill. The highborn audiences were interested in the plays themselves and began to include editions of their favorite plays in their libraries. With this demand for printed copies of the plays, the conception began of the dramatist as an artist in his own right, whether or not he acted himself (as most of them did).

By 1592, when Shakespeare began to make his personal reputation, a set of traditions had developed. This body of traditions gave Shakespeare the basic materials with which to work.

A special type of comedy writing had developed, centered around the name of John Lyly, designed for the sophisticated audience of the court and presented with lavish dances and decorative effects. This type of play was characterized by a delicately patterned artificiality of speech. The dialogue was studded with complicated references to Latin and Italian literature that the renaissance had made fashionable.

Shakespeare used this method extensively. In the early plays (before *The Merchant of Venice*) he was experimenting and wrote much that is nothing more than conventional. Later on, as his mature style developed, the writing becomes integral with and indispensable to the play and no longer appears artificial. In *Romeo and Juliet,* an early play, the following lines are spoken by Lady Capulet in urging Juliet to accept the Count Paris for her husband. These lines are brilliant but artificial, and the play seems to pause in order that this trick bit of word-acrobatics may be spoken.

> Read o'er the volume of young
> Paris' face,
> And find delight, writ there
> with beauty's pen.
> Examine every married linea-
> ment,
> And see how one another lends
> content:
> And what obscured in this fair
> volume lies,
> Find written in the margent of
> his eyes.
> This precious book of love, this
> unbound lover,
> To beautify him only needs a
> cover!

The other most important dramatic tradition was that of tragedy. The Elizabethan audiences liked spectacular scenes; they also had a great relish for scenes of sheer horror. This led to a school of tragic writing made popular by Kyd and Marlowe.

These plays were full of action and color and incredible wickedness, and the stage literally ran with artificial blood. Shakespeare's early tragedies are directly in this tradition, but later the convention becomes altered and improved in practice, just as that of comedy had done. The scene in *King Lear* where Gloucester has his eyes torn out stems from this convention. Lear, however, is a comparatively late play and the introduction of this scene does not distort or interrupt its organization.

Shakespeare's stylistic development falls into a quite well-defined progression. At first he wrote plays according to the habit of his rivals. He very quickly began experimenting with his technique. His main concern seems to be with tricks of language. He was finding out just what he could do. These early plays use a great deal of rhyme, seemingly just because Shakespeare liked writing rhyme. Later on, rhyme is used only when there is a quite definite dramatic purpose to justify it. Between the early plays and those which may be called mature, *(The Merchant of Venice* is the first of the mature plays) there is a basic change in method. In the early works Shakespeare was taking his patterns from previous plays and writing his own pieces, quite consciously incorporating one device here and another there.

In the later period these tricks of the trade had been tested and

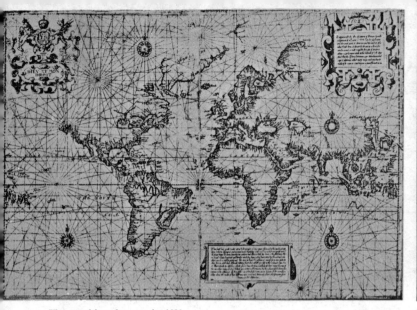
The world as known in 1600

Elizabethan coins

absorbed; they had become not contrived methods but part of Shakespeare's mind. This meant that, quite unconsciously, while his total attention was focused on the emotional and intellectual business of writing a masterpiece, he wrote in terms of the traditional habits he had learned and used in the earlier period. (*Henry IV, Julius Caesar, Henry V,* and *Hamlet* are the plays of this advanced stage.)

The group of plays between 1606 and 1609 shows a further new development. Having reached mastery of his medium in terms of dramatic technique (with *Othello*) and of power over the tension of thought in moving easily through scenes of comedy, pathos, and tragedy, he turned again to the actual literary quality of his plays and began to enlarge his scope quite beyond and apart from the theatrical traditions of his day. The early results of this new attempt are the two plays *King Lear* and *Macbeth*. The change in these plays is in the direction of concentration of thought. The attempt is, by using masses of images piled one on another, to convey shadings and intensities of emotion not before possible. He was trying to express the inexpressible. For example the following is from the last part of

an introduction
to Shakespeare

Lady Macbeth's famous speech in Act One, Scene v:

> Come, thick night,
> And pall thee in the dunnest smoke of hell,
> That my keen knife see not the wound it makes,
> Nor heaven peep through the blanket of the dark,
> To cry, hold, hold!

Compare the concentrated imagery of this speech with Hamlet's soliloquy at the end of Act III, Scene ii.

> 'Tis now the very witching time of night,
> When churchyards yawn, and hell itself breathes out
> Contagion to this world: now could I drink hot blood,
> And do such bitterness as the day
> Would quake to look on.

The sentiment of these two speeches is similar, but the difference in method is striking and produces a difference again in the type of affect. The Lear-Macbeth type of writing produces a higher tension of subtlety but tends to collect in masses rather than to move in lines as the lighter, more transparent writing of Hamlet does.

Shakespeare's last plays were conceived for the new indoor theater at Blackfriars and show this is in a more sophisticated type of staging. In *The Tempest,* last and most celebrated of these late comedies, there is dancing, and much complicated staging (such as the disappearing banquet, the ship at sea, and so on). The writing of plays for the

more distinguished audience of Blackfriars, and the increased stage resources there provided, influenced the form of the plays.

The writing of these plays forms a culmination. In his early apprenticeship Shakespeare had been extravagant in word-acrobatics, testing the limits of his technique. In the Lear-Macbeth period of innovation he had tried the limits of concentrated emotion to the point almost of weakening the dramatic effectiveness of the plays. In *The Tempest* his lines are shaken out into motion again. He seems to have been able to achieve the subtlety he was after in verse of light texture and easy movement, no longer showing the tendency to heaviness or opacity visible in *King Lear* and *Macbeth*.

THE THEATER

The first public theater in London was built in the year 1576 for James Burbage and was called simply The Theatre. Before this time players' companies had performed for the public in the courtyards of the city inns. For a more select public they frequently played in the great halls of institutions, notably the Inns of Court. The stage and auditorium of the Elizabethan theater were based on these traditions and combined features of both the hall and the inn-yard. The auditorium was small. There was a pit where the orchestra seats would be in a modern playhouse; this section was for the lowest classes who stood during the performances. Around the

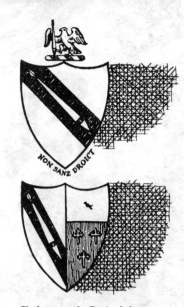

Shakespeare's Coat of Arms   Wood cut camp illustration

wall was a gallery for the gentry. The galleries and the tiring-house behind the fore-stage were roofed; the rest was open to the sky. The stage consisted of a very large platform that jutted out so that the pit audience stood on three sides of it. Behind this, under the continuation behind the stage of the gallery, was the inner stage; this was supplied with a curtain, but the open fore-stage was not. Above this inner stage was a balcony (really a continuation of the gallery), forming still another curtained stage. This gallery was used for kings addressing subjects from balconies, for the storming of walls, for Juliet's balcony and bedroom, for Cleopatra's monument and so on. Costumes and properties were extravagant (such as guillotines, fountains, ladders, etc.); extensive music was constantly used and such sound effects as cannon, drums, or unearthly screams were common; but there was no painted scenery as we know it; there was no darkness to focus attention on the stage, no facilities for stage-lighting. All these things are in marked contrast to the modern stage conventions and thus a serious problem of adaptation is posed when it comes to producing the plays under present day conditions.

The advantages are not all with the modern stage. It is true that the modern or picture stage can do more in the way of realistic effects, but this kind of realism is not important to good

drama. In fact there has been a recent trend away from realistic scenery in the theater back to a conventional or stylized simplicity.

One effect of Shakespeare's stage upon his work was to make the scenes in the plays more person-scenes than place-scenes. As a matter of fact in many cases the places assigned in the texts to various scenes were not in the original and have only been added by an editor who did not understand this very fact.

It used to be said that *Antony and Cleopatra* could not be staged and was written to be read rather than acted. The grounds for this statement were that in the fourth act there were no less than fourteen scenes. To some, a scene means a change of place and requires a break in the play while scenery is shifted. To Shakespeare these scenes meant no such thing; they meant, simply, that there were fourteen different groupings of people, successively and without any break, carrying on the action of the play. The scene headings when added should have been (1) Caesar, (2) Antony and Cleopatra, (3) the common soldiers, etc., instead of (1) Before Alexandria, (2) Alexandria, a room in the palace, etc. By this you may see that with all its limitations, the Elizabethan stage had a measure of flexibility that the modern stage could envy.

Fashions in staging Shakespeare have altered radically in the last few years. At the close

of the nineteenth century, Sir Herbert Beerbohm Tree staged a spectacular series of pageant productions. All the tricks of romantic realistic staging were used and, if necessary, the play was twisted, battered, and re-written to accommodate the paraphernalia.

The modern method is to produce the plays as nearly according to the text as possible and work out a compromise to achieve the sense of space and of flexibility necessary, yet without departing so far from the stage habits of today as to confuse or divert the audience. This technique was inaugurated by Granville-Barker in the early twentieth century. With the exception of such extravagant stunts as Orson Welles' production of *Julius Caesar* in modern dress (set in Chicago and complete with tommy-guns), the prevailing practice now is to use simple, stylized scenery adapted to the needs of producing the play at full length.

Much can be done in the way of learning Shakespeare through books, but the only sure way is to see a well produced performance by a good company of actors. Whatever genius Shakespeare may have possessed as a psychologist, philosopher, or poet, he was first of all a man of the theater, who knew it from the inside, and who wrote plays so well-plotted for performance that from his day up to the present, no great actor has been able to resist them.

Fool's Bauble

King Lear and Three Daughters

an introduction to The Tragedy

King Lear is generally considered to be Shakespeare's greatest tragedy, and it is not hard to see why. In it Shakespeare's command of the medium of poetic drama is at its height; the play has immense sweep and power, and the profundity of all the greatest tragedy. Actors and audiences, critics and readers return continually to *King Lear*, and find it continually rewarding. Yet at the same time, and perhaps because of this greatness, there is a remarkable degree of disagreement about the play. For example it has been maintained that, because of the greatness of its conception, it is unsuitable for the stage. This idea arose during a period when it was generally thought that Shakespeare was a great poet rather than a great playwright, and that at his best—as in *King Lear* —his plays are hampered by the limitations of stage representation. So we have Charles Lamb saying (and it must be remembered that Lamb was an avid theatregoer) that to put *King Lear* on the stage is to reduce its power: "To see Lear acted—to see an old man tottering about the stage with a walking-stick, turned out of doors by his daughters in a rainy night, has nothing in it but what is painful

and disgusting. We want to take him into shelter and relieve him. That is all the feeling that the acting of Lear ever produced in me. But the Lear of Shakespeare cannot be acted. The contemptible machinery by which they mimic the storm which he goes out in, is not more inadequate to represent the horrors of the real elements, than any actor can be to represent Lear: they might more easily propose to personate the Satan of Milton upon a stage, or one of Michael Angelo's terrible figures. The greatness of Lear is not in corporal dimension, but in intellectual: the explosions of his passion are as terrible as a volcano: they are storms turning up and disclosing to the bottom that sea, his mind, with all its vast riches. It is his mind which is laid bare. This case of flesh and blood seems too insignificant to be thought on, even as he himself neglects it. On the stage we see nothing but corporal infirmities and weakness, the impotence of rage; while we read it, we see not Lear, but we are Lear . . ."

However admirable Lamb's apprehension of the greatness of the play is, we must always recall that Shakespeare himself would have been baffled by this view. He was a working man of the theatre, and therefore his

concern was with producing an actable, stageable play. Perhaps what is at the basis of Lamb's protest is the feeling that what is visible on the stage must somehow have the same degree of grandeur as the poetry. But for Shakespeare, it is just because stage and actors are by their nature limited that the dramatic poetry must do the work. We may be confronted with a bare stage, but when we hear

"Blow, winds, and crack your
    cheeks. Rage, blow
You cataracts and hurricanes,
    spout
Till you have drenched our
    steeples, drowned the cocks.
You sulph'rous and thought-
    executing fires,
Vaunt-couriers to oak-cleaving
    thunderbolts,
Singe my white head!"

we have an imaginative creation of turbulence and storm that no visual approximation on a stage could ever give.

Another area of debate concerns the final meaning of the play. *King Lear* has been called both a statement of intense, unrelieved pessimism, and of man's greatness and dignity in the face of suffering. The reader may see these views argued out at greater length in the commentary to V,iii; the point here is simply that *King Lear*, above all

Fool and Courtesan

King Lear, Fool & Servants

# of King Lear

the rest of Shakespeare's plays, cannot be reduced to a formula, or tidy explanation.

In *King Lear,* as in the rest of his drama, Shakespeare made liberal use of the literary sources he found to hand. Like any great artist he borrowed freely and transformed his borrowings into something far greater than the originals. Shakespeare had several versions of the Lear story to draw on when he wrote the play in 1604-5. There was, in the first place, a legend of long standing and various forms in which a king demands declarations of love from his three daughters, becomes angry at the youngest daughter's reticence, punishes her, and is himself punished. Tolstoy (who hapened to disapprove of Shakespeare's *King Lear*) has said that all the great truths of literature can be conveyed in the simple terms of a folk tale, and perhaps the folk tale here does give the essence of Shakespeare's play: love cannot be demanded, or suffering will result. In literary form, the medieval historian Geoffrey of Monmouth wrote, somewhat vaguely, of an historical Lear, and he occurs later in Holinshed's *Chronicles* (1587) as ruling "in the year of the world 3105." We know that Shakespeare used Holinshed's history

continually in the construction of his plays, and he was perhaps intrigued by the primitive, pre-Christian setting of the Lear narrative. This setting is important; in many of his plays Shakespeare is somewhat circumscribed by the known historical background (as in *Julius Caesar* or *Henry V*), but with *King Lear* he is free to create his own tale. There are further versions of Lear in the 16th century *Mirrour For Magistrates* and Spenser's *Faerie Queene*, both of which Shakespeare knew. Finally, a version had already appeared on the Elizabethan stage in the 1590's, when Shakespeare was learning his craft, and he may well have acted in it. The play was entitled *The True Chronicle History of King Leir;* it was anonymous, and very bad. The sub-plot of Gloucester, Edgar and Edmund, Shakespeare found in Sidney's *Arcadia,* where it serves as an episode in that long prose romance. Again Shakespeare's brilliance lies in the way he adapted Sidney's story of the "Paphlagonian king" to his own use in *King Lear* as a balancing and enriching counterpoint to the main plot.

One of the most striking things about *King Lear* is the way in which Shakespeare presents the conflict between good and evil

11

in terms of two groups of characters who are carefully separated and put into opposition early in the play. Lear's opening unfairness to Cordelia is simply a trigger-mechanism to set the plot in motion; it is clear that Lear, although misguided, is a good man, and Kent's loyalty further establishes his goodness. At the outset, then, we have one faction composed of Lear, Cordelia, the Fool, Kent, Edgar, and later Gloucester, all of whom are morally good. In opposition to them stand Goneril and Regan, Cornwall, Edmund and Oswald, all of whom are morally bad, or amoral. Normally, such a clear cut division between "good" and "bad" characters leads to oversimplified, artificial drama. Shakespeare is a great enough playwright to risk this sort of division, in the interests of bringing two attitudes to life into dramatic conflict. We might say that drama consists in the creation of attitudes-in-action, and the conflicts that arise between them.

The conflict between the good and evil factions in *King Lear* lies in their opposed attitudes to what man is, and therefore what man's obligation to other men, or society, is. Nowhere are these attitudes made completely explicit, since this is a drama, and not an ethical debate. However

an introduction to the tragedy of King Lear

they are implicit in what the characters say and do everywhere in the play. The nearest thing to a statement of principle comes from the villain Edmund, in his soliloquy at I,ii,1, and there he gives expression to what we may well see as the point of view of the whole of the evil party.

"Nature," Edmund says, is his "goddess." He speaks of nature as having a "law" which he opposes to "the plague of custom," according to which society is ruled. This would have seemed a much more powerful and ominous statement to the Elizabethan audience than it does to us. The Elizabethan conception of society was of an ordered, divinely conceived organism which reflected the hierarchy and order of the rest of the created universe. Within society the bonds and obligations, the combination of love for "thy neighbour" and duty toward him, were divinely ordained. They included such things as the parent's love for the child, the child's for the parent, the subject's for the king, and indeed all the "holy cords" (as Kent calls them) that make the human community cohere. Edmund dismisses all these with the phrase "plague of custom," holding them, as many more recent representatives of his point of view have done, to be simply those rules with which the weak group protects itself from the strong individual. Although this was an unorthodox, or revolutionary position at the time, it had its precedents in the 16th century. Of these, the most fa-

miliar to the Elizabethans had been given expression in the writings of Niccolo Machiavelli (1469-1527), the Italian political philosopher. In his great work, *The Prince,* Machiavelli had described the struggle for power within society not as though it were bound to the laws of God or a higher morality, but as he saw it in practice. In other words he described man as a "natural" organism, and society, not as a divinely directed community, but as the arena in which "natural" man struggled for power and supremacy. Thus Machiavelli's name (although this was not his intention) became attached to the new view of man as a natural rather than spiritual being. Since, in this view, "nature" imposes no moral laws or directions on its creatures, man need abide by none. He may be completely amoral in the satisfaction of his appetites and his drive to power, and on the Elizabethan stage this conception produced the new, "Machiavellian" villain, of which Edmund is an example.

In *King Lear* there is a continuing conflict between man as "natural," and man as responsible to some transcedent, spiritual law. Shakespeare gives us the evil party, all behaving with direct, cold-blooded amorality in the pursuit of their ambitions. Like Edmund, they take "Nature" for their goddess. But "Nature" is not only the powerful, instinctive force that Edmund admires. It is also animal nature, and throughout the play Shakespeare continually uses bestial imagery to describe the

evil party, and Goneril and Regan in particular. The effect of the continued association of the evil sisters with the animal world is powerful, as A. C. Bradley has pointed out: "Goneril is a kite; her ingratitude has a serpent tooth: she has struck her father most serpentlike upon the heart: her visage is wolfish: she has tied sharp-toothed unkindness like a vulture upon her father's breast: for her husband she is a gilded serpent: to Gloucester her cruelty seems to have the fangs of a boar. She and Regan are dog-hearted: they are tigers, not daughters; each is an adder to the other; the flesh of each is covered with the fell of a beast . . . As we read, the souls of all the beasts in turn seem to us to have entered the bodies of these mortals, horrible in their venom, savagery, lust, deceitfulness, cruelty, filthiness."

Man, then, if directed solely by "natural" law, becomes natural in the worst sense of the word. Given the attitude of the evil party, "Man's life" as Lear points out, "is cheap as beast's." Opposed to this we have the idea of human society based on a standard of value that transcends the animal world, where the bonds of duty and love and reverence bind the human community together. This idea recurs again and again in the play, although it is nowhere made as explicit as Edmund's deification of "Nature." It lies, in the opening scene, behind Cordelia's assertion that she loves Lear "according to her bond," which she will not elaborate on because it needs no elaboration. The "bond" is filial duty and love, and representative in this play of every mode of human love and obligation. It lies behind Kent's headstrong defence of Lear, and his hatred of Oswald:

"Such smiling rogues as these
Like rats oft bite the holy cords atwain
Which are too intrinse t' unloose." (II,ii,68)

It lies behind Lear's great speech to Goneril and Regan when he pleads with them not to "reason" about giving him their love—not to try to estimate his need in material, measurable terms, since it is spiritual (II,iv, 259). It is also present at the end of the play when Lear and Cordelia are reunited. Their reunion is a vindication of the "bond" of love. It also brings about their deaths—their failure in the "natural" world—but here the final comment ought, perhaps, to be Lear's:

"Upon such sacrifices, my Cordelia
The gods themselves throw incense."

Note on the text

Editions of *King Lear* are based on the 1608 Quarto (the "Pied Bull" Quarto) and the 1623 Folio, the former having a good many errors and the latter a good many omissions. This edition is mainly based on the Folio (as are all recent editions) with additions from the Quarto. There are seven instances in which Quarto readings have been preferred:

I,iv,257 "Yet have I left a daughter" for "I have another daughter."

II,i,46 "their thunders" for "the thunder."
II,i,90 "is cracked" for "its cracked."
II,ii,72 "Bring" for "Being."
II,iv,295 "bleak" for "high."
III,iv,46 "thy cold bed" for "thy bed."
V,iii,326 "oldest have" for "oldest hath."

Dramatis Personae

LEAR, King of Britain
KING OF FRANCE
DUKE OF BURGUNDY
DUKE OF CORNWALL
DUKE OF ALBANY
EARL OF KENT
EARL OF GLOUCESTER
EDGAR, son to Gloucester
EDMUND, bastard son to Gloucester
CURAN, a courtier
OLD MAN, tenant to Gloucester
Doctor
Lear's Fool
OSWALD, steward to Goneril
A Captain under Edmund's command
Gentlemen
A Herald
Servants to Cornwall
GONERIL ⎫
REGAN   ⎬   daughters to Lear
CORDELIA ⎭
Knights attending on Lear, Officers,
Messengers, Soldiers, Attendants

KING LEAR

ACT I SCENE I

In the opening scenes of his plays Shakespeare has a double task before him: he must introduce his characters (the 'exposition'), and he must do it in such a way as to excite the attention and anticipation of the audience. In the opening of KING LEAR Shakespeare presents us with two characters who combine to make up what is usually called the sub-plot: Gloucester and Edmund. Kent is on stage as well but, in the light of what is being said, our attention is focused on the father and son. In many of Shakespeare's plays two stories develop at once, and in some sort of relation. That involving the hero is the plot, or main plot, and in the other the sub-plot. We shall see that Gloucester's story, in the sub-plot, is a close parallel to the story of Lear; both men misunderstand their children, mistaking the good for the evil, and both suffer terribly for their misunderstanding. The stories illuminate one another. The second requirement for the opening scene is that of capturing the audience's interest. That is done here by the introduction, almost at once, of Edmund's illegitimacy. The notion of two brothers, one legitimate and one illegitimate, intrigues the audience at once. They anticipate some sort of conflict, and of course it will be revealed in the next scene.

Notice further the way in which Gloucester speaks, in his presence, of his illegitimate child. He has "often blushed to acknowledge him," he is a "whoreson," but "there was good sport at his making." The tone suggests that Gloucester is little concerned with the morality of the arrangement, or indeed with the morality of marriage and parenthood. He speaks with what Coleridge called a "most degrading and licentious levity." At this point we may see little objection to this free and easy attitude, but later in the play Gloucester will be made to realize, in a peculiarly horrifying way, the importance of the parent's relation to the child. Both he and Lear begin the play with a highly defective understanding of their own children. The fact that Edmund is on stage during Gloucester's account of his birth is important in the way the scene is played; Edmund will be revealed in the next scene as a conscious, cold-blooded schemer, who plots both his brother's and his father's destruction. Here, therefore, the actor who plays Edmund, though he has little to say, may communicate a

---

ACT ONE, scene one.

(KING LEAR'S PALACE.)

Enter KENT, GLOUCESTER, *and* EDMUND.

Kent. I thought the King had more affected the 1
Duke of Albany than Cornwall. 2

Gloucester. It did always seem so to us; but now, in the division of the kingdom, it appears not which of the dukes he values most, for equalities are so 5 weighed that curiosity in neither can make choice of either's moiety.

Kent. Is not this your son, my lord?

Gloucester. His breeding, sir, hath been at my 9 charge. I have so often blushed to acknowledge him that now I am brazed to't. 11

Kent. I cannot conceive you. 12

Gloucester. Sir, this young fellow's mother could; whereupon she grew round-wombed, and had indeed, sir, a son for her cradle ere she had a husband for her bed. Do you smell a fault? 16

Kent. I cannot wish the fault undone, the issue of it being so proper. 18

Gloucester. But I have a son, sir, by order of law, 19 some year elder than this who yet is no dearer in my 20 account: though this knave came something saucily 21 to the world before he was sent for, yet was his mother fair, there was good sport at his making, and the whoreson must be acknowledged. Do you know 24 this noble gentleman, Edmund?

Edmund. No, my lord.

Gloucester. My Lord of Kent. Remember him hereafter as my honorable friend.

Edmund. My services to your lordship.

Kent. I must love you, and sue to know you better.

Edmund. Sir, I shall study deserving. 31

Gloucester. He hath been out nine years, and away 32
he shall again.   [*Sound a sennet.* s.d.
The King is coming.

Enter one bearing a coronet, then KING LEAR, *then the*
DUKES OF CORNWALL *and* ALBANY, *next* GONERIL, s.d.
REGAN, CORDELIA, *and* Attendants.

Lear. Attend the lords of France and Burgundy,
    Gloucester.

Gloucester. I shall, my lord.   [*Exit with* EDMUND.

Lear. Meantime we shall express our darker purpose. 37
Give me the map there. Know that we have divided
In three our kingdom; and 'tis our fast intent 39
To shake all cares and business from our age,
Conferring them on younger strengths while we
Unburdened crawl toward death. Our son of Cornwall,
And you our no less loving son of Albany,
We have this hour a constant will to publish 44
Our daughter's several dowers, that future strife 45
May be prevented now. The princes, France and
    Burgundy,

15

---

1. "affected": loved

2. "Albany": the area once ruled over by 'Albanacte,' now Scotland.

5. "equalities . . . moiety": i.e., the portions appear so equal that neither could rightly choose that awarded to the other.

9. "breeding": upbringing.

11. "brazed": made brazen, hardened.

12. "conceive": Kent uses conceive in the sense of 'understand;' Gloucester puns on the sexual sense (to become pregnant) in the next line.

18. "proper": handsome.

19. "by order of law": legitimately born.

21. "account": estimation. "saucily": impertinently, in the sense of not having been invited.

24. "whoreson": meant as i) affectionate abuse, ii) literally true.

31. "study deserving": i.e., I shall try to be worthy of your interest, but the actor may also introduce an ironic note, characteristic of the Edmund we shall come to know during the play, suggesting 'I shall do everything I can to succeed.'

32. "out": away, presumably in military training.

Stage Direction "sennet": a musical phrase played on the trumpet indicating a ceremonial entrance.

Stage Direction "coronet": small crown, presumably for the most deserving of Lear's daughters.

37. "darker purpose": secret intention, i.e., of giving the largest share of his kingdom to the daughter who loves him most. Some critics see 'darker' as having an ironic sense, unknown to Lear, suggesting to the audience the evils that will follow from his division of the kingdom.

39. "fast intent": firm intention.

44. "constant will to publish": firm intention of announcing.

45. "several": respective.

KING LEAR

ACT I SCENE I

good deal of the bitter pride of a bastard whose illegitimacy is being discussed, and of his cold superiority to the easygoing, lecherous frivolity of his father. The line "Sir, I shall study deserving" is probably delivered with acid irony.

Lear enters and announces his intention of dividing his kingdom between his daughters and their husbands. This decision will itself be seen as an ominous one by the Elizabethan audience. Generally in Shakespeare's plays, and especially those dealing with power and rule, division leads to strife and civil disorder. For the Elizabethan the state was an organic, divinely ordered whole, and internal, civil strife was an unmitigated evil. Lear's assertion that the partition of his kingdom is undertaken "that future strife/May be prevented now" is therefore ironic: the play ends in a welter of civil strife. Moreover Lear's renunciation of power is ambiguous. He says that he will renounce "rule,/Interest of territory, cares of state," and the audience wonders what he imagines his position will be. Can he retain the grandeur of kingship while giving up its power? As George Orwell has pointed out, one of the ideas presented in KING LEAR is that "to make oneself powerless is to invite attack." In a world inhabited by Goneril, Regan, Edmund and Cornwall, good will never triumph unaided; without power it will always be victimized.

Another point in Lear's speech from 37 to 55 should be noted here, since it is meant to alert the audience to the significant way in which the play's opening relates it to the tradition of the Morality plays. 'Moralities' were religious plays, beginning in the Middle Ages but continuing almost to Shakespeare's day, in which a central figure—called Everyman, or Mankind, and representing humanity in general—is summoned by the figure of Death. As Death approaches, Everyman is forced to realize that the things he had valued, such as wealth, power and high office, are finally worthless.

Great rivals in our youngest daughter's love,
Long in our court have made their amorous sojourn, 48
And here are to be answered. Tell me, my daughters
(Since now we will divest us both of rule,
Interest of territory, cares of state), 51
Which of you shall we say doth love us most,
That we our largest bounty may extend
Where nature doth with merit challenge. Goneril, 54
Our eldest-born, speak first.
 Goneril. Sir, I love you more than word can wield 56
  the matter;
Dearer than eyesight, space, and liberty; 57
Beyond what can be valued, rich or rare;
No less than life, with grace, health, beauty, honour;
As much as child e'er loved, or father found;
A love that makes breath poor, and speech unable. 61
Beyond all manner of so much I love you.
 Cordelia. [*Aside.*] What shall Cordelia speak?
  Love, and be silent.
 Lear. Of all these bounds, even from this line to
  this,
With shadowy forests and with champains riched, 65
With plenteous rivers and wide-skirted meads, 66
We make thee lady. To thine and Albany's issues 67
Be this perpetual.—What says our second daughter,
Our dearest Regan, wife of Cornwall?
 Regan. I am made of that self mettle as my sister, 70
And prize me at her worth. In my true heart
I find she names my very deed of love; 72
Only she comes too short, that I profess
Myself an enemy to all other joys
Which the most precious square of sense possesses, 75
And find I am alone felicitate 76
In your dear Highness' love.
 Cordelia.   [*Aside.*] Then poor Cordelia;
And yet not so, since I am sure my love's
More ponderous than my tongue. 79
 Lear. To thee and thine hereditary ever
Remain this ample third of our fair kingdom,
No less in space, validity, and pleasure 82
Than that conferred on Goneril.—Now, our joy,
Although our last and least; to whose young love 84
The vines of France and milk of Burgundy 85
Strive to be interest; what can you say to draw 86
A third more opulent than your sisters? Speak.
 Cordelia. Nothing, my lord.
 Lear. Nothing?
 Cordelia. Nothing.
 Lear. Nothing will come of nothing. Speak again.
 Cordelia. Unhappy that I am, I cannot heave
My heart into my mouth. I love your Majesty
According to my bond, no more nor less. 94
 Lear. How, how, Cordelia? Mend your speech a
  little,
Lest you may mar your fortunes.
 Cordelia.   Good my lord,
You have begot me, bred me, loved me. I
Return those duties back as are right fit, 98
Obey you, love you, and most honour you.
Why have my sisters husbands if they say
They love you all? Haply, when I shall wed, 101

48. "amorous sojourn": courtship.

51. "interest": possession.

54. "nature . . . challenge": where natural or filial love is matched with other merits.

56. "wield": express.

57. "space": in which to exercise the liberty.

61. "breath": the power to speak.

65. "champains riched": rich fields.

66. "wide-skirted": far-reaching.

67. "issues": descendants.

70. "self mettle": same quality.

72. "very deed of love": the reality of my love. Deed is used in the legal sense.

75. "square of sense": the measurement that sense makes; 'square' is from a carpenter's square, or measure.

76. "felicitate": made happy.

79. "More ponderous": greater.

82. "validity": value.

84. "least": smallest: actresses playing Goneril and Regan are generally overpowering, while Cordelia is usually represented as slight.

85. "vines": vineyards.
"milk": pasture land.

86. "Strive to be interest": have expressed their interest.

94. "bond": obligation; also here, in an important sense, the natural bond between father and daughter.

98. "Return . . . fit": I am properly dutiful in return.

101. "love you all": give you all their love.

KING LEAR

ACT I SCENE I

The Elizabethans were familiar with this representative character, and when Lear announces that he will "Unburdened crawl towards death," they recognized him as a kind of Everyman figure. But Lear does not really give up his power and privilege; he still desires it, at least until the end of the play. He is an Everyman who, like many, pays lip-service to the idea of renunciation but cannot live with the fact of it. Although both Lear and Everyman suffer for their illusions, Lear is a great tragic hero, and Everyman a simple character in a simple, didactic play. However through the parallel to Everyman, Shakespeare suggested to the Elizabethans the universality of Lear; his sufferings, despite their nightmarish, volcanic quality, are still human sufferings, or a magnified, heroic version of suffering in general. If Lear did not have some element of Everyman, the play would not have the enduring emotional appeal that so many actors and critics, audiences and readers, have found in it.

In any Shakespearean play the sort of language the characters use suggests important distinctions between them, and that is true in this scene. Lear's utterances—at this point in the play—are commanding and imperious: "Attend the lords of France and Burgundy . . . Give me the map there . . . We our largest bounty may extend . . . We make thee lady." He is the assertive, feudal lord, and we are prepared for the overpowering anger that is to come. There is an even more significant difference between the language used by the sisters, Goneril and Regan

That lord whose hand must take my plight shall carry 102
Half my love with him, half my care and duty.
Sure I shall never marry like my sisters,
To love my father all.
Lear. But goes thy hearth with this?
Cordelia.   Ay, my good lord.
Lear. So young, and so untender?
Cordelia. So young, my lord, and true.
Lear. Let it be so, thy truth then be thy dower!
For, by the sacred radiance of the sun,
The mysteries of Hecate and the night, 111
By all the operation of the orbs 112
From whom we do exist and cease to be,
Here I disclaim all my paternal care,
Propinquity and property of blood,
And as a stranger to my heart and me
Hold thee from this for ever. The barbarous 117
    Scythian,
Or he that makes his generation messes 118
To gorge his appetite, shall to my bosom
Be as well neighboured, pitied, and relieved,
As thou my sometime daughter.
Kent.   Good my liege —
Lear. Peace, Kent!
Come not between the dragon and his wrath.
I loved her most, and thought to set my rest 124
On her kind nursery.—Hence and avoid my 125
    sight!—
So be my grave my peace as here I give 126
Her father's heart from her! Call France. Who stirs!
Call Burgundy. Cornwall and Albany,
With my two daughters' dowers digest the third; 129
Let pride, which she calls plainness, marry her.
I do invest you jointly with my power,
Preeminence, and all the large effects
That troop with majesty. Ourself, by monthly course, 133
With reservation of an hundred knights, 134
By you to be sustained, shall our abode
Make with you by due turn. Only we shall retain
The name, and all th' addition to a king. The sway, 137
Revenue, execution of the rest,
Belov'd sons, be yours; which to confirm,
This coronet part between you.
Kent.   Royal Lear,
Whom I have ever honoured as my king,
Loved as my father, as my master followed,
As my great patron thought on in my prayers —
Lear. The bow is bent and drawn; make from the
    shaft. 144
Kent. Let it fall rather, though the fork invade 145
The region of my heart. Be Kent unmannerly
When Lear is mad. What wouldst thou do, old man?
Think'st thou that duty shall have dread to speak
When power to flattery bows? To plainness
    honour's bound
When majesty falls to folly. Reserve thy state, 150
And in thy best consideration check 151
This hideous rashness. Answer my life my judgment 152
Thy youngest daughter does not love thee least,
Nor are those empty-hearted whose low sounds

102. "plight": pledge of marital devotion.

111. "Hecate": goddess of witchcraft.

112. "operation of the orbs": influence of the stars.

117. "barbarous Scythian": the Scythians were proverbially a cruel people.

118. "makes . . . messes": devours his own offspring.

124. "set my rest": count on for my repose.

125. "nursery": care.

126. "give": give away, or release (from Cordelia's care).

129. "digest": include.

133. "Ourself": the royal plural.

134. "With reservation": reserving to himself.

137. "th' addition": prerogatives and honours; Lear's vagueness here as to the form of royalty he does wish to retain provides the bone of contention later in the play.

144. "make . . . shaft": i.e., shoot!

145. "fork": two-pronged head.

150. "Reserve thy state": retain your authority.

151. "consideration": deliberation.

152. "Answer . . . judgment": i.e., I'll stake my life on my opinion.

KING LEAR

ACT I SCENE I

on one hand, and Cordelia on the other. Goneril and Regan's speeches (beginning at 56 and 70) are stilted and careful utterances giving the effect of having been composed for the occasion. Goneril, after announcing that language cannot do justice to her love ("I love you more than word can wield the matter") launches into a polished rhetorical account of her feelings for her father, designed to do her the utmost credit. The audience spots the false diffidence (the apology for her "speech unable") as an oratorical trick at once. Regan is equally specious, fulsome and pious. Her speech is also noticeable for a kind of irony that Shakespeare uses frequently. Dramatic irony may take many forms (and we shall notice other varieties later on) but here it lies in the speaker saying something that carries a fuller meaning than she intends, but which alerts the audience to some future development. Often the fuller, or ironic, meaning is the reverse of what the speaker means to say. Here, for example, when Regan says she is of "the selfsame mettle" as Goneril, and must be "prized at her worth" she means, and Lear understands, that she is like Goneril in her character and her love for Lear. The resemblance is there, but it lies not in love for, but cruelty toward her father. The audience senses this, although it is not revealed to Lear until later in the play. The speeches of Regan and Goneril, in their elaborate, formal quality, are in complete contrast to the brief, compact statements of Cordelia. She speaks simply and truly and is disbelieved; they speak with complicated, florid dishonesty and are believed.

To be misled by Goneril and Regan is an error, but Lear's gravest error in this scene, and the flaw in his judgment that sets in motion the whole tragic process, is his misunderstanding of love. He regards it as a commodity that can be bought with gifts—in this case the parts of his kingdom. When Lear asks "Which of you shall say doth love us most" he acts not only as a stupid and demanding parent, but as one who completely misunderstands the most vital relation between human beings. We have already seen one father, Gloucester, who has treated love as a matter of sensual satisfaction. Lear's fault is far greater than sensual appetite; he thinks that love can be demanded as an offering to his own pride.

When Lear asks Cordelia what she can offer in this verbal competition to "draw/A third more opulent than your sisters," she answers "Nothing," and the word

Reverb no hollowness. 155
Lear.   Kent, on thy life, no more!
Kent. My life I never held but as a pawn
To wage against thine enemies; ne'er fear to lose it, 157
Thy safety being motive. 158
Lear.   Out of my sight!
Kent. See better, Lear, and let me still remain
The true blank of thine eye. 160
Lear. Now by Apollo —
Kent.   Now by Apollo, King,
Thou swear'st thy gods in vain.
Lear.   O vassal! Miscreant! 162
                    [*Grasping his sword.*
Albany, Cornwall. Dear sir, forbear!
Kent. Kill thy physician, and thy fee bestow
Upon the foul disease. Revoke thy gift,
Or, whilst I can vent clamour from my throat,
I'll tell thee thou dost evil.
Lear.   Hear me, recreant, 167
On thin allegiance, hear me!
That thou hast sought to make us break our vows, 169
Which we durst never yet, and with strained pride 170
To come betwixt our sentence and our power, 171
Which nor our nature nor our place can bear,
Our potency made good, take thy reward. 173
Five days we do allot thee for provision
To shield thee from disasters of the world,
And on the sixth to turn thy hated back
Upon our kingdom. If, on the tenth day following,
Thy banished trunk be found in our dominions, 178
The moment is thy death. Away. By Jupiter,
This shall not be revoked.
Kent. Fare thee well, King. Sith thus thou wilt 181
          appear,
Freedom lives hence, and banishment is here.
[*To Cordelia.*] The gods to their dear shelter take
          thee, maid,
That justly think'st and hast most rightly said.
[*To Regan and Goneril.*] And your large speeches
          may your deeds approve, 185
That good effects may spring from words of love.
Thus Kent, O princes, bids you all adieu;
He'll shape his old course in a country new. [*Exit.* 188
          Flourish. Enter GLOUCESTER, *with* FRANCE *and*
                    BURGUNDY; *Attendants.*
Gloucester. Here's France and Burgundy, my noble
          lord.
Lear. My Lord of Burgundy,
We first address toward you, who wish this king
Hath rivalled for our daughter. What in the least
Will you require in present dower with her,
Or cease your quest of love?
Burgundy.   Most royal Majesty,
I crave no more than hath your Highness offered,
Nor will you tender less.
Lear.   Right noble Burgundy,
When she was dear to us, we did hold her so;
But now her price is fallen. Sir, there she stands.
If aught within that little seeming substance, 199
Or all of it, with our displeasure pieced 200

155. "Reverb no hollowness": i.e., make no noise, as a hollow vessel does when it is struck.

157. "wage": bet, set against.
158. "motive": the cause.

160. "true blank": center of the target, as a guide to Lear's aim.

162. "Miscreant": infidel.

167. "recreant": traitor.

169. "That": in that.
170. "strained": forced or excessive.
171. "To come . . . power": i.e., to oppose my right to pass sentence.
173. "Our . . . good": if I am to be powerful.

178. "trunk": body.

181. "Sith": since.

185. "approve": make good, confirm.

188. "shape his old course": continue his old ways.

199. "little seeming substance": frail body.

200. "pieced": added.

18

KING LEAR

ACT I SCENE I

is given additional emphasis by being repeated four times in the exchange at 88-91. Shakespeare sometimes makes a single word bear a great weight of meaning in a passage, as "nothing" does here. Lear has regarded love as a "something," having material, measurable values, which can be exchanged for possessions, as Goneril and Regan exchange it. Cordelia's "nothing" in answer to Lear's question has a double meaning. She means, first of all, that she can say "nothing" to match the substantial and false protestations of her sisters. But her second meaning has to do with Lear's view of love as a commodity. Cordelia's love is of the spirit; it is no thing, or "nothing" materially. It cannot be exchanged, or bought, or used. Lear's progress through the play is, in part, from ignorance of this fact to hard-won knowledge of it. Lear's answer at 91 is also important in the play on the word "nothing." "Nothing will come of nothing" is a common phrase, a translation of a line from the philosopher Lucretius: EX-NIHILO NIHIL FIT. But Lucretius' philosophy was the classical exposition of materialism, and a denial of spiritual value. Throughout the play the evil faction—Goneril, Regan, Edmund and Cornwall—act and think as though life were simply a matter of the material world, of physical appetite and the struggle for domination. At this point Lear also acts as though this were true—"Nothing will come of nothing" means that nothing can be made of, or gained from a love which is spiritual, which cannot here be "given" to him as a prize or possession.

Cordelia uses another word which has a pervasive meaning in the play when she says that she loves Lear "according to her bond." By this she means all those obligations dependent upon the fact that Lear has "begot, bred, loved" her, in fact the whole network of love and obligation (in its most important respects an immaterial one: a "nothing") that binds a family together. The point was made in the introduction that there are really two conceptions of human society in the play. On the one hand the evil faction views society as a matter of natural competition and supremacy, on the analogy (as the animal imagery of the play suggests throughout) of the animal world. On the other hand there is the conception of society represented by Cordelia's "bond"; like the family, it is an organic whole, held together by spiritual unity and ethical obligation. While the play treats of the family, or two families, and their disruption, the idea of the whole of society is implicit in the notion

And nothing more, may fitly like your Grace, | 201
She's there, and she is yours.
Burgundy.   I know no answer.
Lear. Will you, with those infirmities she owes, | 203
Unfriended, new adopted to our hate,
Dow'red with our curse, and strangered with our oath,
Take her, or leave her?
Burgundy.   Pardon me, royal sir.
Election makes not up on such conditions. | 207
Lear. Then leave her, sir, for by the pow'r that made me
I tell you all her wealth. [*to France.*] For you, great King,
I would not from your love make such a stray | 210
To match you where I hate; therefore beseech you
T' avert your liking a more worthier way
Than on a wretch whom nature is ashamed
Almost t' acknowledge hers.
France.   This is most strange,
That she whom even but now was your best object,
The argument of your praise, balm of your age, | 216
The best, the dearest, should in this trice of time
Commit a thing so monstrous to dismantle | 218
So many folds of favour. Sure her offence
Must be of such unnatural degree
That monsters it, or your fore-vouched affection | 221
Fall'n into taint; which to believe of her | 222
Must be a faith that reason without miracle | 223
Should never plant in me.
Cordelia.   I yet beseech your Majesty,
If for I want that glib and oily art
To speak and purpose not since what I well intend | 226
I'll do't before I speak, that you make known
It is no vicious blot, murder, or foulness,
No unchaste action or dishonoured step,
That hath deprived me of your grace and favour;
But even for want of that for which I am richer — | 231
A still-soliciting eye, and such a tongue | 232
That I am glad I have not, though not to have it
Hath lost me in your liking.
Lear.   Better thou
Hadst not been born than not t' have pleased me better.
France. It is but this? A tardiness in nature | 236
Which often leaves the history unspoke. | 237
That it intends to do. My lord of Burgundy,
What say you to the lady? Love's not love
When it is mingled with regards that stands | 240
Aloof from th' entire point. Will you have her?
She is herself a dowry.
Burgundy.   Royal King,
Give but that portion which yourself proposed,
And here I take Cordelia by the hand,
Duchess of Burgundy.
Lear. Nothing. I have sworn. I am firm.
Burgundy. I am sorry then you have so lost a father
That you must lose a husband.
Cordelia.   Peace be with Burgundy.
Since that respects of fortune are his love, | 249
I shall not be his wife.

---

201. "fitly like": appeal to.

203. "owes": possesses.

207. "Election . . . conditions": i.e., I cannot choose on these terms.

210. "make . . . stray": go so far.

216. "argument": subject.
218. "to dismantle": to take off.

221. "monsters": makes monstrous. "fore-vouched": already sworn.
222. "taint": bad odor, or decay.
222-4. "which to believe . . . me"; i.e., I should need a miracle to persuade me that she is the cause of the 'taint'.

226. "and purpose not": i.e., with no intention of fulfilling what I say.

231. "for want of": for lack of.

232. "still-soliciting": continually asking or importuning.

236. "tardiness in nature": natural reticence.
237. "the history unspoke": the real facts unspoken.

240-1. "mingled . . . point": i.e., full of irrelevant considerations.

249. "respects": considerations.

KING LEAR

ACT I SCENE I

of family; the disorder of one is the same as the disorder of the other. In a sense it is true to say that in KING LEAR all human relationships are exemplified by the parent-child relationship. This will become clearer later in the play when, as a result of Lear's daughters' hatred of him, all human relations are distorted.

Lear's anger at what appears to him to be Cordelia's lack of filial affection is monumental, and produces the inflamed speech beginning at 109. The speech poses a theatrical problem, as one director has pointed out: "Lear begins the play, as it were, at the top of his voice. The actor's problem is to be able to give full expression to the passion in Scene one, and yet have something in reserve for the even greater, yet different, flights of anger and sorrow later on." There are also some ironic touches in this speech, which give us hints as to the subsequent development of the action. "Truth then be thy dower!" Lear says to Cordelia in his rage. She will have, that is, nothing in the way of material possessions, which seems to Lear at the moment to be a harsh punishment. But the possessions he gives to his other daughters they rapidly take away from him, and he will come to realize that the "truth" Cordelia possesses is the only possession finally worth having. His disclaimer here of "propinquity of blood" is an angry phrase, but it is just this that Goneril and Regan will disclaim in fact when

France. Fairest Cordelia, that art most rich being poor,
Most choice forsaken, and most loved despised,
Thee and thy virtues here I seize upon.
Be it lawful I take up what's cast away.
Gods, gods! 'Tis strange that from their cold'st neglect
My love should kindle to inflamed respect.
Thy dow'rless daughter, King, thrown to my chance,
Is queen of us, of ours, and our fair France.
Not all the dukes of wat'rish Burgundy
Can buy this unprized precious maid of me.
Bid them farewell, Cordelia, though unkind.
Thou losest here, a better where to find.   262

   Lear. Thou hast her, France; let her be thine, for we
Have no such daughter, nor shall ever see
That face of hers again. Therefore be gone
Without our grace, our love, our benison.   266
Come, noble Burgundy.

       [*Flourish. Exeunt* LEAR, BURGUNDY, CORNWALL,
            ALBANY, GLOUCESTER *and* Attendants.

   France. Bid farewell to your sisters.

   Cordelia. The jewels of our father, with washed eyes 269
Cordelia leaves you. I know you what you are;
And, like a sister, am most loath to call
Your faults as they are named. Love well our father. 272
To your professed bosoms I commit him;   273
But yet, alas, stood I within his grace,
I would prefer him to a better place.   275
So farewell to you both.

   Regan. Prescribe not us our duty.

   Goneril.   Let your study
Be to content your lord, who hath received you
At fortune's alms. You have obedience scanted,   279
And well are worth the want that you have wanted.   280

   Cordelia. Time shall unfold what plighted cunning 281
hides,
Who covers faults, at last with shame derides.   282
Well may you prosper.

   France.   Come, my fair Cordelia.
               [*Exit* FRANCE *and* CORDELIA.

   Goneril. Sister, it is not little I have to say of what most nearly appertains to us both. I think our father will hence to-night.

   Regan. That's most certain, and with you; next month with us.

   Goneril. You see how full of changes his age is. The observation we have made of it hath not been little. He always loved our sister most, and with what poor judgment he hath now cast her off appears too grossly. 292

   Regan. 'Tis the infirmity of his age; yet he hath ever but slenderly known himself.   294

   Goneril. The best and soundest of his time hath been but rash; then must we look from his age to receive not alone the imperfections of long-ingraffed condi- 297
tion, but therewithal the unruly waywardness that infirm and choleric years bring with them.

   Regan. Such unconstant starts are we like to have 300
from him as this of Kent's banishment.

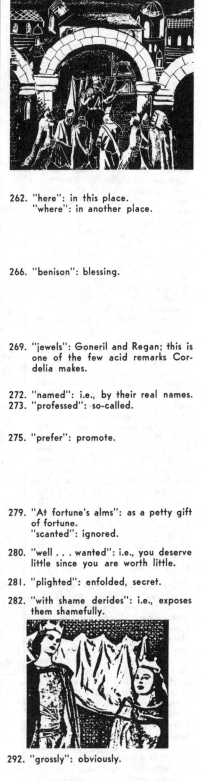

262. "here": in this place.
     "where": in another place.

266. "benison": blessing.

269. "jewels": Goneril and Regan; this is one of the few acid remarks Cordelia makes.

272. "named": i.e., by their real names.
273. "professed": so-called.

275. "prefer": promote.

279. "At fortune's alms": as a petty gift of fortune.
     "scanted": ignored.

280. "well . . . wanted": i.e., you deserve little since you are worth little.

281. "plighted": enfolded, secret.

282. "with shame derides": i.e., exposes them shamefully.

292. "grossly": obviously.

294. "slenderly known himself": knows little of his real self.

297. "long-ingraffed": long-standing.

300. "unconstant starts": erratic acts.

20

KING LEAR

ACT I SCENE I

they send Lear into the storm. Finally, when Lear speaks of the "barbarous Scythian" who will be nearer to him than Cordelia, he speaks a truth he does not realize. The barbarous Scythians are his elder daughters.

ACT I SCENE II

One of the most useful conventions of the Elizabethan theatre is the soliloquy, in which the character is alone on the stage and is able to talk, as it were, directly to the audience. He is free to tell the truth about himself—at least as he sees it—thereby simplifying the playwright's job of character construction, and informing the audience as to what they may expect from him. One of the major uses to which the Elizabethan playwrights put this convention lay in bringing on the villain to explain his own villany. Shakespeare does this here with Edmund.

Like many of the characters in this play, Edmund may be viewed in two ways, although these 'views' are never really separated when we are watching or reading the play. The character is, first of all, simply a character: a person in a certain situation with certain emotions, ideas, likes, dislikes, and all the rest of the things that go to make up the idea of 'character'. But Shakespeare's creations are often more than particular individuals. They also function in the context of the play in a way that suggests more general ideas and attitudes: they represent a point of view. One of Shakespeare's greatest virtues as a playwright is his ability to create characters who have this 'double' existence. If his characters were ONLY individuals, of a certain place and time, they would not fascinate successive generations, and never be of universal interest. On the other hand if they were ONLY ideas, or dramatized attitudes (e.g., character X 'stands for' capitalism, character Y for communism, and so on) then the plays would be dramatized arguments, with the characters as illustrative puppets; and many of our plays are of just this kind.

KING LEAR is in some ways a highly philosophical play—not in the sense that it argues a certain philosophical position, but that it dramatizes various and conflicting attitudes toward the values of life. Consequently the personages of the play are often a combination of particular individuals, and of ideas given dramatic embodiment.

Goneril. There is further compliment of leave-taking 302
between France and him. Pray you let us hit to- 303
gether; if our father carry authority with such disposition as he bears, this last surrender of his will but 305
offend us.

Regan. We shall further think of it.

Goneril. We must do something, and i' th' heat. 308

[*Exeunt.*

Scene two.

(THE EARL OF GLOUCESTER'S CASTLE.)
Enter EDMUND, *alone, with a letter.*

Edmund. Thou, Nature art my goddess; to thy law 1
My services are bound. Wherefore should I
Stand in the plague of custom, and permit 3
The curiosity of nations to deprive me, 4
For that I am some twelve or fourteen moonshines 5
Lag of a brother? Why bastard? Wherefore base, 6
When my dimensions are as well compact, 7
My mind as generous, and my shape as true,
As honest madam's issue? Why brand they us
With base? with baseness? Bastardy base? Base?
Who, in the lusty stealth of nature, take
More composition and fierce quality 12
Than doth, within a dull, stale tired bed,
Go to th' creating a whole tribe of fops
Got 'tween asleep and wake? Well then, 15
Legitimate Edgar, I must have your land.
Our father's love is to the bastard Edmund
As to th' legitimate. Fine word, 'legitimate.'
Well, my legitimate, if this letter speed,
And my invention thrive, Edmund the base 20
Shall top th' legitimate. I grow, I prosper.
Now, gods, stand up for bastards.

Enter GLOUCESTER.

Gloucester. Kent banished thus? and France in
choler parted?
And the King gone to-night? prescribe his pow'r? 24
Confined to exhibition? All this done 25
Upon the gad? Edmund, how now? What news? 26
Edmund. So please your lordship, none.
Gloucester. Why so earnestly seek you to put up 28
that letter?
Edmund. I know no news, my lord.
Gloucester. What paper were you reading?
Edmund. Nothing, my lord.
Gloucester. No? What needed then that terrible
dispatch of it into your pocket? The quality of noth-
ing hath not such need to hide itself. Let's see.
Come, if it be nothing, I shall not need spectacles.
Edmund. I beseech you, sir, pardon me. It is a let-
ter from my brother that I have not all o'er-read;
and for so much as I have perused, I find it not fit
for your o'erlooking. 39

---

302. "compliment": ceremony.

303-4. "hit together": agree.

305-6. "surrender . . . us": i.e., his giving of his kingdom to us will cause difficulty.

308. "i' th' heat": in a hurry.

1. "Nature": physical as distinct from spiritual nature; see commentary for discussion of this word's importance in the play.

3. "plague of custom": the repression of convention.

4. "curiosity": careful social distinctions.

5. "moonshines": months.

6. "Lag of": short of (in age).

7. "compact": made.

12. "composition": constitutional strength.
"fierce": sharp, high-spirited.

15. "Got": conceived.

20. "my invention thrive": my plan work.

24. "prescribe": limit.

25. "exhibition": allowance.

26. "Upon the gad": on the spur of the moment.

28. "put up": hide.

39. "o'erlooking": reading.

KING LEAR

ACT I SCENE II

So with Edmund, who is both a character, and also the representative of an attitude.

As a character, Edmund defines himself with the words "bastard" and "base," which recur like a refrain throughout his speech. We know of Edgar's illegitimacy from the opening scene. We might well expect bitterness from a youth placed in such a position, and bitterness is perhaps the dominant note in this speech. From the point of view of character alone Edmund is, as we say today, overcompensating for the stigma of bastardy. Far from evading the term, he flaunts it, and boasts of the "fierce quality" that goes into the conception of the illegitimate, as opposed to the "tired bed" of legitimate, married procreation. We see his desire to get the better of Edgar, to "top the legitimate," as a natural consequence of his position as a "base" outsider.

But Edmund is much more than a psychological study in the aggression produced by illegitimacy. He is also an exemplification of one of the central attitudes in the play (and it is the attitude, generally, of the evil faction), suggested here in his use of the word "Nature" (see introduction). The "Nature" that Edmund addresses as a deity is related to his own "natural" begetting: it is beyond human and social law or sanction; it is the natural law that makes man a part of the animal kingdom, and therefore without morality. There is no ethical direction for this kind of "nature;" it is governed by the needs of appetite— whether the appetite be for physical gratification, or wealth, or power. It is therefore committed to complete and destructive competition, no matter how it disguises this in pursuit of its ends. Such laws as Cordelia's "bond," the obligation that exists between human beings, and that asserts their spiritual value, are, for Edmund, the plague of custom," the empty inventions of society.

The Elizabethan audience would recognize Edmund's position as conflicting with the accepted morality of the time, and with the general idea of society as a divinely-created organism, which subjected the individual to a higher law, based on man-as-spirit rather than on man-as-animal. But the audience would also have, just as we have, a strong if perhaps not entirely consious fascination for the amoral lawbreaker, the "outsider" who refuses to be bound by the rules, which he regards as the creation of the "tribe of fops." The Elizabethan Machiavellian had, as our rebels and criminals sometimes have today, a certain allure on the stage.

Gloucester. Give me the letter, sir.

Edmund. I shall offend, either to detain or give it. The contents, as in part I understand them, are to blame. 43

Gloucester. Let's see, let's see.

Edmund. I hope, for my brother's justification, he wrote this but as an essay or taste of my virtue. 46

Gloucester. (reads) 'This policy and reverence of 47 age makes the world bitter to the best of our times; 48 keeps our fortunes from us till our oldness cannot relish them. I begin to find an idle and fond bond- 50 age in the oppression of aged tyranny, who sways, 51 not as it hath power, but as it is suffered. Come 52 to me, that of this I may speak more. If our father would sleep till I wake him, you should enjoy half 54 his revenue for ever, and live the beloved of your brother,   EDGAR.'

Hum! Conspiracy? 'Sleep till I wake him, you should enjoy half his revenue.' My son Edgar! Had he a hand to write this? A heart and brain to breed it in? When came you to this? Who brought it?

Edmund. It was not brought me, my lord; there's the cunning of it. I found it thrown in at the case- 62 ment of my closet.

Gloucester. You know the character to be your brother's?

Edmund. If the matter were good, my lord, I durst 66 swear it were his; but in respect of that, I would 67 fain think it were not.

Gloucester. It is his.

Edmund. It is his hand, my lord; but I hope his heart is not in the contents.

Gloucester. Has he never before sounded you in this business?

Edmund. Never, my lord. But I have heard him oft maintain it to be fit that, sons at perfect age, and 75 fathers declined, the father should be as ward to the son, and the son manage his revenue.

Gloucester. O villain, villain! His very opinion in the letter. Abhorred villain, unnatural, detested, brut- ish villain; worse than brutish! Go, sirrah, seek him. I'll apprehend him. Abominable villain! Where is he?

Edmund. I do not well know, my lord. If it shall please you to suspend your indignation against my brother till you can derive from him better testi- mony of his intent, you should run a certain course; 86 where, if you violently proceed against him, mistak- ing his purpose, it would make a great gap in your own honour and shake in pieces the heart of his obedience. I dare pawn down my life for him that he hath writ this to feel my affection to your honour, 91 and to no other pretence of danger. 92

Gloucester. Think you so?

Edmund. If your honour judge it meet, I will place 94 you where you shall hear us confer of this and by an auricular assurance have your satisfaction, and that 96 without any further delay than this very evening.

Gloucester. He cannot be such a monster.

Edmund. Nor is not, sure.

43. "are to blame": are improper, blameworthy.

46. "essay or taste": trial or test.

47. "policy and reverence": policy of being reverent.

48. "best . . . times": i.e., our youth.

50. "fond": foolish.

51. "sways": governs.
52. "suffered": permitted.

54. "till I waked him": i.e., he would sleep forever.

62-3. "casement . . . closet": window of my room.

66. "matter": contents.

67. "of that": i.e., the contents.

75. "at perfect age": at maturity.

86. "run a certain course": be certain of what you do.

91. "feel": feel out or test.

92. "pretence of danger": dangerous motive.

94. "meet": proper.

96. "auricular assurance": heard evidence.

KING LEAR

ACT I SCENE II

Gloucester enters, and Shakespeare begins the development of the sub-plot. In its general outlines, the Edmund-Gloucester story is a reflection of the story of Lear and his daughters. In both cases we have an old father, presumably basically good, but with a failing that sets the plot in motion. Lear so far misunderstands the nature of parenthood that he demands love as a kind of filial fee. Gloucester's error is sexual laxity; for him 'family' means simply a social arrangement, and Edmund's occurrence outside it matter for a coarse joke. These errors may not seem particularly evil to us, but notice that both of them are affronts to the "bond" of the family, and the family in this play may be seen as a compact example of human society generally, with its obligations and virtues. In both the Lear and Gloucester plots we have parents who grossly misunderstand their children; in each case they reward the evil children and punish the good; and in each case their ultimate help and sustaining power come from the rejected children. Finally both men are made to undergo extremes of suffering which are purgatorial in that they produce, if not happiness in any ordinary sense of the word, at least enlightenment, a new vision of human values, at the play's end.

The forged letter (28) provides the opportunity for some 'stage business' for the actors. Gloucester's line "Why so earnestly seek you to put up that letter?" is one of Shakespeare's frequent built-in-dialogue stage directions: the actor who plays Edmund must do a good deal of guilty maneuvering in order to get himself caught by the not overly-sharp Gloucester. All this gives Edmund an opportunity for his suggestive dialogue, condeming Edgar while seeming to defend him. Note the pious "It is his hand, my lord; but I hope his heart is not in the contents." Here as elsewhere Edmund's Machiavellian brilliance overcomes the honest stupidity of his victims. We might adapt Fal-

Gloucester. To his father, that so tenderly and entirely loves him. Heaven and earth! Edmund, seek him out; wind me into him, I pray you; frame the business after your own wisdom. I would unstate myself to be in a due resolution.

Edmund. I will seek him, sir, presently; convey the business as I shall find means, and acquaint you withal.

Gloucester. These late eclipses in the sun and moon portend no good to us. Though the wisdom of nature can reason it thus and thus, yet nature finds itself scourged by the sequent effects. Love cools, friendship falls off, brothers divide. In cities, mutinies; in countries, discord; in palaces, treason; and the bond cracked 'twixt son and father. This villain of mine comes under the prediction, there's son against father; the King falls from bias of nature, there's father against child. We have seen the best of our time. Machinations, hollowness, treachery, and all ruinous disorders follow us disquietly to our graves. Find out this villain, Edmund, it shall lose thee nothing; do it carefully. And the noble and true-hearted Kent banished; his offence, honesty. 'Tis strange.

[*Exit.*

Edmund. This is the excellent foppery of the world, that when we are sick in fortune, often the surfeits of our own behaviour, we make guilty of our disasters the sun, the moon, and stars; as if we were villains on necessity; fools by heavenly compulsion; knaves, thieves, and treachers by spherical predominance; drunkards, liars, and adulterers by an enforced obedience of planetary influence; and all that we are evil in, by a divine thrusting on. An admirable evasion of whoremaster man, to lay his goatish disposition on the charge of a star. My father compounded with my mother under the Dragon's Tail, and my nativity was under Ursa Major, so that it follows I am rough and lecherous. Fut! I should have been that I am, had the maidenliest star in the firmament twinkled on my bastardizing. Edgar —

Enter EDGAR.

and pat he comes, like the catastrophe of the old comedy. My cue is villainous melancholy, with a sigh like Tom o' Bedlam. — O, these eclipses do portend these divisions. Fa, sol, la, mi.

Edgar. How now, brother Edmund; what serious contemplation are you in?

Edmund. I am thinking, brother, of a prediction I read this other day, what should follow these eclipses.

Edgar. Do you busy yourself with that?

Edmund. I promise you, the effects he writes of succeed unhappily; as of unnaturalness between the child and the parent; death, dearth, dissolutions of ancient amities; divisions in state, menaces and maledictions against king and nobles; needless diffidences, banishment of friends, dissipation of cohorts, nuptial breaches, and I know not what.

Edgar. How long have you been a sectary astronomical?

102. "wind me into him": i.e., tell me his plots.

103-4. "I would . . . resolution": I would give up my power to be sure.

105. "presently": immediately. "convey": conduct.

108-10. "wisdom . . . effects": i.e., the scientific knowledge of nature may reason concerning these things, yet nature itself is still the victim of them.

114. "under the prediction": is one of the things predicted by ill-omens.

122. "foppery": silliness.

123. "sick in fortune": in trouble. "surfeits": excesses.

127. "treachers . . . predominance": traitors because of the effect of the planets.

131. "goatish": the goat was frequently used to represent lechery by the Elizabethans.

132. "compounded": joined in the creation (of me).

133-4. "Dragon's Tail," "Ursa Major": constellations; Ursa Major was held to combine the powers of Venus (love or lust) and Mars (war).

138. "catastrophe": the conclusion of a play; here the reference is to a conventional character who comes in 'pat' to finish the action of the drama.

140. "Tom o' Bedlam": one who begs on the roads, and has been released from the London madhouse, Bethlehem ('Bedlam') Hospital. The character is later to provide Edgar with a disguise.

141. "Fa, sol": musical notes, probably put in by Shakespeare to indicate that Edmund is to hum innocently as Edgar approaches.

149. "succeed unhappily": turn out badly.

153. "diffidences": lack of trust.

153-4. "dissipation of cohorts": desertion of supporters.

155-6. "sectary astronomical": a devotee of astrology.

23

KING LEAR

ACT I SCENE II

staff's remark about himself to fit Edmund: he is not only evil himself, but the cause of evil in others —here Gloucester, whom he infects with hatred for his son. It is necessary, of course, for Shakespeare to make both Gloucester and Edgar somewhat obtuse, in order to be taken in by Edmund's ruse of the supposed plot on Gloucester's life. Why, for example, does Edgar need to write Edmund an incriminating letter, when he lives in the same house with him? And why should Edmund forge such a letter when Gloucester does not know Edgar's handwriting? And how is it that Gloucester does not know his son's handwriting? And finally why does not Edgar—who is represented as a man of honesty and courage—confront Gloucester at once with the accusation instead of lending plausibility to it by going into hiding? None of these inconsistencies worried Shakespeare, and the reason is significant: because of the power of his dramatic creation of poetry and character and situation, we simply do not notice them while we are watching the play. In the theatre we concentrate on what is dramatically important, on what Shakespeare meant us to attend to—the clever, cold-blooded villainy of Edmund, Gloucester's misguided belief in him, and the beginning of Edgar's journey which will lead him, in various disguises, to Lear on the heath, to Dover and the succour of his father, and lastly to the throne.

ACT I SCENE III

This short scene carries on the development of the main plot from the end of Scene one. Brief though it is, it has two noticeable functions.

1) Oswald, Goneril's steward and accomplice, is introduced. Just as Lear is supported by Kent, so the sisters have Oswald. He is perhaps a portrait of the unprincipled time-server (apparently in full supply in the Elizabethan court), and Kent's comment sums him up: "That such a slave as this should wear a sword/Who wears no honesty" (II,ii,76). He also serves a dramatic purpose in the design of the play; to show the lesser supporters of evil is to remind us that evil is not simply a quality of the play's primary villains: it is also a quality of society, or a part of it, as well.

2) Shakespeare very deftly sketches in Goneril's method of

Edmund. Come, come, when saw you my father last?

Edgar. The night gone by.

Edmund. Spake you with him?

Edgar. Ay, two hours together.

Edmund. Parted you in good terms? Found you no displeasure in him by word nor countenance?

Edgar. None at all.

Edmund. Bethink yourself wherein you may have offended him; and at my entreaty forbear his presence until some little time hath qualified the 167 heat of his displeasure, which at this instant so rageth in him that with the mischief of your person 168 it would scarcely allay. 169

Edgar. Some villain hath done me wrong.

Edmund. That's my fear. I pray you have a conti- 172 nent forbearance till the speed of his rage goes slower; and, as I say, retire with me to my lodg- ing, from whence I will fitly bring you to hear my 175 lord speak. Pray ye, go; there's my key. If you do stir abroad, go armed.

Edgar. Armed, brother?

Edmund. Brother, I advise you to the best. Go armed. I am no honest man if there be any good meaning toward you. I have told you what I have seen and heard; but faintly, nothing like the image 182 and horror of it. Pray you, away.

Edgar. Shall I hear from you anon?

Edmund. I do serve you in this business.

[*Exit* EDGAR.

A credulous father, and a brother noble,
Whose nature is so far from doing harms
That he suspects none; on whose foolish honesty
My practices ride easy. I see the business. 189
Let me, if not by birth, have lands by wit; 190
All with me's meet that I can fashion fit. [*Exit.* 191

167. "qualified": moderated.

168. "mischief": injury.

169. "allay": be reduced.

172-3. "continent forbearance": i.e., keep carefully out of the way.

175. "fitly": when it is convenient.

182-3. "image and horror": i.e., the real thing.

189. "practices": deceptions.

190. "wit": intelligence.

191. "meet": acceptable, permissable. "can fashion fit": can make work.

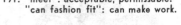

Scene three.

(THE DUKE OF ALBANY'S PALACE.)

Enter GONERIL *and* OSWALD, *her* Steward.

Goneril. Did my father strike my gentleman for
    chiding of his fool?

Oswald. Ay, madam.

Goneril. By day and night, he wrongs me! Every
    hour
He flashes into one gross crime or other
That sets us all at odds. I'll not endure it.
His knights grow riotous, and himself upbraids us
On every trifle. When he returns from hunting,
I will not speak with him. Say I am sick.
If you come slack of former services, 9
You shall do well; the fault of it I'll answer.

[*Horns within.*

9. "come . . . services": i.e., serve him worse than you have been doing.

KING LEAR

ACT I SCENE III

operation which was, and always will be, a familiar one. It consists in provoking the weak or the insecure into attack, so that they may be destroyed under the color of 'reasonable' policy. Lear's weakness is his kingly pride and anger, as Goneril well knows. "I'd have it come to question" she plans, in order that "it" may "breed occasions" on which she, with a full show of righteousness, may discipline Lear. Nobility, like beauty, is in the eye of the beholder. Lear, who is "authority" for Kent, and beloved by the Fool and Cordelia, is for Goneril the "idle old man," and the "old fool" who is a child again. As to the childishness, she is right; it is the nobility that she cannot see.

ACT I SCENE IV

Kent enters disguised. Several of the characters in the play are, from time to time, disguised. Kent adopts the role of Lear's servant, Edgar becomes in turn Tom o'Bedlam, a peasant, and an anonymous knight, the Fool may be seen as wearing his court jester's motley as a form of protection against the world, and there is a sense in which Lear, mad and garlanded with wild flowers (IV,vi) may be said to have been driven unconsciously to disguise his real, royal self. This recurrence of disguise is not without its significance in the play. The first example of it, Kent, has found that to exist in a world where evil is dominant, the good man must hide his real identity; Edgar makes the same decision (II,iii). Here, as in other instances, we see the world of KING LEAR as a kind of abstract of society. When society functions in its normal, healthy way, each member has his identity and plays his part. But when the social order is perverted by the evil and anti-social powers its members no longer function simply and honestly, but have to adopt some kind of protective mask in order to exist. Lear, unable to accept the new order which has robbed him of his identity as king and father, has the change forced upon him: he goes

Oswald. He's coming, madam; I hear him.
Goneril. Put on what weary negligence you please,
You and your fellows. I'd have it come to question. 13
If he distaste it, let him to my sister, 14
Whose mind and mine I know in that are one,
Not to be overruled. Idle old man,
That still would manage those authorities 17
That he hath given away. Now, by my life,
Old fools are babes again, and must be used
With checks as flatteries, when they are seen abused. 20
Remember what I have said.
Oswald.   Well, madam.
Goneril. And let his knights have colder looks
        among you.
What grows of it, no matter; advise your fellows so.
I would breed from hence occasions, and I shall, 24
That I may speak. I'll write straight to my sister
To hold my course. Prepare for dinner. [*Exeunt.* 26

Scene four.

(A HALL IN THE SAME.)
Enter KENT, *disguised.*

Kent. If but as well I other accents borrow
That can my speech defuse, my good intent 2
May carry through itself to that full issue 3
For which I razed my likeness. Now, banished Kent, 4
If thou canst serve where thou dost stand condemned,
So may it come, thy master whom thou lov'st
Shall find thee full of labours. 7
    Horns within. Enter LEAR, Knight, *and* Attendants.
Lear. Let me not stay a jot for dinner; go get it 8
ready. [*Exit an Attendant.*] How now, what art
thou?
Kent. A man, sir.
Lear. What dost thou profess? What wouldst thou
with us?
Kent. I do profess to be no less than I seem, to 14
serve him truly that will put me in trust, to love him
that is honest, to converse with him that is wise and
says little, to fear judgment, to fight when I cannot
choose, and to eat no fish. 18
Lear. What art thou?
Kent. A very honest-hearted fellow, and as poor as
the King.
Lear. If thou be'st as poor for a subject as he's for
a king, thou art poor enough. What wouldst thou?
Kent. Service.
Lear. Who wouldst thou serve?
Kent. You.
Lear. Dost thou know me, fellow?
Kent. No, sir, but you have that in your countenance which I would fain call master.

13. "come to question": come up for discussion.
14. "distaste": dislike.

17. "authorities": the right to command.

20. "With . . . abused": with punishments as well as praise, when they do not understand their own position.

24. "occasions": issues.

26. "hold my course": do as I do.

2. "defuse": make diffuse, disguise.

3. "full issue": final result.

4. "razed my likeness": erased my own appearance.

7. "labours": i.e., of assistance.

8. "stay": wait.

14. "profess": do, as a profession or job.

18. "eat no fish": be a Protestant. Here and elsewhere Shakespeare cares little for the accuracy of his portrayal of pre-Christian England.

KING LEAR

ACT I SCENE IV

mad. In a somewhat different sense, the protective disguise of Kent is the result of Lear's own lack of knowledge. While his judgment is blinded he mistakes disloyal daughters for loyal ones, friends for enemies. His real supporters must aid him secretly.

Kent also exemplifies the loyalty shown to Lear by the group (Kent, the Fool, and Cordelia) associated with him in the play. Lear has, up to now, been remarkable for his misunderstanding of those around him, and his hot temper. But he is also a tragic hero, or will become one. He has greatness, and one of the ways in which Shakespeare establishes this is by the extent of love and loyalty Lear inspires in his supporters. "You have," Kent says to him, "that in your face which I would fain call master." At the beginning of the play Lear does exhibit considerable power, even though it takes the form of pride and anger. We have only to listen to his abusive phrases to hear it: "Come not between the dragon and his wrath! . . . Therefore be gone . . . Call the clotpoll back . . . You whoreson dog, you slave, you cur!" The point of these flashes of rage is to underline the fact that Lear—despite his egocentricity and stupidity concerning his daughters—is a man of power and authority. Yet his real greatness is revealed only after this outward power and authority have been stripped from him and he has been sent, humiliated, into the storm. There his "authority" is of a deeper kind, arising from new-found knowledge. Until then Shakespeare reminds us through Kent that Lear, irascible and erratic as he is, is still (as he later calls himself) "every inch a king."

The incident with the steward Oswald (45-94) points up the "great abatement of kindness" toward Lear that his daughter Goneril has ordered. Lear begins, perhaps for the first time, to win our sympathy when he admits that he has "blamed" his own "jealous curiosity," i.e., his readiness to take offence over minor matters, in the case of Goneril's servants rudeness to him. It is, however, typical that from this mood of self-enquiry (which will increase as the play continues) Lear moves immediately back to violent anger and strikes Oswald, after which Kent trips the steward up. This is, of course, exactly what Oswald invites (as the actor must make clear on the stage) and what Goneril has planned. Both Kent and Lear react directly, passionately, and, as it happens, stupidly. Their violence is boyishly naive compared to the calculated violence of the Machiavellians, which is far more brutal and effective.

Lear. What's that?

Kent. Authority.

Lear. What services canst thou do?

Kent. I can keep honest counsel, ride, run, mar a [33] curious tale in telling it and deliver a plain message [34] bluntly. That which ordinary men are fit for I am qualified in, and the best of me is diligence.

Lear. How old art thou?

Kent. Not so young, sir, to love a woman for sing- [38] ing, nor so old to dote on her for anything. I have years on my back forty-eight.

Lear. Follow me; thou shalt serve me. If I like thee no worse after dinner, I will not part from thee yet. Dinner, ho, dinner! Where's my knave? my [43] fool? Go you and call my fool hither.

[*Exit an* Attendant.

Enter OSWALD.

You, you, sirrah, where's my daughter? [45]

Oswald. So please you — [*Exit.*

Lear. What says the fellow there? Call the clotpoll back. [*Exit Knight.*] Where's my fool? Ho, I think the world's asleep.

Enter Knight.

How now? Where's that mongrel?

Knight. He says, my lord, your daughter is not well.

Lear. Why came not the slave back to me when I called him?

Knight. Sir, he answered me in the roundest man- [55] ner, he would not.

Lear. He would not?

Knight. My lord, I know not what the matter is; but to my judgment your Highness is not entertained with that ceremonious affection as you were wont. There's a great abatement of kindness appears as well in the general dependants as in the Duke himself also and your daughter.

Lear. Ha? Say'st thou so?

Knight. I beeseech you pardon me, my lord, if I be mistaken; for my duty cannot be silent when I think your Highness wronged.

Lear. Thou but remem'rest me of mine own con- [68] ception. I have perceived a most faint neglect of late, which I have rather blamed as mine own jealous [70] curiosity than as a very pretense and purpose of unkindness. I will look further into't. But where's my fool? I have not seen him this two days.

Knight. Since my young lady's going into France, sir, the fool hath much pined away.

Lear. No more of that; I have noted it well. Go you and tell my daughter I would speak with her.

[*Exit* Knight.

Go you, call hither my fool. [*Exit an* Attendant.

Enter OSWALD.

O, you, sir, you! Come you hither, sir. Who am I, sir?

Oswald. My lady's father.

Lear. 'My lady's father'? My lord's knave, you whoreson dog, you slave, you cur!

33. "keep honest counsel": i.e., keep what I am told to myself.

34. "curious": complicated. Kent 'mars' it because he is uncomplicated, or 'blunt'.

38-9. Kent means that he is not so young that he only loves women for the way they sing, nor is he so old that he loves them for any sort of reason: he is neither a child, nor senile.

43. "knave": boy.

45. "sirrah": generally a term of disrespect.

55. "roundest": bluntest, rudest.

68. "remem'rest": remind.

70. "jealous": suspicious.

26

KING LEAR

ACT I SCENE IV

Lear calls for his Fool, and it is pointed out to him that since Cordelia's departure "the fool hath much pined away." This at once establishes the Fool as a member of the Lear party, so that when he does arrive on stage we are prepared to see him take Lear's part, even though most of what he says is acid criticism of Lear's judgment. In this he plays a traditional role; he is, as Goneril points out, an "all-licensed fool," the court jester who alone is able, through his wit, to attack the king.

Something ought to be said at this point about the role of the fool or clown in Elizabethan drama in general and Shakespeare's plays in particular. The character of the Fool derives ultimately, of course, from the medieval court jester, whose presence as a monarch's attendant extended well into the 16th century. The honor and reverence which surrounded the throne could, on occasion, be called into question by the gibes of the "all-licensed" fool; this served as a healthy counterbalance to the 'divinity' of the king's position, reminding him that although his function was regarded as being divinely ordained, he was in his own person as fallible as anyone else.

In the drama the fool was, of course, used to provide comedy. All the theatrical companies employed comic actors who specialized in the fool's role, and in Shakespeare's early plays fools and clowns appear a good deal (sometimes as servants, or petty officials) and are given much to do in the way of fairly low level, vaudeville antics. However as Shakespeare developed and his art matured, he widened and deepened the role, returning to the original conception of the fool as one who deflates pomposity, and through apparent nonsense expresses sense, particularly when those around him are being stupid. In the comedy TWELFTH NIGHT, for example, the fool, Feste, does not simply make jokes; his often bitter comments ridicule by implication the notions of his social betters. Shakespeare seems to have had the character of Feste in mind in the writing of KING LEAR, where the Fool recalls Feste's bittersweet song on the vicissitudes of life, "With a heigh ho, the wind and the rain" (III,ii, 74).

Fools in comedy were acceptable enough, but fools in tragedy were another matter. According to the best classical tradition, the fool and his jests were excluded from tragic plays, where it was felt that their clowning would dissipate the mood of tragic solemnity. Two of

---

Oswald. I am none of these, my lord; I beseech your pardon.

Lear. Do you bandy looks with me, you rascal?
                                        [*Strikes him.*

Oswald. I'll not be strucken, my lord.

Kent. Nor tripped neither, you base football player. 88
                                        [*Trips up his heels.*

Lear. I thank thee, fellow. Thou serv'st me, and I'll love thee.

Kent. Come, sir, arise, away. I'll teach you differ- 91 ences. Away, away. If you will measure your lubber's length again, tarry; but away. Go to! Have you wisdom? So.   [*Pushes him out.*

Lear. Now, my friendly knave, I thank thee. There's earnest of thy service.   [*Gives money.* 96

Enter Fool.

Fool. Let me hire him too. Here's my coxcomb. 97
                                        [*Offers Kent his cap.*

Lear. How now, my pretty knave? How dost thou?

Fool. Sirrah, you were best take my coxcomb.

Kent. Why, fool?

Fool. Why? For taking one's part that's out of favour. Nay, an thou canst not smile as the wind sits, 102 thou'lt catch cold shortly. There, take my coxcomb. Why, this fellow has banished two on's daughters, 104 and did the third a blessing against his will. If thou follow him, thou must needs wear my coxcomb — How, now, nuncle? Would I had two coxcombs and 107 two daughters.

Lear. Why, my boy?

Fool. If I gave them all my living, I'ld keep my cox- 110 combs myself. There's mine; beg another of thy daughters.

Lear. Take heed, sirrah — the whip.

Fool. Truth's a dog must to kennel; he must be whipped out, when the Lady Brach may stand by th' 115 fire and stink.

Lear. A pestilent gall to me. 117

Fool. Sirrah, I'll teach thee a speech.

Lear. Do.

Fool. Mark it, nuncle.

Have more than thou showest,
Speak less than thou knowest,
Lend less than thou owest, 123
Ride more than thou goest, 124
Learn more than thou trowest, 125
Set less than thou throwest; 126
Leave thy drink and thy whore,
And keep in-a-door,
And thou shalt have more 129
Than two tens to a score.

Kent. This is nothing, fool.

Fool. Then 'tis like the breath of an unfee'd law- 132 yer — you gave me nothing for't. Can you make no use of nothing, nuncle?

Lear. Why, no, boy. Nothing can be made out of nothing.

Fool [*to Kent*] Prithee tell him, so much the rent 137 of his land comes to; he will not believe a fool.

Lear. A bitter fool.

88. "football": in Shakespeare's day a street game of low social status.

91. "differences": i.e., the differences in rank among those he serves.

96. "earnest": payment.

97. "coxcomb": a fool's cap, often with a cock's comb attached to the top.

102. "smile . . . sits": adapt yourself to the prevailing wind, or pressure, which comes in this case from Goneril and Regan.

104. "banished": i.e., he has made enemies of them.

107. "nuncle": an abbreviation of mine uncle; intimacies of address such as this were permitted to a 'licensed fool'.

110. "living": possessions.

115. "Brach": hound bitch.

117. "pestilent gall": Lear is perhaps speaking of Oswald, perhaps of the Fool's home truths. "He listens and finds cheer in the Fool's chatter and song, snarls now and then like an old lion if a sting goes too deep; yet his thoughts, we can tell, are far away" (Granville-Barker).

123. "owest": own.

124. "goest": walk.

125. "Learn": listen.
"trowest": believe, give credit to.

126. "Set . . . throwest": bet less than you will win, i.e., have the odds in your favor.

129-30 "have . . . score": since 'two tens' are a 'score' the Fool's meaning seems to be that—by taking all the proper precautions—one ends by only breaking even.

132. "breath": voice, opinion. The Fool's meaning is that a lawyer who is not paid for what he says, says nothing of any value.

137-8. "rent of his land": i.e., nothing, since he has given his land away.

27

KING LEAR

ACT I SCENE IV

the most powerful Elizabethan literary figures—the courtier-critic Sir Philip Sidney and the great comic playwright Ben Jonson—criticized what they felt to be the improper use of fools in tragic drama. Luckily for us Shakespeare seems to have cared little for academic or formal criticism; his genius was able to employ the fool in such a way as to complement and intensify the tragic mood. In his SHAKESPEAREAN TRAGEDY A. C. Bradley permits himself an intriguing fantasy when he imagines that Shakespeare, while composing KING LEAR, and "going home from an evening at the Mermaid Tavern, where he had listened to Jonson fulminating against fools in general and perhaps criticizing the Clown in TWELFTH NIGHT in particular, had said to himself: 'Come, my friends, I will show you once for all that the mischief is in you, and not in the fool or the audience. I will have a fool in the most tragic of my tragedies. He shall not play a little part. He shall keep from first to last the company in which you most object to see him, the company of a king. Instead of amusing the king's idle hours, he shall stand by him in the very tempest and whirlwind of passion. Before I have done you shall confess, between laughter and tears, that he is of the very essence of life, that you have known him all your days though you never recognized him till now, and that you would as soon go without Hamlet, as miss him.' "

The Fool in KING LEAR plays a difficult role, both from the point of view of the actor who must interpret, and the audience or reader who tries to understand him. The most obvious of the Fool's functions is to point out to King Lear (who does not understand him) and the audience the way in which Lear's distorted judgment has reversed the natural order of things. The rider should ride the beast of burden; Lear lets the ass ride him (164). The father should punish the children; Lear lets the children whip him (176). The king should teach the fool; Lear asks the Fool to teach him (142). The Fool needles Lear to the point of direct, aggressive insult, calling Lear a fool to his face: "All thy other titles thou has given away; that thou wast born with," and Kent supports him.

The Fool also functions as a kind of chorus—an ancient dramatic device in which a group or individual comments on the play's situation in order to clarify it for the audience. The Fool does this continually. Take, for example, his comment on the world in which the Gonerils and Regans rule: "Truth's

---

Fool. Dost thou know the difference, my boy, between a bitter fool and a sweet one?

Lear. No, lad; teach me.

Fool.
    That lord that counselled thee
      To give away thy land,
    Come place him here by me —
      Do thou for him stand.   146
    The sweet and bitter fool
      Will presently appear;
    The one in motley here,
      The other found out there.   150

Lear. Dost thou call me fool, boy?

Fool. All thy other titles thou hast given away; that thou wast born with.

Kent. This is not altogether fool, my lord.

Fool. No, faith; lords and great men will not let 155 me. If I had a monopoly out, they would have part on't. And ladies too, they will not let me have all the fool to myself; they'll be snatching. Nuncle, give me an egg, and I'll give thee two crowns.

Lear. What two crowns shall they be?

Fool. Why, after I have cut the egg i' th' middle and 162 eat up the meat, the two crowns of the egg. When thou clovest thy crown i' th' middle and gav'st away both parts, thou bor'st thine ass on thy back o'er the dirt. 164 Thou hadst little wit in thy bald crown when thou gav'st thy golden one away. If I speak like myself 166 in this, let him be whipped that first finds it so.
[*Sings.*] Fools had ne'er less grace in a year,   168

    For wise men are grown foppish,   169
    And know not how their wits to wear,   170
    Their manners are so apish.

Lear. When were you wont to be so full of songs, sirrah?

Fool. I have used it, nuncle, e'er since thou mad'st thy daughters thy mothers; for when thou gav'st them the rod, and put'st down thine own breeches,
[*Sings*] Then they for sudden joy did weep,

    And I for sorrow sung,
    That such a king should play bo-peep   179
    And go the fools among.
Prithee, nuncle, keep a schoolmaster that can teach thy fool to lie. I would fain learn to lie.

Lear. An you lie, sirrah, we'll have you whipped.

Fool. I marvel what kin thou and thy daughters are. They'll have me whipped for speaking true; thou'lt have me whipped for lying; and sometimes I am whipped for holding my peace. I had rather be any kind o' thing than a fool, and yet I would not be thee, nuncle: thou hast pared thy wit o' both sides and 189 left nothing i' th' middle. Here comes one o' the parings.

Enter GONERIL.

Lear. How now, daughter? What makes that front- 192 let on? You are too much of late i' th' frown.

Fool. Thou wast a pretty fellow when thou hadst no need to care for her frowning. Now thou art an O without a figure. I am better than thou are now: I 196 am a fool, thou art nothing. [*to Goneril*] Yes, for-

---

146. "Do . . . stand": making Lear stand for his foolish counsellor.

150. "the other": i.e., Lear's counsellor (and hence Lear himself) is the 'real' fool, as opposed to the professional Fool in motley.

155-6. "will not let me": i.e., they will not let him be 'altogether' fool since they share so much of his foolishness themselves.

162-4. "thou . . . dirt": i.e., reversing normal behaviour; see commentary.

166-7. "If I speak . . . so": i.e., if I speak like a fool, punish him that says so, since what I have said is not really foolish.

168. "grace": favor.

170. "wits to wear": be intelligent.

179. "play bo-peep": i.e., play as a child.

189-90. "pared . . . middle": whittled your wits from both sides and left nothing.

192-3. "frontlet": decoration for the brow, here a frown.

196. "without a figure": without a digit, therefore without any value.

28

KING LEAR

ACT I SCENE IV

a dog must to kennel; he must be whipped out, when the Lady Brach may stand by the fire and stink." It is a homely and effective image. Power and position have gone to "the Lady Brach"— the hunter bitch—and there could be no more compact and acid phrase to apply to Lear's elder daughters. Here and elsewhere the Fool uses the animal imagery which has such an important imaginative function in the play (see introduction). The world in which he and Lear now find themselves is a world of animal struggle, rather than human order. Lear's daughter is a "fox," and the Fool recommends to Lear the moral of the animal tale in which "The hedge-sparrow fed the cuckoo so long/ That it's had it head bit off by it young."

The Fool has another important function, and that is to try to interpret the mentality of Regan and Goneril to the King. Goneril is right to attack "the all-licensed fool" (see 198 and 203) since he sees, far more clearly than either Kent or Lear, the way in which her mind works and the attitude which she and her group represent. Where Lear simply does not understand Goneril, and reacts to her with blank amazement ("Are you our daughter?"), the Fool understands perfectly, as he shows in the example of the cuckoo biting off the head of the hedge-sparrow which fed it. He knows that for Lear's party—Kent and himself—the "candle" is indeed about to go out and leave them "darkling" in the night, and in the storm.

As a dramatic character, the Fool is more important than he seems at first sight. A character who has dramatic interest is usually one in whom we see some sort of clash or conflict. The Fool is just such a character. On the one hand he understands the Machiavellian reasoning of Goneril's party, and realizes that Lear cannot hope to survive pitted against such total, and efficient, egotism: "Thou hadst little wit in thy bald crown when thou gav'st thy golden one away." In his song (121) the Fool outlines the sort of careful and hardheaded attitude that can survive in the Regan-Goneril world, and, as a disciple of common sense, the Fool wants to survive (see III,ii,10). On the other hand the Fool's loyalty is to Lear, and he is torn between survival and self-interest and his love for Lear and the humanity Lear stands for. This is what accounts for the note of bitterness, and sometimes melancholy, in the Fool's lines. His position is indeed an ambiguous one, as he points out to the King: They [the daugh-

sooth, I will hold my tongue. So your face bids me, though you say nothing. Mum, mum.

> He that keeps nor crust nor crumb,
> Weary of all, shall want some. — 201

[*Points at Lear.*] That's a shealed peascod. 202

Goneril. Not only, sir, this your all-licensed fool, 203
But other of your insolent retinue
Do hourly carp and quarrel, breaking forth
In rank and not-to-be-endured riots. Sir,
I had thought by making this well known unto you
To have found a safe redress, but now grow fearful,
By what yourself too late have spoke and done,
That you protect this course, and put it on 210
By your allowance; which if you should, the fault
Would not 'scape censure, nor the redresses sleep, 212
Which, in the tender of a wholesome weal,
Might in their working do you that offence,
Which else were shame, that then necessity
Will call discreet proceeding. 216

Fool. For you know, nuncle,
> The hedge-sparrow fed the cuckoo so long
> That it's had it head bit off by it young. 219
So out went the candle, and we were left darkling. 220

Lear. Are you our daughter?

Goneril. I would you would make use of your good
wisdom.
(Whereof I know you are fraught) and put away 223
These dispositions which of late transport you 224
From what you rightly are.

Fool. May not an ass know when the cart draws the
horse?
Whoop, Jug, I love thee! 227

Lear. Does any here know me? This is not Lear.
Does Lear walk thus? speak thus? Where are his
eyes?
Either his notion weakens, his discernings 230
Are lethargied — Ha! Waking? 'Tis not so. 231
Who is it that can tell me who I am?

Fool. Lear's shadow.

Lear. I would learn that; for, by the marks of sov- 234
ereignty,
Knowledge, and reason, I should be false persuaded
I had daughters.

Fool. Which they will make an obedient father.

Lear. Your name, fair gentlewoman?

Goneril. This admiration, sir, is much o' th' savour 239
Of other your new pranks. I do beseech you
To understand my purposes aright.
As you are old and reverend, should be wise.
Here do you keep a hundred knights and squires,
Men so disordered, so debosh'd, and bold 244
That this our court, infected with their manners,
Shows like a riotous inn. Epicurism and lust 246
Makes it more like a tavern or a brothel
Than a graced palace. The shame itself doth speak 248
For instant remedy. Be then desired
By her that else will take the thing she begs
A little to disquantity your train, 251
And the remainders that shall still depend 252
To be such men as may besort your age, 253

201. "want": need.

202. "shealed peascod": shelled peapod.

203. "all-licensed": referring to the tradition according to which the court fool was 'licensed' to say anything, no matter how impertinent; the Fool avails himself generously of this license.

210. "put it on": encourage it.

212. "redresses sleep": punishments lie dormant.

212-16. "Goneril speaks in an officious and elaborate way; the meaning is "in the interests of our well-being, we may have to correct you more harshly than would normally be proper."

219. "it": its; a common Shakespearean usage.

220. "darkling": in the dark (with reference to what will happen to Lear and the Fool).

223. "fraught": equipped.

224. "dispositions": moods.

227. "Whoop, Jug": here and elsewhere Shakespeare gives the Fool (and Edgar as Poor Tom) phrases and refrains from old songs, all of which were presumably familiar to the audience.

230. "notion": understanding.

231. "Waking": Lear pretends to pinch himself to see if he is really awake.

234. "marks of sovereignty": evidences of kingship.

239. "admiration": the air of being baffled that Lear ironically assumes.

244. "debosh'd": debauched.

246. "Epicurism": the luxurious habits (wrongly) attributed to the philosopher Epicurus and his followers.

248. "speak": require.

251. "disquantity your train": reduce the number of your followers.

252. "depend": be attached to you.

253. "besort": be proper to.

KING LEAR

ACT I SCENE IV

ters] will have me whipped for speaking true; thou'lt have me whipped for lying." The truth which the Fool sees is too painful to utter, and there is a note of something like anguish in "Prithee nuncle, keep a schoolmaster that can teach thy fool to lie. I would fain learn to lie." Lear, of course, can see none of this; his affection for the Fool ignores the sharp accuracy of the Fool's pronouncements. Thus the character of the Fool, who loves Lear but cannot make him see his true position, has a good deal of pathos in it.

The first open conflict between Lear and his daughters begins near the end of this scene, with Lear's "How now, daughter? . . . You are too much of late i' the frown," and Goneril's answering denunciation, and goes on to Lear's exit at 313, in the first of his consuming rages. Shakespeare again points up the difference between the two in the language of their speeches. Goneril's are precise and careful; we can see the hard, self-righteous face and hear the prim enunciation: "I had thought by making this well known unto you/To have found safe redess . . ." Lear is immediately put at fault. Goneril says she "grows fearful/By what yourself too late have spoke and done,/That you protect this course, and put it on . . ." The iron will shows through the polite phrases toward the end of the speech—"Be then desired/By her that else will take the thing she begs . . ."—where the sudden, cold fury of the "will take" shows us the real Goneril, and the falseness of the assumed politeness. Opposed to this we have Lear's enraged reply. Where Goneril's

Which know themselves, and you. 254

Lear.   Darkness and devils!
Saddle my horses; call my train together.
Degenerate bastard, I'll not trouble thee: 256
Yet have I left a daughter.

Goneril. You strike my people, and your disordered rabble
Make servants of their betters.

Enter ALBANY.

Lear. Woe that too late repents. — O, sir, are you come?
Is it your will? Speak, sir. — Prepare my horses.
Ingratitude! thou marble-hearted fiend,
More hideous when thou show'st thee in a child
Than the sea-monster.

Albany.   Pray, sir, be patient.

Lear. Detested kite, thou liest. 265
My train are men of choice and rarest parts, 266
That all particulars of duty know
And in the most exact regard support 268
The worships of their name. O most small fault, 269
How ugly didst thou in Cordelia show!
Which, like an engine, wrenched my frame of nature 271
From the fixed place; drew from my heart all love
And added to the gall. O Lear, Lear, Lear!
Beat at this gate that let thy folly in.
                              [*Strikes his head.*
And thy dear judgment out. Go, go, my people.

Albany. My lord, I am guiltless, as I am ignorant
Of what hath moved you.

Lear.   It may be so, my lord.
Hear, Nature, hear; dear goddess, hear:
Suspend thy purpose if thou didst intend
To make this creature fruitful.
Into her womb convey sterility,
Dry up in her the organs of increase,
And from her derogate body never spring 283
A babe to honour her. If she must teem, 284
Create her child of spleen, that it may live 285
And be a thwart disnatured torment to her. 286
Let it stamp wrinkles in her brow of youth,
With cadent tears fret channels in her cheeks, 288
Turn all her mother's pains and benefits 289
To laughter and contempt, that she may feel
How sharper than a serpent's tooth it is
To have a thankless child. Away, away!   [*Exit.*

Albany. Now, gods that we adore, wherof comes this?

Goneril. Never afflict yourself to know more of it, 294
But let his disposition have that scope
As dotage gives it.

Enter LEAR.

Lear. What, fifty of my followers at a clap? 297
Within a fortnight?

Albany.   What's the matter, sir?

Lear. I'll tell thee. [*To Goneril.*] Life and death, I am ashamed
That thou hast power to shake my manhood thus!
That these hot tears, which break from me perforce, 301

254. "know themselves": i.e., know their place.

256. "Degenerate bastard": unnatural or misbegotten child.

265. "kite": bird of prey.

266. "parts": abilities.

268. "exact regard": careful way.

269. "worships": dignity.

271. "engine": i.e., of torture, the rack.

283. "derogate": degraded.

284. "teem": be fruitful.

285. "spleen": the acid supposed to cause ill-humor in the body.

286. "disnatured": unnatural.

288. "cadent": flowing.

289. "pains and benefits": cares and joys.

294. "afflict": trouble.

297. "fifty": presumably Lear had been told offstage that his train was to be "disquantitied" by this number.

301. "perforce": against my will.

KING LEAR

ACT I SCENE IV

language is formal and cold, Lear's is passionate; it is the language of emotion rather than reason. Lear's curse on Goneril at 278 is overpowering in its violence; we can see that Kent was right in I,i, to see Lear as in some sense deranged. Lear seems to call on the same "Nature" that is a "goddess" to Edmund, the force of the natural, biological world that can "dry up" Goneril's fertility and "stamp wrinkles in her brow of youth." He does not yet understand—though suffering will soon make him understand—that man's life is significantly different from the 'natural' life of the animals; see here his attempted distinction between "Man's life" and "beast's" II,iv,264.

Should make thee worth them. Blasts and fogs upon
   thee!
Th' untented woundings of a father's curse   303
Pierce every sense about thee! Old fond eyes,   304
Beweep this cause again I'll pluck ye out   305
And cast you, with the waters that you loose,
To temper clay. Yea, is it come to this?   307
Ha! Let it be so. Yet have I left a daughter,
Who I am sure is kind and comfortable.   309
When she shall hear this of thee, with her nails
She'll flay thy wolfish visage. Thou shalt find
That I'll resume the shape which thou dost think   312
I have cast off for ever.
        [*Exit* LEAR *with* KENT *and* Attendants.
Goneril.   Do you mark that?
Albany. I cannot be so partial, Goneril,   314
To the great love I bear you —   315
Goneril. Pray you, content. — What, Oswald, ho!
[*To Fool.*] You, sir, more knave than fool, after your
   master!
Fool. Nuncle Lear, nuncle Lear, tarry. Take the fool
with thee.
         A fox, when one has caught her,
         And such a daughter,
         Should sure to the slaughter,
         If my cap would buy a halter.
         So the fool follows after.   [*Exit.*
Goneril. This man hath had good counsel — a hun-   325
   dred knights!
'Tis politic and safe to let him keep
At point a hundred knights — yes, that on every
   dream,   327
Each buzz, each fancy, each complaint, dislike,   328
He may enguard his dotage with their pow'rs
And hold our lives in mercy. — Oswald, I say!   330
Albany. Well, you may fear too far.
Goneril.   Safer than trust too far.
Let me still take away the harms I fear,   332
Not fear still to be taken. I know his heart.   333
What he hath uttered I have writ my sister.
If she sustain him and his hundred knights,
When I have showed th' unfitness —
         Enter OSWALD.
              How now, Oswald?
What, have you writ that letter to my sister?
Oswald. Ay, madam.
Goneril. Take you some company, and away to   339
   horse.
Inform her full of my particular fear,   340
And thereto add such reasons of your own
As may compact it more. Get you gone,   342
And hasten your return. [*Exit Oswald.*] No, no, my
   lord,
This milky gentleness and course of yours,
Though I condemn not, yet under pardon,
You are much more ataked for want of wisdom   346
Than praised for harmful mildness.   347
Albany. How far your eyes may pierce I cannot tell;
Striving to better, oft we mar what's well.
Goneril. Nay then —
Albany. Well, well; th' event.   [*Exeunt.* 351

303. "untented": uncurable; to 'tent' a wound was to probe and clean it.

304. "fond": foolish.

305. "Beweep": "if you" is understood.

307. "temper": soften.

309. "comfortable": able to comfort.

312. "shape": i.e., of authority.

314-15. "partial . . . To": biassed by.

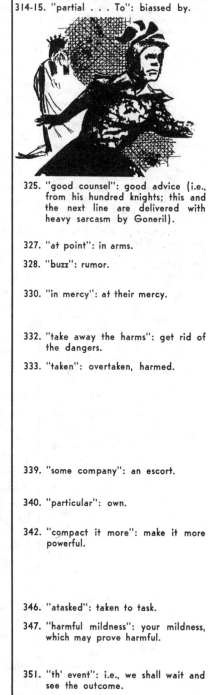

325. "good counsel": good advice (i.e., from his hundred knights; this and the next line are delivered with heavy sarcasm by Goneril).

327. "at point": in arms.

328. "buzz": rumor.

330. "in mercy": at their mercy.

332. "take away the harms": get rid of the dangers.

333. "taken": overtaken, harmed.

339. "some company": an escort.

340. "particular": own.

342. "compact it more": make it more powerful.

346. "ataked": taken to task.

347. "harmful mildness": your mildness, which may prove harmful.

351. "th' event": i.e., we shall wait and see the outcome.

KING LEAR

ACT I SCENE V

Having failed with Goneril, Lear will now turn to Regan. Since Kent leaves almost at once, this short scene is a duologue between Lear and the Fool. The Fool continues his criticism of Lear, beginning with the involved joke about the "brains in heels"—the point being that Lear has no brains—to which Lear replies with what, on the stage, can only be a hollow and automatic laugh. The Fool's next joke, however, is meant for the audience. Regan, he says, will use Lear "kindly" (see glossary) and although Lear misses the pun, we see that the Fool means the word in a sense altogether different from the ordinary one; the dramatic effect is to alert the audience to the forthcoming display of cruelty on Regan's part.

While the Fool delivers his witticisms, Lear's mind is working furiously elsewhere. He begins to see, if only in a confused way, his folly toward Cordelia—"I did her wrong"—but, afraid to dwell on that, he reverts to his unreasoning though legitimate, anger at Goneril. He contemplates reversing his judgment of I,i, and retaking the command he so lightly gave away ("To take 't again perforce"); but the Fool, understanding Lear's position so much better than Lear himself, points out that Lear's wisdom falls far short of his age (42); power surrendered is power lost.

A further piece of dramatic anticipation, suggesting what is to come, occurs at the end of the scene in Lear's reference to the madness he fears. We must remember that what has shaken Lear is not simply a matter of a daughter's unkindness. The testings of the daughters in the first scene was not simply a father's whimsy; it was also (no matter how misguided) an overpowering demand for love. In the expression of his fear of madness, Lear shows the intensity of the shock that Goneril has administered to him.

Scene five.

(A COURT BEFORE THE SAME.)
Enter LEAR, KENT, *and* Fool.

Lear. Go you before to Gloucester with these let- 1
ters. Acquaint my daughter no further with anything
you know than comes from her demand out of the let- 3
ter. If your diligence be not speedy, I shall be there
afore you.

Kent. I will not sleep, my lord, till I have delivered
your letter.   [*Exit.*

Fool. If a man's brains were in's heels, were't not 8
in danger of kibes?   9

Lear. Ay, boy.

Fool. Then I prithee be merry. Thy wits shall not
go slipshod.   12

Lear. Ha, ha, ha.

Fool. Shalt see thy other daughter will use thee
kindly; for though she's as like this as a crab's like 15
an apple, yet I can tell what I can tell.

Lear. What canst tell, boy?

Fool. She will taste as like this as a crab does to a crab.
Thou canst tell why one's nose stands i' th' middle
on's face?

Lear. No.

Fool. Why, to keep one's eyes of either side 's nose,
that what a man cannot smell out he may spy into.

Lear. I did her wrong.   24

Fool. Canst tell how an oyster makes his shell?

Lear. No.

Fool. Nor I neither; but I can tell why a snail has
a house.

Lear. Why?

Fool. Why, to put 's head in; not to give it away to
his daughters, and leave his horns without a case.   31

Lear. I will forget my nature. So kind a father! — 32
Be my horses ready?

Fool. Thy asses are gone about 'em. The reason why
the seven stars are no moe than seven is a pretty
reason.

Lear. Because they are not eight.

Fool. Yes indeed. Thou wouldst make a good fool.

Lear. To take 't again perforce — Monster ingrati- 38
tude!

Fool. If thou wert my fool, nuncle, I'd have thee
beaten for being old before thy time.

Lear. How's that?

Fool. Thou shouldst not have been old till thou
hadst been wise.

Lear. O, let me not be mad, not mad, sweet heaven!
Keep me in temper; I would not be mad!   46

        Enter a Gentleman.

How now, are the horses ready?

Gentleman. Ready, my lord.

Lear. Come, boy.

Fool. She that's a maid now, and laughs at my de- 50
parture,

Shall not be a maid long, unless things be cut shorter.
                       [*Exeunt.*

---

1. "Gloucester": the place, not the character. The "letters" are intended for Regan.

3. "demand out of": questions concerning.

8. "man's brains . . . heels": a proverbial saying, which the Fool uses as the basis for a joke.

9. "kibes": chilblains.

12. "slipshod": shod in slippers. Since Lear has no "brains" they will never have "kibes" and he need never wear the kibe-sufferer's slippers.

15. "kindly": the Fool uses the word in a double sense i) affectionately and ii) after her kind, i.e., in Regan's case, cruelly.
"crab": crabapple.

24. "her": Cordelia; see Granville-Barker's remark above, I,iv,117.

31. "case": shelter.

32. "nature": i.e., as a father.

38. "take 't again": Lear is considering retaking his position by force.

46. "in temper": in a tempered or balanced state.

50-1. The Arden editor gives the following note to these two lines: "This is addressed to the audience. Several editors assume that Shakespeare was not responsible for the couplet. The maid who sees only the funny side of the Fool's gibes, and does not realize that Lear is going on a tragic journey is such a simpleton that she won't know how to preserve her virginity."

KING LEAR

ACT II SCENE I

In this scene the sub-plot of Edmund and Gloucester is combined with the main plot of Lear and his daughters; Edmund is joined to Regan and Cornwall, making the evil faction complete, and Gloucester, through Edmund's trickery, is turned against Edgar.

Curan's entry into the play at this point is required only to give the rumor of dissension between the Dukes of Albany and Cornwall. This puts into our minds, at an early point in the play, the suggestion of conflict to come. Lear's plan in dividing his kingdom had been, he said, to avoid "future strife"; here, as in every other aspect of his plan, the old king is seen to have been wrong.

The character of Edmund is expanded in this scene, where we see him fulfill the Elizabethan audience's expectations of the Machiavellian villain. Machiavelli's political writings had suggested (although this had not been their intention) to the Elizabethan dramatist a particular kind of villain—someone totally without moral scruple, engaged in a struggle for power, who, himself clear-headed, uses the muddle-headedness of others to achieve his ends. Shakespeare's plays, like those of other Elizabethans, are full of such villains. Iago, who plays on Othello's jealousy, and Richard III and Macbeth, who murder their way to the throne, are outstanding examples, as is Edmund. We have already suggested the enduring fascination of villains of the Machiavellian type. Members of the audience, themselves law-abiding, seem always to have been intrigued by the portrayal of the figures who live beyond the law, in total disregard of civil and moral authority, and who do so explicitly and consciously. It is, perhaps, their consciousness of what they are doing that is a large part of their fascination. Most actors who play the part of Edmund have given the character a certain attractiveness, and indeed it is tempting to do so, especially early in the play. When, for example, Gloucester (whom, at the beginning, we have no great cause to respect) babbles on about the effect of the stars on man's fortunes, we are liable to prefer Edmund's common sense, pragmatic, 'realistic' attitude. It ought to be said, however, that we are probably more favorably disposed to characters of this sort than an Elizabethan audience would be. In our own age (and perhaps ever since the Romantic idea of the nobility of revolt) we tend to see the rebel, the nonconformist, as in some ways an heroic and admirable figure. The Elizabethans, with their much more

ACT TWO, scene one.

(A COURT IN THE CASTLE OF THE EARL OF GLOUCESTER.)
Enter EDMUND *and* CURAN *severally.*   s.d.

Edmund. Save thee, Curan.   1

Curan. And you, sir. I have been with your father, and given him notice that the Duke of Cornwall and Regan his Duchess will be here with him this night.

Edmund. How comes that?

Curan. Nay, I know not. You have heard of the news abroad — I mean the whispered ones, for they are yet but ear-kissing arguments?   8

Edmund. Not I. Pray you, what are they?

Curan. Have you heard of no likely wars toward,   10
'twixt the
Dukes of Cornwall and Albany?

Edmund. Not a word.

Curan. You may do, then, in time. Fare you well,
sir.   [*Exit.*

Edmund. The Duke be here to-night? The better   14
best!
This weaves itself perforce into my business.
My father hath set guard to take my brother,
And I have one thing of a queasy question   17
Which I must act. Briefness and fortune, work!   18
Brother, a word: descend. Brother, I say!

Enter EDGAR.

My father watches. O sir, fly this place.
Intelligence is given where you are hid.
You have now the good advantage of the night.
Have you not spoken 'gainst the Duke of Cornwall?
He's coming hither; now i' th' night, i' th' haste,
And Regan with him. Have you nothing said
Upon his party 'gainst the Duke of Albany?   26
Advise yourself.   27

Edgar.   I am sure on't, not a word.

Edmund. I hear my father coming. Pardon me:
In cunning I must draw my sword upon you.   29
Draw, seem to defend yourself; now quit you well.—   30
Yield! Come before my father! Light ho, here! —
Fly, brother. — Torches, torches! — So farewell.

[*Exit* EDGAR.

Some blood drawn on me would beget opinion
Of my more fierce endeavour. [*Wounds his arm.*] I
have seen drunkards
Do more than this in sport. — Father, father!
Stop, stop! No help?

Enter GLOUCESTER *and* Servants *with torches.*

Gloucester. Now, Edmund, where's the villain?

Edmund. Here stood he in the dark, his sharp
sword out,
Mumbling of wicked charms, conjuring the moon
To stand auspicious mistress.   39

Gloucester.   But where is he?

Stage Direction "severally": from different entrances.

1. "Save thee": abbreviated from 'God save thee'.

8. "ear-kissing": whispered.

10. "toward": imminent.

14. "better best": i.e., all the better.

17. "queasy question": unknown outcome.

18. "Briefness": speed.

26. "Upon his party": about his feud.

27. "Advise yourself": i.e., try to recall.

29. "In cunning": as a trick.

30. "quit you": acquit yourself.

39. "auspicious mistress": as a favorable influence; perhaps Edmund recalls Gloucester's belief in the effect of the stars on human behavior.

33

KING LEAR

ACT II SCENE I

powerful sense of human society as requiring a moral order, would see the amoral Edmund as a villain from the start. Their attitude would be ambivalent: on the one hand they might admire Edmund the 'outsider' (the illegitimate child) who puts himself against the established, orthodox code; but on the other hand, and primarily, they would realize that his amoral individualism could only lead to the destruction of the larger social organizations, the family, and the state itself, and these units were more valuable to Elizabethan audiences than to modern ones. In KING LEAR the family, like the state, stands for the values of love, duty, service and obligation. The families of both Lear and Gloucester are disrupted by those (like Edmund) who admit no moral obligation to them.

It is typical of Edmund that he sees everything that happens as providing a possible tactical advantage for himself: "The Duke be here tonight? . . . This weaves itself perforce into my business". He can improvise brilliantly with the opportunities that others give him, and he sets to work immediately in this scene to carry through his plot against his brother Edgar. This involves acting out a duel with Edgar, and Edmund takes complete charge of stage-managing this ("Draw. Seem to defend yourself . . . Yield!"), then priming his father with both insinuation and direct suggestion to ensure that the old man rightly interprets what he has seen. Edmund says that Edgar tried to "Persuade me to the murder of your lordship" until he, Edmund, "told him . . . how manifold and strong a bond/ The child was bound to th' father." The irony of Edmund representing himself as the loyal defender of the "bond" of filial duty and love will be apparent to the audience, but lost on Gloucester. Edmund then implants the notion of himself being rebuked as an "unpossessing bastard" who would never be believed by "the world" in denouncing Edgar's betrayal, a suggestion that leads directly to Gloucester's offer of all his land to this "loyal and natural boy" who has defended him. The scene, on the stage, has the effect of showing us how deft and able Edmund is in the manipulation of those around him, as well as how he benefits, in his freedom of action, from his total lack of any moral sense.

Edmund. Look, sir, I bleed.
Gloucester.   Where is the villain, Edmund?
Edmund. Fled this way, sir, when by no means he
    could —
Gloucester. Pursue him, ho! Go after. [*Exit some*
    Servants.] By no means what?
Edmund. Persuade me to the murder of your lord-
    ship;
But that I told him the revenging gods
'Gainst parricides did all their thunders bend;
Spoke with how manifold and strong a bond
The child was bound to th' father — sir, in fine,   48
Seeing how loathly opposite I stood   49
To his unnatural purpose, in fell motion   50
With his prepared sword he charges home
My unprovided body, latched mine arm;   52
And when he saw my best alarumed spirits   53
Bold in the quarrel's right, roused to th' encounter,
Or whether gasted by the noise I made,   55
Full suddenly he fled.
Gloucester.   Let him fly far.
Not in this land shall he remain uncaught;
And found — dispatch. The noble Duke my master,   58
My worthy arch and patron, comes to-night: 59
By his authority I will proclaim it
That he which finds him shall deserve our thanks,
Bringing the murderous coward to the stake;
He that conceals him, death.
Edmund. When I dissuaded him from his intent
And found him pight to do it, with curst speech   65
I threatened to discover him. He replied,   66
'Thou unpossessing bastard; dost thou think,   67
If I would stand against thee, would the reposal   68
Of any trust, virtue, or worth in thee
Make thy words faithed? No. What I should deny   70
(As this I would, ay, though thou didst produce
My very character) I'll turn it all   72
To thy suggestion, plot, and damnèd practice;   73
And thou must make a dullard of the world,   74
If they not thought the profits of my death   75
Were very pregnant and potential spirits   76
To make thee seek it.'
Gloucester.   O strange and fast'nèd villain!   77
Would he deny his letter, said he? [I never got
    him.]   [*Tucket within.* s.d.
Hark, the Duke's trumpets. I know not why he
    comes.
All ports I'll bar; the villain shall not 'scape;
The Duke must grant me that. Besides, his picture
I will send far and near, that all the kingdom
May have due note of him; and of my land,
Loyal and natural boy, I'll work the means
To make thee capable.   85

Enter CORNWALL, REGAN, *and* Attendants.

Cornwall. How now, my noble friend? Since I came
    hither
(Which I can call but now) I have heard strange
    news.
Regan. If it be true, all vengeance comes too short
Which can pursue th' offender. How dost, my lord?

48. "in fine": at last.

49. "loathly opposite": firmly opposed.

50. "fell": death-dealing.

52. "unprovided": unarmed.
    "latched": stabbed.

53. "best alarumed": fully roused.

55. "gasted": frightened (as in 'aghast').

58. "dispatch": he will be dispatched, executed.

59. "arch": chief.

65. "pight": determined.
    "curst": angry.

66. "discover": uncover, unmask.

67. "unpossessing": i.e., possessed of no rights.

68. "reposal": placing.

70. "faithed": believed.

72. "character": i.e., the 'characters' of my handwriting.

73. "practice": treachery.

74. "make . . . world": consider the world stupid.

75. "not thought": did not think.

76. "pregnant and potential": fruitful and potent.

77. "fast'ned": hardened, confirmed.

Stage Direction "Tucket within": A trumpet played offstage.

85. "capable": legally able to inherit.

Gloucester. O madam, my old heart is cracked, is cracked.

Regan. What, did my father's godson seek your life?
He whom my father named, your Edgar? 92

Gloucester. O lady, lady, shame would have it hid.

Regan. Was he not companion with the riotous knights
That tended upon my father?

Gloucester. I know not, madam. 'Tis too bad, too bad.

Edmund. Yes, madam, he was of that consort. 97

Regan. No marvel then though he were ill affected. 98
'Tis they have put him on the old man's death, 99
To have th' expense and waste of his revenues. 100
I have this present evening from my sister
Been well informed of them, and with such cautions
That, if they come to sojourn at my house,
I'll not be there.

Cornwall.   Nor I, assure thee, Regan.
Edmund, I hear that you have shown your father
A childlike office. 106

Edmund.   It was my duty, sir.

Gloucester. He did bewray his practice, and received
This hurt you see, striving to apprehend him.

Cornwall. Is he pursued?

Gloucester.   Ay, my good lord.

Cornwall. If he be taken, he shall never more
Be feared of doing harm. Make your own purpose, 111
How in my strength you please. For you, Edmund,
Whose virtue and obedience doth this instant
So much commend itself, you shall be ours.
Natures of such deep trust we shall much need;
You we first seize on.

Edmund.   I shall serve you, sir,
Truly, however else.

Gloucester.   For him I thank your Grace.

Cornwall. You know not why we came to visit you?

Regan. Thus out of season, threading dark-eyed night.
Occasions, noble Gloucester, of some prize, 120
Wherein we must have use of your advice.
Our father he hath writ, so hath our sister,
Of differences, which I best thought it fit
To answer from our home. The several messengers 124
From hence attend dispatch. Our good old friend, 125
Lay comforts to your bosom, and bestow 126
Your needful counsel to our business,
Which craves the instant use.

Gloucester.   I serve you, madam.
Your Graces are right welcome. [*Exeunt. Flourish.*

92. "named": i.e., in baptism.

97. "consort": company.

98. "ill affected": treacherous.

99. "put him on": urged on him.

100. "expense and waste": the wasteful expenditure.

106. "childlike": dutiful; for the audience the line is heavily ironic.

111-12. "Make . . . please": i.e., make your own plan and use my authority as you wish.

120. "prize": importance.

124. "To answer . . . home": deal with away from home.

125. "attend dispatch": wait to go.

126. "Lay . . . bosom": be consoled.

KING LEAR

ACT II SCENE II

The meeting of Kent and Oswald returns us to the play's conflict on another level, that of the servants, or secondary members of the two parties. As one might expect, the characteristics of the leaders are repeated in their followers. Oswald must be played on the stage as Kent describes him—"a lily-livered . . . superserviceable, finical rogue." Since Shakespeare did not write elaborate stage directions or descriptions of what he wanted his actors to do, he often uses one character's description of another —as here—to suggest to the actor (and the director, in our day) what sort of performance he wants.

Kent we already know, and he is a compound of two qualities: devotion to his master, Lear, and a forthright honesty which is incapable of ambiguity or diplomacy. His readiness to risk chastisement in the interests of truth has already been demonstrated in his denunciation of Lear's actions in I,i. He is, as we have seen, much like Lear in his direct, uncompromising, and often thoughtless approach. Lear's anger is matched by Kent's physical violence; both men suffer for their directness. In both cases we are meant to contrast this directness—the lack of deliberation and planning—with the more effective and less admirable behavior of their opponents. Strategically Kent and Lear are wrong; morally they are right.

Scene two.

(BEFORE GLOUCESTER'S CASTLE.)

Enter KENT, *and* OSWALD, *severally.*

Oswald. Good dawning to thee, friend. Art of this house?

Kent. Ay.

Oswald. Where may we set our horses?

Kent. I' th' mire.

Oswald. Prithee, if thou lov'st me, tell me.

Kent. I love thee not.

Oswald. Why then, I care not for thee.

Kent. If I had thee in Lipsbury Pinfold, I would 9
make thee care for me.

Oswald. Why dost thou use me thus? I know thee
not?

Kent. Fellow, I know thee.

Oswald. What dost thou know me for?

Kent. A knave, a rascal, an eater of broken meats; 15
a base, proud, shallow, beggarly, three-suited, hun- 16
dred-pound, filthy worsted-stocking knave; a lily- 17
livered, action-taking, whoreson, glass-gazing, super- 18
serviceable, finical rogue; one-trunk-inheriting 19
slave; one that wouldst be a bawd in way of good 20
service, and art nothing but the composition of a
knave, beggar, coward, pander, and the son and
heir of a mongrel bitch; one whom I will beat into
clamorous whining if thou deny'st the least syllable
of thy addition. 25

Oswald. Why, what a monstrous fellow art thou,
thus to rail on one that is neither known of thee nor
knows thee!

Kent. What a brazen-faced varlet art thou to deny
thou knowest me! Is it two days ago since I tripped
up thy heels and beat thee before the King? [*Draws
his sword.*] Draw, you rogue, for though it be night,
yet the moon shines. I'll make a sop o' th' moon- 33
shine of you. You whoreson cullionly barbermonger, 34
draw!

Oswald. Away, I have nothing to do with thee.

Kent. Draw, you rascal. You come with letters
against the King, and take Vanity the puppet's part 38
against the royalty of her father. Draw, you rogue,
or I'll so carbonado your shanks. Draw, you rascal. 40
Come your ways! 41

Oswald. Help, ho! Murder! Help!

Kent. Strike, you slave! Stand, rogue! Stand, you
neat slave! Strike! [*Beats him.* 44

Oswald. Help, ho! Murder, murder!

Enter EDMUND, *with his rapier drawn,* CORNWALL,
REGAN, GLOUCESTER, *Servants.*

Edmund. How now? What's the matter? Part!

Kent. With you, goodman boy, if you please! Come, 47
I'll flesh ye; come on, young master. 48

Gloucester. Weapons? Arms? What's the matter
here?

9. "Lipsbury Pinfold": a slang term, combining Pinfold as a 'pen for animals' and Lipsbury 'between the lips or teeth'; Kent means he would like to have Oswald imprisoned in his teeth.

15. "broken meats": scraps from a master's table.

16-17. "three-suited": with three suits; i.e., a fop, see III,iv,133. "hundred pounds": the amount a man needed to be declared fit for jury duty, i.e., a solid citizen.

17. "worsted-stockings": woolen stocking, as opposed to the silks of the real aristocrat.

18. "action-taking": resorting to law. "glass": mirror. "superserviceable": over-ready to serve someone of higher rank.

19. "finical": finicky, fastidious. "one-trunk-inheriting": i.e., one trunk, or box holds all he owns.

20-1. "bawd . . . service": a pander to an employer.

25. "addition": i.e., the titles which I have given you.

33-4. "sop o' th' moonshine": a sop was something set floating in a drink; Kent will 'float' Oswald in the light of the moon.

34. "cullionly barbermonger": rascal who goes to too often to the barber.

38. "Vanity the puppet": Vanity was a stock figure in the medieval morality plays; Kent has Goneril in mind.

40. "carbonado": flay into strips for cooking.

41. "Come your ways": Come on!

44. "neat": prim.

47. "goodman": contemptuous form of address.

48. "flesh": i.e., cut into your flesh, also a hunting term, like 'blood', signifying a youth's first taste of blood.

36

KING LEAR

ACT II SCENE II

The abuse which Kent showers on Oswald would have been particularly welcome to the Elizabethan audience, especially the groundlings—the lower orders who stood in the pit and delighted in the rough and tumble of physical or verbal combat. On one level Kent's abuse is the sort of free-wheeling and creative invective that our theatre—and our language—has largely lost. The richness of the Elizabethan language was not only a matter of the glittering artifice of the Elizabethan lyrics, or Shakespeare's more exalted 'poetic' passages. The exuberant earthiness of the language of the streets and bear pits and taverns was also a part of it. Kent's "knave, beggar, coward, pander and the son and heir of a mongrel bitch" would be recognized at once by the audience as a brilliant and compressed transcript of the sort of thing they might hear at any time in the streets of London. We find this kind of thing in Shakespeare because he considered poetry, and especially dramatic poetry, a wide and flexible medium, far wider and more flexible than we consider it to be today. For Shakespeare any powerful emotion, whether fashionable or repellent, proper or improper, was capable of being turned into poetry—as he here makes Kent's insults into wonderfully vivid dramatic poetry. At another level Kent is simply telling us the truth about Oswald and, by implication, any follower of the Goneril-Regan party: "one that would be a bawd in the way of good service," i.e., one that would perform any immoral act (here, pandering or procuring) for advancement.

The debate between Kent and Cornwall is also significant. When asked Oswald's "fault", Kent can only reply "His countenance likes me not", or as we should say 'I don't like his face'. In fact Kent's dislike of Oswald is too basic and far-reaching to be easily phrased. It is intuitive, deeper than specific 'reasons' can account for. "Anger hath a privilege" Kent says (voicing a sentiment we have all felt when angry), yet he can give no immediate reason for his anger. Perhaps the line "That such a slave should wear a sword" comes closest—in a world in which his master Lear is disdained, Oswald seems to Kent to represent the time-server and sycophant who 'gets on.'

Cornwall's view is also interesting. For him, any attitude must be some sort of Machiavellian disguise, or trick. Hence his suspicion that Kent is an actor "who doth affect a saucy roughness." For Cornwall the face must necessarily be some sort of hypocritical mask.

Cornwall. Keep peace, upon your lives.
He dies that strikes again. What is the matter?
Regan. The messengers from our sister and the King.
Cornwall. What is your difference? Speak.
Oswald. I am scarce in breath, my lord.
Kent. No marvel, you have so bestirred your valour. 57
You cowardly rascal, nature disclaims in thee. A 58
tailor made thee.
Cornwall. Thou art a strange fellow. A tailor make a man?
Kent. A tailor, sir. A stonecutter or a painter could 62
not have made him so ill, though they had been
but two years o' th' trade.
Cornwall. Speak yet, how grew your quarrel?
Oswald. This ancient ruffian, sir, whose life I
have spared at suit of his gray beard— 67
Kent. Thou whoreson zed, thou unnecessary letter! 68
My lord, if you will give me leave, I will tread this
unbolted villain into mortar and daub the wall of a 70
jakes with him. Spare my gray beard? you wagtail. 71
Cornwall. Peace, sirrah!
You beastly knave, know you no reverence?
Kent. Yes, sir, but anger hath a privilege.
Cornwall. Why art thou angry?
Kent. That such a slave as this should wear a
    sword,
Who wears no honesty. Such smiling rogues as
    these
Like rats oft bite the holy cords atwain 78
Which are too intrinse t' unloose; smooth every 79
    passion
That in the natures of their lords rebel, 80
Bring oil to fire, snow to the colder moods;
Renege, affirm, and turn their halcyon beaks 82
With every gale and vary of their masters,
Knowing naught, like dogs, but following.
A plague upon your epileptic visage! 85
Smile you my speeches, as I were a fool?
Goose, if I had you upon Sarum Plain, 87
I'd drive ye cackling home to Camelot. 88
Cornwall. What, art thou mad, old fellow?
Gloucester. How fell you out? Say that.
Kent. No contraries hold more antipathy
Than I and such a knave.
Cornwall. Why dost thou call him knave? What is 93
    his fault?
Kent. His countenance likes me not.
Cornwall. No more perchance does mine, nor his,
    nor hers.
Kent. Sir, 'tis my occupation to be plain: 96
I have seen better faces in my time
Than stands on any shoulder that I see
Before me at this instant.
Cornwall.   This is some fellow
Who, having been praised for bluntness, doth affect
A saucy roughness, and constrains the garb 101
Quite from his nature. He cannot flatter, he;
An honest mind and plain — he must speak truth.
An they will take it, so; if not, he's plain.

57. "bestirred": stirred up, used.

58. "disclaims": wants no responsibility for.

62. "stonecutter": sculptor—like the painter, one who 'makes' men.

67. "at suit": at the (implied) plea of.

68. "zed": last and least useful letter of the alphabet.

70. "unbolted": unsifted, unworked.

71. "jakes": privy.

78. "holy cords": sacred bonds (of family, state, and religion).

79. "intrinse": intrinsic, vital. "smooth": feed, flatter.

80. "rebel": i.e., against civilized restraint.

82. "Renege": deny. "halcyon beaks": kingfisher beaks; it was once supposed that these birds always pointed into the wind, like weather vanes.

85. "epileptic": contorted, as in a fit.

87. "Sarum Plain": Salisbury.

88. "Camelot": legendary seat of King Arthur; this may have been Winchester, in which case the 'goose' reference above is clear—'Winchester goose' was a specially abusive Elizabethan phrase.

96. "occupation": business, habit.

101-2. "constrains . . . nature": assumes the fashion (of 'bluntness' contrary to his real nature.

37

KING LEAR

ACT II SCENE II

Kent, because of his loyalty and directness, is in fact a useful tool of the evil party. Regan has been informed by Goneril of the method to be used against Lear; he must be provoked into an outburst (like Kent's here) in order to render him vulnerable. The putting of Kent in the stocks will provide just such a provocation, as Gloucester points out (135-143). Kent has given Lear's enemies the sort of opportunity they need.

Gloucester's role in the scene is also interesting. Until now, he has been shown in unfortunate light. His first appearance on the stage suggested that he was both morally weak and insensitive. Like Lear, Gloucester has erred, but he will suffer for it, and acquire in the course of the play far more courage and dignity than he begins with. His sympathy here for Kent foreshadows this. Lear and Gloucester may be headstrong and stupid, but they are never cruel or malignant. Gloucester's behavior here indicates his funda-

These kind of knaves I know which in this plainness
Harbour more craft and more corrupter ends
Than twenty silly-ducking observants
That stretch their duties nicely.   108
 Kent. Sir, in good faith, in sincere verity,
Under th' allowance of your great aspect,   110
Whose influence, like the wreath of radiant fire
On flick'ring Phoebus' front —   112
 Cornwall.   What mean'st by this?
 Kent. To go out of my dialect, which you discom- 113
mend so much. I know, sir, I am no flatterer. He 114
that beguiled you in a plain accent was a plain
knave, which, for my part, I will not be, though I
should win your displeasure to entreat me to't.   117
 Cornwall. What was th' offence you gave him?
 Oswald. I never gave him any.
It pleased the King his master very late
To strike at me, upon his misconstruction;   121
When he, compact, and flattering his displeasure,   122
Tripped me behind; being down, insulted, railed,
And put upon him such a deal of man   124
That worthied him, got praises of the King   125
For him attempting who was self-subdued;   126
And, in the fleshment of this dread exploit,   127
Drew on me here again.
 Kent.   None of these rogues and cowards
But Ajax is their fool.   129
 Cornwall.   Fetch forth the stocks!
You stubborn ancient knave, you reverent braggart,   130
We'll teach you.
 Kent.   Sir, I am too old to learn.
Call not your stocks for me, I serve the King —
On whose employment I was sent to you;
You shall do small respect, show too bold malice
Against the grace and person of my master,   135
Stocking his messenger.
 Cornwall. Fetch forth the stocks. As I have life and
  honour,
There shall he sit till noon.
 Regan. Till noon? Till night, my lord, and all night
  too.
 Kent. Why, madam, if I were your father's dog,
You should not use me so.
 Regan.   Sir, being his knave, I will.
 Cornwall. This is a fellow of the selfsame colour   142
Our sister speaks of. Come, bring away the stocks.   143
        [*Stocks brought out.*
 Gloucester. Let me beseech your Grace not to do so.
His fault is much, and the good King his master
Will check him for't. Your purposed low correction
Is such as basest and contemned'st wretches   147
For pilf'rings and most common trespasses
Are punished with.
The King his master needs must take it ill
That he, so slightly valued in his messenger,   151
Should have him thus restrained.
 Cornwall.   I'll answer that.
 Regan. My sister may receive it much more worse,
To have her gentleman abused, assaulted,
For following her affairs. Put in his legs.
       [KENT *is put in the stocks.*

108. "nicely": too-correctly.

110. "allowance": permission.
"aspect": appearance.

112. "Phoebus' front": the sun's fore-head; Kent is now deliberately polished in his speech.

113. "my dialect": my usual way of speaking.

114. "He": see line 93.

117. "I should . . . to't": i.e., since you dislike it, you have almost persuaded me to adopt it.

121. "misconstruction": misunderstanding.

122. "compact": i.e., in on the plan.

124. "deal of man": show of manliness.

125. "worthied him": did him credit.

126. "For . . . self-subdued": attacking him (Oswald) who attempted no resistance.

127. "fleshment of": excitement of.

129. "Ajax": a conventionally stupid type in drama; Kent means that cowards like Oswald must always make their enemies out to be Ajaxes.

130. "reverent": old.

135. "grace": honor.

142. "colour": kind.

143. "bring away": bring on.

147. "contemned'st": who draw the heaviest sentences.

151. "so slightly valued in": so little respected in.

KING LEAR

ACT II SCENE II

mental goodness; at the moment he is the dupe of Regan and Cornwall, but he is becoming a sympathetic figure.

The scene ends with evil clearly in the acendant, and Kent in the stocks. Yet, paradoxically, the feeling at the end is not particularly somber. This is in part because of the humane behavior of Gloucester in trying to comfort Kent, but Kent's own attitude is also responsible for it. Kent has neither brilliance nor imagination, but he does have courage and endurance. He submits to the indignity of the stocks with a good grace: "Some time I shall sleep out, the rest I'll whistle." Kent also reminds us at this point of Cordelia's existence, and the possibiltiy of her return. The lowest points in this play often produce some suggestion of hope and redemption (see Edgar's lines at IV,i,1). It is "misery" that is in the best position, Kent says philosophically, to see "miracles."

ACT II SCENE III

Edgar has been outlawed; now both the loyal children have been rejected by their parents. Edgar's choice of "the basest and most poorest shape" is deliberate on Shakespeare's part: it is in the most direct contrast with the pomp and power of what has become, in effect, the new "court" party—Goneril, Regan, Edmund and Cornwall. One of the themes of the play is that of purhation. The good characters must undergo rejection and suffering before they return from the heath and the storm. Edgar, who here asumes the lowest guise he can, will end as king (V,iii,320-324).

The form that Edgar chooses was well known in Elizabethan England—the relatively non-violent inmates of Bethlehem (Bedlam) Hospital who were allowed to wander and beg. Here is a contemporary description from Dekker's BELL-MAN OF LONDON (1608): "He swears he hath been in Bedlam, and will talk frantically of purpose: you see pins stuck in sundry places of his naked flesh, especially in his arms, which pain

---

Cornwall. Come, my lord, away!

      [*Exit with all but* GLOUCESTER *and* KENT.

Gloucester. I am sorry for thee, friend. 'Tis the
    Duke's pleasure,

Whose disposition all the world well knows   158

Will not be rubbed nor stopped. I'll entreat for thee. 159

Kent. Pray do not, sir. I have watched and travelled 160
    hard.

Some time I shall sleep out, the rest I'll whistle.

A good man's fortune may grow out at heels.   162

Give you good morrow.

Gloucester. The Duke's to blame in this. 'Twill be
      ill taken.   [*Exit.*

Kent. Good King, that must approve the common 165
    saw,

Thou out of heaven's benediction com'st   166
To the warm sun.

Approach, thou beacon to this under globe,   168

That by thy comfortable beams I may

Peruse this letter. Nothing almost sees miracles   170

But misery. I know 'tis from Cordelia,

Who hath most fortunately been informed

Of my obscured course. And shall find time   173

From this enormous state, seeking to give

Losses their remedies. — All weary and o'erwatched, 175

Take vantage, heavy eyes, not to behold   176

This shameful lodging. Fortune, good night;

Smile once more, turn thy wheel.   [*Sleeps.* 178

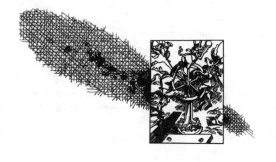

Scene three.

(A WOOD.)

Enter EDGAR.

Edgar. I heard myself proclaimed,   1

And by the happy hollow of a tree   2

Escaped the hunt. No port is free, no place

That guard and most unusual vigilance

Does not attend my taking. Whiles I may 'scape,   5

I will preserve myself; and am bethought   6

To take the basest and most poorest shape

That ever penury, in contempt of man,

Brought near to beast: my face I'll grime with filth,

Blanket my loins, elf all my hairs in knots,   10

And with presented nakedness outface   11

---

158. "disposition": inclination.

159. "rubbed": turned aside (a bowling term).

160. "watched": gone without sleep.

162. "out at heels": i.e., it is no disgrace to suffer misfortunes (with a reference to Kent's heels encased in the stocks).

165. "approve . . . saw": show the truth of the proverbial saying.

166-7. The intended meaning of the proverb is 'better to worse', the sun here standing for worldly discomfort.

168. "beacon": sun.

170-1. "Nothing . . . misery": i.e., those who are miserable may expect miracles.

173. "obscured": disguised.

173-5. "And shall . . . remedies": this passage is obscure, possibly due to the omission of a phrase in the original printing. The sense seems to be 'who will find the opportunity to deliver us from this unnatural state of affairs, putting right what is wrong'.

175. "o'erwatched": having been too long awake.

176. "vantage": advantage (i.e., of sleep).

178. "wheel": the medieval image of Fortune as a giant wheel, continually revolving, to which the members of humanity cling; it occurs frequently in Shakespeare's plays.

1. "proclaimed": i.e., as a criminal.

2. "happy": lucky.

5. "attend my taking": attempt my capture.

6-7. "am bethought . . . take": have decided to take.

10. "elf": elves were held to knot the manes of horses into 'elf locks'.

11. "presented": exposed.

KING LEAR

ACT II SCENE III

he gladly puts himself to, only to make you believe he is out of his wits. He calls himself by the name of Poor Tom, and coming near anybody cries out, 'Poor Tom is a-cold.' " The resemblance to Edgar's impersonation is remarkable.

ACT II SCENE IV

In this long and important scene, which ends Act II and brings us to one of the climaxes of the play, there is a brutally direct confrontation between the father and his elder daughter. Lear (and the audience) learn the depth of Goneril and Regan's hardness.

The scene opens before Gloucester's castle, with Lear discovering Kent in the stocks. The dialogue from 11 to 21, with the repetition of assertion and denial on the part of Kent and Lear, illustrates the stubbornness of Lear's misunderstanding of his situation, and of the nature of the forces that are replacing him in authority.

The Fool sees his earlier line—"Truth's a dog must to kennel; he must be whipped out"—born out by the sight of Kent in the stocks. The Fool's laughter at Kent (7-11) has in it an undercurrent of meaning for the whole play, for the imagery is again drawn from the animal world. Horses, dogs, bears, and monkeys are the animals that occur to the Fool, and we are reminded that in the world of Goneril and Regan men behave, and are therefore treated, as though they were animals. The Fool has a good deal to say in the earlier part of the scene, and his role is again that of a kind of chorus, or commentator. As usual, he is the one to point out the danger Lear is in; he understands the Machiavellian world of which Lear is only beginning to have an inkling. He rebukes Kent's obtuseness in asking why the King's support has been reduced: "there's not a nose among twenty but can smell him htat's stinking." The first of his little songs (47-52) reduces parental relationships to matters of money and power with a cynicism worthy of Edmund. it is rich parents who have "kind" children. The second song (76-83, and see glossary) looks forward to Lear in the storm. Here the Fool also comments, by implication, on his own curious position—divided between love for Lear on the one

---

The winds and persecutions of the sky.
The country gives me proof and precedent   13
Of Bedlam beggars, who, with roaring voices,   14
Strike in their numbed and mortified bare arms   15
Pins, wooden pricks, nails, sprigs of rosemary;   16
And with this horrible object, from low farms,   17
Poor pelting villages, sheepcotes, and mills,   18
Sometimes with lunatic bans, sometime with prayers,   19
Enforce their charity. Poor Turlygod, poor Tom,   20
That's something yet: Edgar I nothing am.   [*Exit.*

Scene four.

(BEFORE GLOUCESTER'S CASTLE. KENT IN THE STOCKS.)
Enter LEAR, Fool, *and* Gentleman.

Lear. 'Tis strange that they should so depart from   1
     home,
And not send back my messenger.
Gentleman.   As I learned,
The night before there was no purpose in them
Of this remove.   4
Kent.   Hail to thee, noble master.
Lear. Ha!
Mak'st thou this shame thy pastime?
Kent.   No, my lord.
Fool. Ha, ha, he wears cruel garters. Horses   7
are tied by the heads, dogs and bears by th' neck,
monkeys by th' loins, and men by th' legs. When a   9
man's over-lusty at legs, then he wears wooden   10
nether-stocks.
Lear. What's he that hath so much thy place mistook
To set thee here?
Kent.   It is both he and she,
Your son and daughter.
Lear. No.
Kent. Yes.
Lear. No, I say.
Kent. I say yea.
Lear. No, no, they would not.
Kent. Yes, they have.
Lear. By Jupiter, I swear no!
Kent. By Juno, I swear ay!
Lear.   They durst not do't;
They could not, would not do't. 'Tis worse than
     murder
To do upon respect such violent outrage.   24
Resolve me with all modest haste which way   25
Thou mightst deserve or they impose this usage,
Coming from us.   27
Kent.   My lord, when at their home
I did commend your Highness' letters to them,   28

---

13. "proof": an example.

14. "Bedlam": see note at I,ii,140.

15. "strike": stick.
"mortified": deadened to pain.

16. "wooden pricks": skewers.

17. "object": image, appearance.

18. "pelting": petty, small.
19. "lunatic bans": insane curses.

20. "Turlygod": another name for Tom o' Bedlam, possibly from the French 'Turlupin', a comic figure.

21. "nothing am": cease to be.

1. "they": Cornwall and Regan.

4. "remove": change of place.

7. "cruel": i) painful, ii) pun on 'crewel', a material used in making garters.

10. "over-lusty at legs": i.e., in tripping Oswald, and 'kicking' generally.

11. "nether-stocks": lower stockings (breeches were often called 'upper-stocks').

24. "upon respect": deliberately.

25. "Resolve": explain to.
"modest": seemly.

27. "Coming from us": i.e., as Lear's representative.

28. "commend": formally deliver.

KING LEAR

ACT II SCENE IV

hand, and his practical sense of the approaching disaster on the other. The song reflects two standards of values. The first is self-interest; he who "seeks for gain" will naturally flee the storm. The second is that of the loyalty which transcends self-serving, according to which the "wise man" who flees is not, finally, wise, but a fool, since he can apprehend no higher ethical standard than self-love.

These songs and ironic comments by the Fool serve yet another dramatic purpose. Regan and Goneril (unlike Edmund) never comment on their own villainy. There is a certain attraction in Edmund, as we have noted, that arises in part from the fact that he is aware of what he is doing, has consciously chosen his line of evil action, and feels himself, however wrongly, justified in it. There is no such self-knowledge, and therefore no such attraction on the part of the evil sisters. So completely do they lack the moral sense that they are unable to see their own position; this is why Shakespeare gives them no speeches or soliloquies which reveal it to the audience. In a sense it is the Fool who speaks, if not for them, of them, in his half-veiled, bitter comments on the world's cruelty.

Ere I was risen from the place that showed
My duty kneeling, came there a reeking post,   30
Stewed in his haste, half breathless, panting forth   31
From Goneril his mistress salutations;
Delivered letters, spite of intermission,   33
Which presently they read; on whose contents   34
They summoned up their meiny, straight took horse,   35
Commanded me to follow and attend
The leisure of their answer, gave me cold looks;
And meeting here the other messenger,   38
Whose welcome I perceived had poisoned mine,
Being the very fellow which of late
Displayed so saucily against your Highness,   41
Having more man than wit about me, drew;   42
He raised the house with loud and coward cries.
Your son and daughter found this trespass worth
The shame which here it suffers.

Fool. Winter's not gone yet, if the wild geese fly   46
    that way.

      Fathers that wear rags
        Do make their children blind,   48
      But fathers that bear bags   49
        Shall see their children kind.
      Fortune, that arrant whore,   51
      Ne'er turns the key to th' poor.   52
But for all this, thou shalt have as many dolours for   53
thy daughters as thou canst tell in a year.   54
Lear. O, how this mother swells up toward my heart!   55
Hysterica passio, down, thou climbing sorrow;
Thy element's below. Where is this daughter?
Kent. With the Earl, sir, here within.
Lear.   Follow me not;
Stay here.   [*Exit.*
Gentleman. Made you no more offence but what you
    speak of?
Kent. None.
How chance the King comes with so small a number?
Fool. An thou hadst been set i' th' stocks for that
question, thou'dst well deserved it.
Kent. Why, fool?
Fool. We'll set thee to school to an ant, to teach thee
there's no labouring i' th' winter. All that follow   67
their noses are led by their eyes but blind men, and
there's not a nose among twenty but can smell him   69
that's stinking. Let go thy hold when a great wheel   70
runs down a hill, lest it break thy neck with following. But the great one that goes upward, let him
draw thee after. When a wise man gives thee better
counsel, give me mine again. I would have none but   74
knaves follow it since a fool gives it.
      That sir which serves and seeks for gain,
        And follows but for form,   77
      Will pack when it begins to rain   78
        And leave thee in the storm.
      But I will tarry; the fool will stay,
        And let the wise man fly.
      The knave turns fool that runs away;   82
        The fool no knave, perdy.   83
Kent. Where learned you this, fool?
Fool. Not i' th' stocks, fool.

30. "reeking": sweating.

31. "Stewed": steaming.

33. "spite of intermission": despite its being an interruption.

34. "presently": immediately.

35. "meiny": followers, attendants.

38. "And": I understood.

41. "Displayed so saucily": showed such insolent behavior.

42. "more man than wit": more manhood than sense.

46. "Winter's . . . way": proverbial, i.e., we are still in trouble.

48. "blind": i.e., to their father's needs.

49. "bags": of gold.

51. "arrant whore": i.e., because so attached to money.

52. "turns the key": opens the door.

53. "dolours": sorrows, with a pun on 'dollar'.

54. "tell": count.

55-6. "mother . . . Hysterico passio": 'mother' and 'Hysterico passio' were the popular and the Latin terms for hysteria. The usual Elizabethan term was 'the suffocation of the mother', an attack attended by the choking which Lear experiences here. The word hysteria is related to the Greek word for womb, hence the translation 'mother'.

67. "winter": i.e., the ant does not work in the winter, and there will be no laboring, or productivity, in the winter of Lear's adversity.

69-70. "smell . . . stinking": anyone can smell a failure.

70. "great wheel": the image here is of both the wheel of Fortune, and the great man (King Lear) in decline.

74-5. "none but knaves": none but the wicked. Here and elsewhere, the Fool gives a practical criticism of Lear's behavior, but adds that only 'knaves' would follow the practical course and abandon him.

77. "form": appearances' sake.

78. "pack": pack up and go.

82-3. "The knave . . . perdy": "The knave who runs away follows the advice given by a fool; but I, the Fool, shall not follow my own advice by turning knave" (Bradley).

83. "perdy": from the French PAR DIEU, by God.

KING LEAR

ACT II SCENE IV

Lear re-enters at 86, and at first he oscillates between anger ("Vengeance, plague, death, confusion!") and an attempt to understand and perhaps forgive ("May be he is not well"). We know perfectly well—and the Fool has warned Lear—that Regan and Goneril are of the same mind ("She's as like this as a crab's like an apple"-I,v,15), and we know that the excuses of "They are sick, they are weary,/They have travelled all night" are just what Lear first recognizes them to be—"the images of revolt and flying off." Lear's attempt to convince himself that all is really well is pathetic, but there is greater pathos in his assumption of Regan's love for him that follows at 126. This speech, with its repetition of his daughter's name ("Regan . . . Beloved Regan . . . O Regan!") is delivered, on the stage, to a stiff and stony-faced figure; we wait for her reply, and Lear's disillusionment. It comes in a speech (138-142) delivered in Regan's typical phrasing, self assured, cold, and so impersonal and complicated as to syntax that Lear himself cannot follow it ("Say, How is that?"). The official, euphemistic language is removed from any direct or heartfelt statement, but as Lear presses, Regan becomes more direct. "O sir, you are old" brings us close to her real meaning. It is not reverence for age but its reverse, contempt, that she exhibits. Lear catches at least this much of her meaning and it induces him to perform the little parody at 151-153. In the phrase "Age is unnecessary" Lear exactly sums up the sisters' point of view. As with Edmund in his deification of the "natural," "whatever is, is right." The weakness of the aged is a fact, and they concern themselves only with facts, not with moral sentiments or obligations. There is a forthright statement of the view at 198: "being weak, seem so." There is a further irony, however, in Lear's bitter mock-prayer to Regan. He has every reason to ask forgiveness of a daughter, but not this one. Lear is still unregenerate, and knows himself and his situation "but slenderly"; the suffering that brings knowledge has yet to come, but Lear will ultimately kneel to Cordelia to ask her forgiveness. A further ele-

Enter LEAR *and* GLOUCESTER.

Lear. Deny to speak with me? They are sick, they
    are weary?
They have travelled all the night? Mere fetches,   87
The images of revolt and flying off!   88
Fetch me a better answer.
Gloucester.   My dear lord,
You know the fiery quality of the Duke,
How unremovable and fixed he is
In his own course.
Lear.   Vengeance, plague, death, confusion!
Fiery? What quality? Why, Gloucester, Gloucester,
I'ld speak with the Duke of Cornwall and his wife.
Gloucester. Well, my good lord, I have informed
    them so.
Lear. Informed them? Dost thou understand me,
    man?
Gloucester. Ay, my good lord.
Lear. The King would speak with Cornwall. The
dear father
Would with his daughter speak, commands —   99
    tends — service.
Are they informed of this? My breath and blood!
Fiery? The fiery Duke, tell the hot Duke that —
No, but not yet. May be he is not well.
Infirmity doth still neglect all office
Whereto our health is bound. We are not ourselves 104
When nature, being oppressed, commands the mind
To suffer with the body. I'll forbear;
And am fallen out with my more headier will   107
To take the indisposed and sickly fit
For the sound man. — Death on my state. Wherefore
Should he sit here? This act persuades me   110
That this remotion of the Duke and her   111
Is practice only. Give me my servant forth.   112
Go tell the Duke and's wife I'ld speak with them!
Now, presently! Bid them come forth and hear me, 114
Or at their chamber door I'll beat the drum
Till it cry sleep to death.   116
Gloucester. I would have all well betwixt you.
                          [*Exit.*
Lear. O me, my heart, my rising heart! But down!
Fool. Cry to it, nuncle, as the cockney did to the 119
eels when she put 'em i' th' paste alive. She knapped 120
'em o' th' coxcombs with a stick and cried, 'Down, 121
wantons, down!' 'Twas her brother that, in pure 122
kindness to his horse, buttered his hay.   123

Enter CORNWALL, REGAN, GLOUCESTER, Servants.

Lear. Good morrow to you both.
Cornwall.   Hail to your Grace
               [KENT *here set at liberty.*
Regan. I am glad to see your Highness.
Lear. Regan, I think you are. I know what reason
I have to think so. If thou shouldst not be glad,
I would divorce me from thy mother's womb,   128
Sepulchring an adultress. [*to Kent*] O, are you free?
Some other time for that. — Beloved Regan,
Thy sister 's naught. O Regan, she hath tied
Sharp-toothed unkindness, like a vulture, here.

87. "fetches": excuses.

88. "images": likenesses.

99. "tends": attends, awaits.

104. "Whereto . . . bound": i.e., which we perform in health.

107. "headier": headstrong.

110. "he": Kent.

111. "remotion": removal, remaining away.

112. "practice": trickery.

114. "presently": at once.

116. "cry . . . death": kill sleep with crying.

119. "cockney": means both city-dweller and cook.

120. "paste": pastry.
"knapped": knocked.

122. "wantons": unruly creatures.

123. "buttered his hay": since the horse would not eat grease, an example of misplaced kindness.

128-9. "I would . . . adultress": i.e., he is not Goneril's father.

42

KING LEAR

ACT II SCENE IV

ment of pathos, and also evidence of Lear's continuing ignorance of his daughters, and of the whole world of REALPOLITIK in which he is caught, comes in his fond belief that the gift of I,i, has won Regan's love: "Thy hald o' the kingdom thou hast not forgot,/ Wherein I thee endowed." We saw in I,i, that Lear's mistake was to imagine that love was a commodity that could be bargained for, and that his rage with Cordelia was just because of her insistence on love as a spiritual non-negotiable thing. Here he repeats that piece of moral blindness with Regan.

At two points in this segment of the scene, however, Lear shows some apprehension of the real meaning of his relation to his daughters. At 175 he speaks of "the offices of nature, bond of childhood" that he assumes must bind Regan to him. "Bond" was also the word Cordelia used in I,i, and it sums up the moral obligations which ought to make the family, the society, and indeed all human relationships more than simply material, selfish and competitive ones. Naturally Regan is outside any such conception, but Lear's pain, though he does not see this altogether clearly himself, arises from the abrogation of this sacred bond on the part of his elder daughters. His second insight lies in his acknowledgement of his own relation to these daughters, here specifically to Goneril, in the speech beginning at 215. The phrasing suggests that

I can scarce speak to thee. Thou'lt not believe
With how depraved a quality — O Regan!   134
  Regan. I pray you, sir, take patience. I have hope   135
You less know how to value her desert
Than she to scant her duty.
  Lear.   Say, how is that?
  Regan. I cannot think my sister in the least
Would fail her obligation. If, sir, perchance
She have restrained the riots of your followers,
'Tis on such ground, and to such wholesome end,
As clears her from all blame.
  Lear. My curses on her!
  Regan.   O, sir, you are old;
Nature in you stands on the very verge   144
Of his confine. You should be ruled, and led
By some discretion that discerns your state   146
Better than you yourself. Therefore I pray you
That to our sister you do make return;
Say you have wronged her.
  Lear.   Ask her forgiveness?
Do you but mark how this becomes the house: 150
'Dear daughter, I confess that I am old.   [*Kneels.*
Age is unnecessary. On my knees I beg
That you'll vouchsafe me raiment, bed, and food."
  Regan. Good sir, no more. These are unsightly
    tricks.
Return you to my sister.
  Lear.   [*rises*] Never, Regan
She hath abated me of half my train,   156
Looked black upon me, struck me with her tongue
Most serpent-like upon the very heart.
All the stored vengeances of heaven fall
On her ingrateful top! Strike her young bones,
You taking airs, with lameness.   161
  Cornwall.   Fie, sir, fie!
  Lear. You nimble lightnings, dart your blinding
    flames
Into her scornful eyes! Infect her beauty,
You fen-sucked fogs drawn by the pow'rful sun   164
To fall and blister.   165
  Regan.   O the blest gods!
So will you wish on me when the rash mood is on.
  Lear. No, Regan, thou shalt never have my curse.
Thy tender-hefted nature shall not give   168
Thee o'er to harshness. Her eyes are fierce, but thine
Do comfort, and not burn. 'Tis not in thee
To grudge my pleasures, to cut off my train,
To bandy hasty words, to scant my sizes,
And, in conclusion, to oppose the bolt   173
Against my coming in. Thou better know'st
The offices of nature, bond of childhood,   175
Effects of courtesy, dues of gratitude.
Thy half o' th' kingdom hast thou not forgot,
Wherein I thee endowed.
  Regan.   Good sir, to th' purpose.
                          [*Tucket within.* s.d.
  Lear. Who put my man i' th' stocks?
  Cornwall.   What trumpet's that?
  Regan. I know't — my sister's. This approves her   180
    letter,
That she would soon be here.

134. "quality": manner.

135-7. "I have . . . duty": Regan hopes— or thinks—that Lear is less capable of appreciating Goneril's merits, than Goneril is of falling short in her duty to him. It is, and is meant to be, a formal and complicated statement which will confuse Lear; hence his next line.

144-5. "very verge . . . confine": i.e., your life is nearly ended.

146-7. "some discretion . . . yourself": i.e., someone who understands your position better than you do.

150. "the house": the royal household.

156. "abated": taken away.

161. "taking": infectious, carrying diseases that 'take' people.

164. "fen-sucked": arising out of swamps.

165. "fall and blister": strike and make corrupt, blister with disease.

168. "tender-hefted": gentle.

173. "oppose the bolt": i.e., bolt the door.

175. "offices of nature": natural, filial duties.

Stage Direction "tucket": trumpet signalling someone's approach.

180. "approves": confirms.

KING LEAR

ACT II SCENE IV

the realization comes almost as a surprise to Lear himself—he says, wonderingly, "but yet thou art my flesh, my blood, my daughter." The recognition of this kinship involves guilt on Lear's part—Goneril is a "disease" in his "corrupted blood"—but Lear is shown here as recognizing just that which the daughters cannot recognize, the connection between father and daughter on which moral obligation (such as Lear's guilt) depends. Although Goneril is evil, Lear sees that she is "what I must call mine." This is a bond that surpasses the "natural" relationship of the amoral world which the evil daughters inhabit.

The debate concerning the number of Lear's retainers may seem to have a minor, and even petty subject, yet it dramatically focuses the conflict between Lear and his daughters. The number of knights is of token or symbolic importance, as both parties to the debate realize. What is at stake is the quality of the daughters' love for Lear. He speaks still in the childish terms of the 'love contest' of I,i; when Regan diminishes the troop to twenty-five he turns again to Goneril: "I'll go with thee. /Thy fifty yet doth double five-and-twenty,/And thou art twice her love." Love is still a matter of measurable, material value.

Notice the way in which the sisters' dialogue proceeds as a kind of duet, gradually increasing the pressure on the old king: "What, fifty followers? . . . What should you need of more? . . . bring but five-and-twenty. To no more/Will I give place . . . No more with me . . . What need you five-and-twenty? Ten? or five?" It is a solid, steady cutting-away of Lear's faith in their love. On the stage it is a dramatic crescendo to the final "What need one?"

Enter OSWALD.

Is your lady come?

Lear. This is a slave, whose easy-borrowed pride 182
Dwells in the fickle grace of her he follows. 183
Out, varlet, from my sight. 184
Cornwall.   What means your Grace?

Lear. Who stocked my servant? Regan, I have good
    hope
Thou didst not know on't.

Enter GONERIL.

Who comes here? O heavens!
If you do love old men, if your sweet sway
Allow obedience, if you yourselves are old, 188
Make it your cause. Send down, and take my part.
[*To Goneril*] Art not ashamed to look upon this
    beard?
O Regan, will you take her by the hand?
Goneril. Why not by th' hand, sir? How have I
    offended?
All's not offence that indiscretion finds 193
And dotage terms so.
Lear.   O sides, you are too tough! 194
Will you yet hold? How came my man i' th' stocks?
Cornwall. I set him there, sir; but his own disorders
Deserved much less advancement. 197
Lear.   You? Did you?
Regan. I pray you, father, being weak, seem so
If till the expiration of your month
You will return and sojourn with my sister,
Dismissing half your train, come then to me.
I am now from home, and out of that provision
Which shall be needful for your entertainment. 203

Lear. Return to her, and fifty men dismissed?
No, rather I abjure all roofs, and choose
To wage against the enmity o' th' air,
To be a comrade with the wolf and owl,
Necessity's sharp pinch. Return with her? 208
Why, the hot-blooded France, that dowerless took
Our youngest born, I could as well be brought
To knee his throne, and, squire-like, pension beg 211
To keep base life afoot. Return with her?
Persuade me rather to be slave and sumpter 213
To this detested groom. 214
Goneril.   At your choice, sir.
Lear. I prithee, daughter, do not make me mad.
I will not trouble thee, my child; farewell.
We'll no more meet, no more see one another.
But yet thou art my flesh, my blood, my daughter;
Or rather a disease that's in my flesh,
Which I must needs call mine. Thou art a boil,
A plague-sore, or embossed carbuncle 221
In my corrupted blood. But I'll not chide thee.
Let shame come when it will, I do not call it.
I do not bid the thunder-bearer shoot, 224
Nor tell tales of thee to high-judging Jove. 225
Mend when thou canst, be better at thy leisure;
I can be patient, I can stay with Regan,
I and my hundred knights.

182. "easy-borrowed": assumed with no justification.

183. "grace": favor.

184. "varlet": low person.

188. "Allow": approves of.

193. "indiscretion": bad judgment.

194. "sides": commonly used for breast, or body; Lear means that his body ought not to be able to contain his emotion.

197. "advancement": promotion.

203. "entertainment": provision.

208. "Necessity's sharp pinch": i.e., the pain which the needy are forced to suffer.

211. "knee": kneel to.
    "squire-like": like a dependent.

213. "sumpter": packhorse.

214. "groom": i.e., Oswald.

221. "embossed": swollen.

224. "thunder-bearer": the god Jupiter.

225. "high-judging": judging from on high.

KING LEAR

ACT II SCENE IV

This produces Lear's great speech at 261 to which special attention ought to be given. It begins with another of those phrases which are central to the meaning of the play—"O reason not the need!" Ostensibly Regan and Goneril have been arguing about the number of followers their father will be allowed, but in fact the subject is how much love they need give, or waste, on their father. There is thus a parallel between this scene and I,i. There Lear was dispensing his love in terms of land, which the daughters had to 'earn' by the amount of rhetoric with which they could vow their love for him. Here the daughters are dispensing love in terms of the followers they will allow Lear. In both cases love is treated as a commodity. In this scene it is a material thing that can be estimated according to material needs. They "reason" Lear's "need" and find it does not really exist. Given their own assumptions, the daughters are logical enough. Lear does not, in actual fact, need his hundred followers for his survival. But to see Lear's situation in this way is to see it as less than human, as the situation of an animal, who needs only the basic necessities of food and shelter. To "reason" the "need," then, is to reduce Lear's situation to a subhuman one—something that Regan and Goneril are quite prepared to do. This is the first point that Lear makes: to deal with human beings simply in terms of material "need" is to make them "cheap as beasts." He then points to the daughters (Lear's "gorgeous" indicates that, on the stage, they should be brilliantly costumed) and asks whether they consider themselves simply in terms of "need." He breaks off here, with the thought only partly developed, but the point has been made. It is the sisters who decide what "need" is, in terms of animal function in the case of others, in terms of what is "gorgeous" in their own.

Lear cries for patience, and the actor ought to suggest the terrible pressure he labours under. If the figure of Lear is not to degenerate into a ranting old man, he must be shown as trying heroically to control himself, making the rages and madness which he does give way to, or which overcome him, all the more moving. Here the effort to reason with the daughters has been too much and, perceiving their absolute intransigence, he breaks down into incoherent threats: "I will do such things/ What they are yet, I know not, but they shall be/The terrors of the earth."

Regan.   Not altogether so.
I looked not for you yet, nor am provided
For your fit welcome. Give ear, sir, to my sister;
For those that mingle reason with your passion   231
Must be content to think you old, and so —
But she knows what she does.
Lear.   Is this well spoken?

Regan. I dare avouch it, sir. What, fifty followers? 234
Is it not well? What should you need of more?
Yea, or so many, sith that both charge and danger   236
Speak 'gainst so great a number? How in one house
Should many people, under two commands,
Hold amity? 'Tis hard, almost impossible.
Goneril. Why might not you, my lord, receive attendance
From those that she calls servants, or from mine?
Regan. Why not, my lord? If then they chanced to   242
    slack ye,
We could control them. If you will come to me
(For now I spy a danger), I entreat you
To bring but five-and-twenty. To no more
Will I give place or notice.
Lear. I gave you all.
Regan.   And in good time you gave it. 247
Lear. Made you my guardians, my depositaries,
But kept a reservation to be followed   249
With such a number. What, must I come to you
With five-and-twenty? Regan, said you so?
Regan. And speak't again, my lord. No more with
    me.
Lear. Those wicked creatures yet do look well-
    favoured
When others are more wicked; not being the worst
Stands in some rank of praise. [*to Goneril*] I'll go 255
    with thee.
Thy fifty yet doth double five-and-twenty,
And thou art twice her love.
Goneril.   Hear me, my lord.
What need you five-and-twenty? ten? or five?
To follow in a house where twice so many
Have a command to tend you?
Regan.   What need one?
Lear. O reason not the need! Our basest beggars   261
Are in the poorest thing superfluous.   262
Allow not nature more than nature needs,   263
Man's life is cheap as beast's. Thou art a lady:
If only to go warm were gorgeous,   265
Why, nature needs not what thou gorgeous wear'st,
Which scarcely keeps thee warm. But, for true
    need —
You heavens, give me that patience, patience I need.
You see me here, you gods, a poor old man,
As full of grief as age, wretched in both.
If it be you that stirs these daughters' hearts
Against their father, fool me not so much   272
To bear it tamely; touch me with noble anger,
And let not women's weapons, water drops,
Stain my man's cheeks. No, you unnatural hags!
I will have such revenges on you both
That all the world shall — I will do such things —

231. "mingle . . . passion": bring reason to bear on your passion.

234. "I dare . . . sir": I will swear by it.

236. "charge and danger": the expense, and the danger of a disturbance.

242. "slack": be slack in service.

247. "good time": just in time; Regan continues to suggest that Lear is senile.

249. "kept a reservation": made it a condition.

255. "Stands . . . praise": is to some small extent praiseworthy (i.e., Goneril is at least better than Regan).

261. "reason": reason about, analyze.

262. "Are . . . superfluous": have at least something which is dispensable, not absolutely necessary.

263. "Allow not": i.e., if one does not allow.

265-6. "If . . . thee warm": "If to be warmly dressed were to be gorgeously dressed, nature would have no use for your fine clothing which, flimsy as it is, scarcely keeps you warm" (F.E. Budd).

272. "fool": mislead.

45

KING LEAR

ACT II SCENE IV

Lear's exit line (283) again suggests his approaching madness, as does the ominous stage direction 'Storm and tempest'; storm and madness are closely related in the play. His line "O fool, I shall go mad!" is powerful enough by itself, but it is given added pathos by contrast to the language of those Lear leaves on the stage. They speak in the flat, unmoved accents of the totally insensitive: "Let us withdraw; 'twill be a storm." To this line Regan answers with the complete self-righteousness of the morally stunted: "This house is little; the old man and 's people/Cannot be well bestowed." Cornwall's last line ends the scene perfectly in its icy inhumanity: "Come out o' th' storm". The two factions are now divided physically, and in a way which is symbolic. Lear, the Fool and Kent have been sent, unprotected, into the open. Goneril, Regan, Edmund and Cornwall are within, the new "court party" secure in its power: "truth must be whipped out when the Lady Brach may stand by the fire and stink."

What they are, yet I know not; but they shall be
The terrors of the earth. You think I'll weep.
No, I'll not weep.   [*Storm and tempest.*
I have full cause of weeping, but this heart
Shall break into a hundred thousand flaws   282
Or ere I'll weep. O fool, I shall go mad!
     [*Exeunt* LEAR, Fool, KENT, *and* GLOUCESTER.
Cornwall. Let us withdraw; 'twill be a storm.
Regan. This house is little; the old man and 's people
Cannot be well bestowed.
Goneril. 'Tis his own blame; hath put himself from 287
rest
And must needs taste his folly.
Regan. For his particular, I'll receive him gladly 289
But not one follower.
Goneril.   So am I purposed.
Where is my Lord of Gloucester?
Cornwall. Followed the old man forth.

Enter GLOUCESTER.

              He is returned.
Gloucester. The King is in high rage.
Cornwall.   Whither is he going?
Gloucester. He calls to horse, but will I know not whither.
Cornwall. 'Tis best to give him way; he leads him- 295
self.
Goneril. My lord, entreat him by no means to stay.
Gloucester. Alack, the night comes on, and the bleak winds
Do sorely ruffle. For many miles about
There's scarce a bush.
Regan.   O, sir, to willful men
The injuries that they themselves procure
Must be their schoolmasters. Shut up your doors.
He is attended with a desperate train,
And what they may incense him to, being apt   303
To have his ear abused, wisdom bids fear.
Cornwall. Shut up your doors, my lord; 'tis a wild night.
My Regan counsels well. Come out o' th' storm.
                   [*Exeunt.*

282. "flaws": pieces, fragments.

287. "from rest": away from where he might rest.

289. "his particular": himself.

295. "give him way": let him be.

303-4. "apt . . . abused": ready to listen to bad advice.

46

KING LEAR

ACT III SCENE I

The central portion of the play is largely an account of Lear's suffering. Lear "contending with the fretful elements"—the storm—is a particularly difficult thing to stage. As Charles Lamb pointed out, we are very liable to see only "an old man tottering about the stage with a walking stick . . . on a rainy night." Therefore to prepare us for the spectacle of Lear in the storm Shakespeare introduces this compact and vivid account by the anonymous "gentleman." The storm itself is of great symbolic importance. Shakespeare uses storm frequently in his plays to signify some sort of violent crisis or upset. Macbeth's murder of Duncan is accompanied by a storm, as is Brutus' preparation for the murder of Caesar. In both cases the disorder in the elements indicates a disorder in the character, and in the society. Thus the storm here is not just a background for Lear's suffering, as 'mood music' might be on our stage. Harmony and order have been destroyed, not only in one m.., but in the family and society. Disorder is general, and the disorder of nature—the storm is a part of the general upheaval. The "gentleman's" line about "the little world of man" reflects the belief that man, and society, were an intimate part of the whole creation. Man was the "microcosm," the "little world" which reflected the "macrocosm," or universe. Therefore, dramatically, an upheaval in one might be represented by an upheaval in the other. Lamb's criticism applies to modern audiences, but the Elizabethan theatre-goer would understand that, despite the lack of realistic storm-effects on the stage, the indication of a storm (probably a piece of metal beaten offstage) was meant to suggest the fierceness of the tumult both in Lear and in the whole society of the play.

ACT THREE, scene one.

(A Heath.)

Storm still. Enter KENT *and a* Gentleman *severally.*

Kent. Who's there besides foul weather?

Gentleman. One minded like the weather, most unquietly.

Kent. I know you. Where's the King?

Gentleman. Contending with the fretful elements; 4
Bids the wind blow the earth into the sea,
Or swell the curled waters 'bove the main, 6
That things might change or cease; tears his white hair,
Which the impetuous blasts, with eyeless rage, 8
Catch in their fury and make nothing of;
Strives in his little world of man to outscorn 10
The to-and-fro-conflicting wind and rain.
This night, wherein the cub-drawn bear would 12
couch,
The lion and the belly-pinched wolf
Keep their fur dry, unbonneted he runs, 14
And bids what will take all. 15

Kent.　　　　　　　　　But who is with him?

Gentleman. None but the fool, who labours to outjest
His heart-struck injuries.

Kent.　　　　　　　　　Sir, I do know you,
And dare upon the warrant of my note 18
Commend a dear thing to you. There is division, 19
Although as yet the face of it is covered
With mutual cunning, 'twixt Albany and Cornwall;
Who have — as who have not, that their great stars 22
Throned and set high?—servants, who seem no less, 23
Which are to France the spies and speculations 24
Intelligent of our state. What hath been seen, 25
Either in snuffs and packings of the Dukes, 26
Or the hard rein which both of them have borne
Against the old kind King, or something deeper,
Whereof, perchance, these are but furnishings — 29
But, true it is, from France there comes a power
Into this scattered kingdom, who already, 31
Wise in our negligence, have secret feet 32
In some of our best ports and are at point
To show their open banner. Now to you:
If on my credit you dare build so far 35
To make your speed to Dover, you shall find
Some that will thank you, making just report
Of how unnatural and bemadding sorrow
The King hath cause to plain. 39
I am a gentleman of blood and breeding,
And from some knowledge and assurance offer
This office to you.

Gentleman. I will talk further with you.

Kent.　　　　　　　　　No, do not.
For confirmation that I am much more
Than my out-wall, open this purse and take 45

4. "Contending": quarreling.

6. "main": the mainland.

8. "eyeless": invisible.

10. "little world of man": "the microcosm, an astrological term meaning the earth, but often applied to man himself as the embodiment in miniature of the elements of the macrocosm, or universe" (Budd). The storm in Lear's mind parallels the storm in nature (see commentary).

12. "cub-drawn": sucked dry by her cubs and hence hungry.

14. "unbonneted": bare-headed.

15. "take all": the gambler's cry on staking the last of his money.

18. "warrant of my note": evidence of what I see (in you).

19. "Commend": entrust.

22. "that their great stars": who have their destines.

23. "Throned": exalted, made powerful. "who . . . less": i.e., who seem to be what they are.

24. "speculations": informers.

25. "Intelligent": i.e., who give intelligence of.

26. "snuffs and packings": the quarrelling and plotting.

29. "furnishings": pretexts, excuses.

31. scattered": divided.

32. "Wise . . . feet": i.e., taking advantage of our negligence, have landed secret forces.

35. "my credit": your trust in me.

39. "plain": lament.

45. "out-wall": external appearance.

KING LEAR

ACT III SCENE I

The scene also anticipates Cordelia's return. At the same time that the triumph of the evil party is confirmed a counter-movement begins, the climax of which will occur in the reunion of Lear and Cordelia, and Lear's return to sanity.

ACT III SCENE II

The scene opens with one of Lear's most reverberating and torrential speeches. The actor must again be careful; the temptation is to start the scene at the top of the voice, leaving him, vocally, fully extended at line 9, although there are three more powerful speeches to come. The speech is a fine example of Shakespeare's mastery of the technique of spoken, or dramatic, poetry. Although the text has full stops at the ends of lines 1 and 6 (probably inserted by early printers) there is no real stop, or pause, in the delivery of the speech between the opening shout of "Blow, winds, and crack your cheeks" to the phrase "Singe my white head" of line 6. This pause is only to allow the actor to take breath, since it is immediately followed by another long, continuing sentence from "And thou, all-shaking thunder" down to "That makes ingrateful man." We must always try to imagine any speech as it should be given from the stage, but even reading this one in silence we get the impression of a cascade of language, of words and phrases that seem to tumble over one another ("cataracts and hurricanoes . . . sulph'rous and thought-executing . . . Vaunt-couriers . . . oak-cleaving thunderbolts") in such a way that it is impossible to imagine the speech given in anything but a rage verging on hysteria. The preceding scene's description of the half-maddened Lear who "Bids the wind blow the earth into the sea" now confronts us on the stage. The Elizabethan stage's lack of technical devices of light and sound for reproducing the storm do not matter here. Lear's language, in its volcanic fury, creates the storm for us.

There is meaning, as well as sound and fury, in the opening speech. Lear identifies himself with the storm as a destructive force.

What it contains. If you shall see Cordelia,
As fear not but you shall, show her this ring,
And she will tell you who that fellow is
That yet you do not know. Fie on this storm!
I will go seek the King.
    Gentleman. Give me your hand. Have you no more
      to say?
    Kent. Few words, but, to effect, more than all yet: 52
That when we have found the King — in which your 53
    pain
That way, I'll this — he that first lights on him
Holla the other.   [*Exeunt.*

Scene two.

(ANOTHER PART OF THE HEATH.)

Storm still. Enter LEAR *and* Fool.

Lear. Blow, winds, and crack your cheeks. Rage,
    blow.
You cataracts and hurricanoes, spout
Till you have drenched our steeples, drowned the 3
    cocks
You sulph'rous and thought-executing fires, 4
Vaunt-couriers to oak-cleaving thunderbolts, 5
Singe my white head. And thou, all-shaking thunder,
Strike flat the thick rotundity o' th' world.
Crack Nature's moulds, all germains spill at once, 8
That makes ingrateful man.
    Fool. O nuncle, court holy-water in a dry house is 10
better than this rain water out o' door. Good nuncle,
in; ask thy daughters' blessing. Here's a night pities
neither wise men nor fools.
    Lear. Rumble thy bellyful. Spit, fire. Spout, rain.
Nor rain, wind, thunder, fire are my daughters.
I tax not you, you elements, with unkindness. 16
I never gave you kingdom, called you children;
You owe me no subscription. Then let fall 18
Your horrible pleasure. Here I stand your slave, 19
A poor, infirm, weak, and despised old man.
But yet I call you servile ministers, 21
That will with two pernicious daughters join
Your high-engendered battles 'gainst a head 23
So old and white as this. O, ho! 'tis foul.
    Fool. He that has a house to put 's head in has a
    good headpiece.
           The codpiece that will house 27
              Before the head has any,
           The head and he shall louse: 29
              So beggars marry many. 30
           The man that makes his toe 31
              What he his heart should make
           Shall of a corn cry woe,
              And turn his sleep to wake.
For there was never yet fair woman but she made
mouths in a glass. 36

52. "to effect": in importance.

53-4. "your pain . . . this": i.e., you go in that direction, I in this.

3. "cocks": weathercocks.

4. "thought-executing": numbing the thought.

5. "Vaunt-couriers": vanguards or messengers.

8. "moulds": forms, patterns. "germains": seeds.

10. "court holy-water": diplomatic or politic behavior; what is used in the court as holy-water is used in church.

16. "tax": accuse.

18. "subscription": loyalty.

19. "pleasure": what you will.

21. "servile": i.e., to Goneril and Regan

23. "high-engendered": exalted, taking place in the heavens.

27. "codpiece": a piece of cloth stitched on to the trunks at the crotch, often slang for phallus.
29. "he": it.

30. "many": i.e., are lousy.

31-4. "toe . . . wake": i.e., the man who prefers a meaner part of his body to the more honorable will regret it.

36. "glass": mirror.

48

KING LEAR

ACT III SCENE II

He wants "Nature's moulds" destroyed, and the word reminds us of Edmund's prayer to "Nature." Edmund saw nature as an amoral force, outside of the "plague of custom" invented by man, and therefore admirable. Lear now sees another aspect of nature—its mindless violence—and in his despair he urges it on in its work of destruction.

The storm also has the effect of forcing Lear into a real consideration of his position, and later (at III,iv,106) into the position of "unaccommodated man" in general. Like most tragic heroes, Lear begins the play secure in the knowledge of his power and place in the world—knowledge which proves to be tragically misguided. His daughters have begun the process of forcing him toward a new appraisal, and the storm completes it. "Here I stand your slave, /A poor, infirm, weak and despised old man" is not a line that the Lear of Act I could have spoken. This is the humility (although it will give way to surges of anger and madness) which is the beginning of knowledge.

The Fool "labours to outjest/ [Lear's] heartstruck injuries." As usual, the Fool takes the line of somewhat soured common sense. Despite his earlier assertions that he "will tarry" in the storm, its violence, which seems to challenge and excite Lear, is too much for him: "Good nuncle, in, ask thy daughter's blessing." The Fool is quite clear on what he is recommending—the hypocrisy of "court holy water" (see glossary) rather than the honesty of open revolt. The brief verse about the "codpiece" (see glossary) which takes precedence over the head is simply an affirmation of the rational view that the wise man attends to the dictates of reason, not passion. But the Fool's common sense carries less and less power as Lear's passion grows toward madness. The suggestions of a Mr. Worldly-Wise, for a good life at any price, for compromise and reasonableness, are out of place in the extremity of spiritual crisis toward which Lear is moving.

For the Fool's prophecy," which ends the scene, see the glossary.

Enter KENT.

Lear. No, I will be the pattern of all patience;
I will say nothing.
    Kent. Who's there?
    Fool. Marry, here's grace and a codpiece; that's a   40
wise man and a fool.
    Kent. Alas, sir, are you here? Things that love
    night
Love not such nights as these. The wrathful skies
Gallow the very wanderers of the dark   44
And make them keep their caves. Since I was man,
Such sheets of fire, such bursts of horrid thunder,
Such groans of roaring wind and rain, I never
Remember to have heard. Man's nature cannot carry
Th' affliction nor the fear.
    Lear.   Let the great gods
That keep this dreadful pudder o'er our heads   50
Find out their enemies now. Tremble, thou wretch,   51
That hast within thee undivulged crimes
Unwhipped of justice. Hide thee, thou bloody hand,
Thou perjured, and thou simular of virtue   54
That art incestuous. Caitiff, to pieces shake,   55
That under covert and convenient seeming
Has practiced on man's life. Close pent-up guilts,   57
Rive your concealing continents and cry   58
These dreadful summoners grace. I am a man   59
More sinned against than sinning.
    Kent.   Alack, bareheaded?
Gracious my lord, hard by here is a hovel;
Some friendship will it lend you 'gainst the tempest.
Repose you there, while I to this hard house   63
(More harder than the stones whereof 'tis raised,
Which even but now, demanding after you,   65
Denied me to come in) return, and force
Their scanted courtesy.   67
    Lear.   My wits begin to turn.
Come on, my boy. How dost, my boy? Art cold?
I am cold myself. Where is this straw, my fellow?
The art of our necessities is strange,   70
And can make vile things precious. Come, your
    hovel,
Poor fool and knave, I have one part in my heart
That's sorry yet for thee.
    Fool. [*sings*]
        He that has and a little tiny wit,   74
          With, heigh-ho, the wind and the rain,
        Must make content with his fortunes fit   76
          Though the rain it raineth every day.
    Lear. True, boy. Come, bring us to this hovel.
                             [*Exit with* KENT.
    Fool. This is a brave night to cool a courtesan. I'll
speak a prophecy ere I go:
When priests are more in word than matter;   81
When brewers mar their malt with water;   82
When nobles are their tailors' tutors,   83
No heretics burned, but wenches' suitors;
When every case in law is right,
No squire in debt nor no poor knight;
When slanders do not live in tongues,
Nor cutpurses come not to throngs;

40. "grace": the king's grace.

44. "Gallow": frighten.

50. "pudder": tumult.

51. "Find . . . now": i.e., discover the godless by their fear.

54. "simular": imitation.

55. "Caitiff": wretch.

57. "practiced": plotted against. "Close": hidden.

58. "Rive": split open. "continents": that which conceals and contains.

59. "grace": pardon.

63. "hard house": cruel household.

65. "demanding after": asking after.

67. "scanted": stingy.
70-1. "art . . . precious": i.e., necessity, like alchemy, can make poor things desirable.
74. "and a": required for the metre, not the sense.
76. "make . . . fit": i.e., must come to terms with his fortunes. The song that the Fool sings here is a variation on a song written by Shakespeare for the clown in the comedy TWELFTH NIGHT; there it had a touch of melancholy, which has increased to bitterness here.
81-95. The Fool's 'prophecy' is regarded by many editors as a non-Shakesperean interpolation, possibly put into the play by the actor who played the Fool. Producers usually have the Fool leave the stage with Kent and Lear, omitting the prophecy. The first four lines refer to present conditions, and the next six to some ideal state of affairs. The last four lines have no apparent relevance to what has gone before. There is, however, an explanation and defence of the speech in Danby's SHAKESPEARE'S DOCTRINE OF NATURE.
81. "more . . . matter": better with words than with thought.
82. "mar": dilute; a common practice.
83. "their tailors' tutors": i.e., spend their time lecturing their tailors' on dress.

KING LEAR

ACT III SCENE III

The purpose of this brief scene is to contrast loyalty and treachery in the persons of Gloucester and Edmund. We have been prepared for Gloucester's commitment to Lear. He has earlier been represented as unintelligent, but in this play intelligence is most frequently associated with evil. Gloucester's moral choice is complete, and arises from love and loyalty, not self-interest. He will stand by Lear, for "If I die for it, as no less is threatened me, the King my old master must be relieved."

Edmund, on the other hand, is represented as the archetypal traitor. Gloucester uses the word "unnatural" and Edmund repeats it, and we must imagine the conscious irony with which he does so on the stage. He has earlier given us his notion of "Nature"; the survival of the fittest, beyond morality. What Gloucester sees as "unnatural," Edmund sees as perfectly natural, as his closing lines show us. "Age" is most certainly "unnecessary" to Edmund, and in his view of the natural law "The younger rises when the old doth fall."

When usurers tell their gold i' th' field, 89
And bawds and whores do churches build —
Then shall the realm of Albion 91
Come to great confusion. 92
Then comes the time, who lives to see't,
That going shall be used with feet. 94
This prophecy Merlin shall make, for I live before 95
his time. [*Exit.*

Scene three.

(A ROOM IN GLOUCESTER'S CASTLE.)

Enter GLOUCESTER *and* EDMUND.

Gloucester. Alack, alack, Edmund, I like not this unnatural dealing. When I desired their leave that I might pity him, they took from me the use of mine 3
own house, charged me on pain of perpetual displeasure neither to speak of him, entreat for him, or any way sustain him.

Edmund. Most savage and unnatural.

Gloucester. Go to; say you nothing. There is division between the Dukes, and a worse matter than 8
that. I have received a letter this night — 'tis dangerous to be spoken — I have locked the letter in my closet. These injuries the King now bears will be revenged home; there is part of a power already footed; we must incline to the King. I will look 14
him and privily relieve him. Go you and maintain 15
talk with the Duke, that my charity be not of him perceived. If he ask for me, I am ill and gone to bed. If I die for it, as no less is threatened me, the King my old master must be relieved. There is strange things toward, Edmund; pray you be 20
careful. [*Exit.*

Edmund. This courtesy forbid thee shall the Duke 22
Instantly know, and of that letter too.
This seems a fair deserving, and must draw me 24
That which my father loses — no less than all.
The younger rises when the old doth fall. [*Exit.*

89. "tell": count.

91. "Albion": England.
92. "confusion": ruin.

94. "going . . . feet": walking will be on foot; a deliberately nonsensical anticlimax.

95. "Merlin": a legendary magician.

3. "pity": show pity to.

8. "division": conflict.

14. "footed": on the march.
"incline to": side with.

15. "privily": secretly.

20. "toward": imminent.

22. "courtesy": aid (to Lear).

24. "fair deserving": an act that deserves approval (from Cornwall).

KING LEAR

ACT III SCENE IV

Some commentators have seen the climax of the play in this scene; it brings together the main plot and the secondary plot (in the person of Gloucester), and it brings Lear to the crisis of his suffering in the storm—his madness. It also shows us Lear both as a particular, individual human being, and as something larger. He is a tragic hero who is also a representative or symbol of human suffering generally: "Lear now clearly assumes a stature that is more than merely personal, he becomes man . . . exposed to a suffering to which the frame of things contributes" (Traversi).

Lear himself makes the point that the storm is, for him, an internal, spiritual crisis—the "tempest in my mind"—rather than simply the physical upheaval which "invades us to the skin." Again he feels the threat of insanity, "O that way madness lies; let me shun that," yet at the same time he is determined to outlast both the storm in nature and the storm in his own mind—"Pour on; I will endure." From this point and until the end of the play the language which Shakespeare gives to Lear suggests both the almost unbearable strain under which he labors, and the great power of his will. If Lear were simply a "poor, infirm, weak and despised old man," as he calls himself at III,ii,20, he would indeed be a pitiful figure, but not quite tragic. For tragedy demands a hero who has, in whatever form, great power and dignity. Although Lear is defeated at the end, as the tragic hero must be, he shows both power and dignity in his will to endure in the face of the tumult taking place both in the outer world and in his own mind.

At 26 we see another development in Lear, in his prayer for the "houseless poverty" and "poor naked wretches" in the storm. Until now Lear's great spirit has issued in pungent and savage attacks—his anger has been personal and limited. But as Traversi in the quotation above points out, Lear in his suffering comes to be a representative of mankind, and now his feeling is not simply for himself, but for suffering in general. This ability to realize the sufferings of others beside himself constitutes an enlargement of spirit; he has learned that suffering is not simply his own special possession; he has learned, in fact, "to feel what wretches feel." There is a point in Coleridge's 'The Rime of the Ancient Mariner' which is analogous to this. The Mariner has killed the

Scene four.

(The Heath, before a Hovel.)

Enter LEAR, KENT, *and* Fool.)

Kent. Here is the place, my lord. Good my lord, enter.
The tyranny of the open night's too rough
For nature to endure.   [*Storm still.*
Lear.   Let me alone.
Kent. Good my lord, enter here.
Lear.   Wilt break my heart?   4
Kent. I had rather break mine own. Good my lord, enter.
Lear. Thou think'st 'tis much that this contentious storm
Invades us to the skin. So 'tis to thee,
But where the greater malady is fixed
The lesser is scarce felt. Thou'dst shun a bear;
But if thy flight lay toward the roaring sea,
Thou'dst meet the bear i' th' mouth. When the   11
    mind's free,
The body's delicate. The tempest in my mind   12
Doth from my senses take all feeling else
Save what beats there. Filial ingratitude,
Is it not as this mouth should tear this hand
For lifting food to't? But I will punish home.   16
No, I will weep no more. In such a night
To shut me out! Pour on; I will endure.
In such a night as this! O Regan, Goneril,
Your old kind father, whose frank heart gave all — 20
O, that way madness lies; let me shun that.
No more of that.
Kent.   Good my lord, enter here.
Lear. Prithee go in thyself; seek thin own ease.
This tempest will not give me leave to ponder
On things would hurt me more, but I'll go in.
[*To the Fool*] In, boy; go first. You houseless poverty —
Nay, get thee in. I'll pray, and then I'll sleep.
                    [*Exit Fool.*

Poor naked wretches, wheresoe'er you are,
That bide the pelting of this pitiless storm,
How shall your houseless heads and unfed sides,
Your looped and windowed raggedness, defend you   31
From seasons such as these? O, I have ta'en
Too little care of this! Take physic, pomp;   33
Expose thyself to feel what wretches feel,
That thou mayst shake the superflux to them   35
And show the heavens more just.
Edgar. [*within*]Fathom and half, fathom and half! 37
Poor Tom!

51

4. "Wilt . . . heart": i.e., physical distress has distracted Lear from his heartbreak.

11. "i' th' mouth": in face to face struggle.
"free": untroubled.

12. "delicate": sensitive to pain.

16. "home": to the root of the evil.

20. "frank": open, generous.

31. "looped": loopholed.

33. "physic": medicine.
"pomp": grandeur, pomposity (personified).

35. "superflux": i.e., that which you find superfluous.

37. "Fathom and half": sailor's shout in taking soundings; Tom's apparently nonsensical remarks are often appropriate, as this one is to the rain and the storm.

KING LEAR

ACT III SCENE IV

albatross, that is, he has committed a crime against nature, for which the albatross is hung around his neck by his crew-mates. Later, at the height of his suffering, and in the grip of terrifying illusions that are not unlike Lear's, the Mariner suddenly notices the sea creatures which surround his ship: "A spring of love gushed from my heart/ And I blessed them unaware." This act of love, coming from the sense of his involvement with other living creatures, in a mysterious way removes the curse from the Mariner, and the albatross falls from his neck. Both the Mariner and Lear have sinned, and both are punished in an extreme way; at the height of their sufferings both are able to re-establish, through an act of selfless prayer, their connection with the world of man (in Lear's case), and nature generally (in the Mariner's). For Lear, of course, this does not terminate the period of pugatorial suffering, which must continue until his reunion with Cordelia, and his death. But it does make Lear less the private and individual sufferer, and more the representative of human suffering in general.

At the end of Lear's speech to the "Poor naked wretches" we are confronted with Edgar in the disguise of Tom o' Bedlam, "poor Tom," who is the embodiment of the wretchedness Lear has spoken of. We have already noticed the significance of Edgar's disguise. He is the complete outcast, and it is therefore dramatically proper that Lear be brought face to face with him at this point of Lear's greatest distance from the well-being of the court and society. Lear immediately sees the Bedlam wanderer as sharing his own plight —"Didst thou give all to thy daughters? And art thou come to this?" A. C. Bradley has said that we may take these lines as the beginning of Lear's own madness, but there are two qualifications that ought to be made to this: i) Lear's madness is not something that begins at any precise point, but rather occurs increasingly from his violence on the heath, to the point at which he enters, according to the stage direction, "mad, bedecked with wild flowers," at IV,vi,80; and he ranges between sanity and insanity throughout; ii) Lear's talk with "poor Tom," although technically 'mad', shows, as all such conditions do in Shakespeare's plays, remarkable instances of intuitive insight; the dramatic power of the exchanges between Lear and "poor Tom" arises from the fact that although both are irrational, both say things that exhibit intense imaginative insight concerning the themes of the play.

Enter Fool.

Fool. Come not in here, nuncle; here's a spirit. Help me, help me!

Kent. Give me thy hand. Who's there?

Fool. A spirit, a spirit. He says his name's poor Tom.

Kent. What art thou that dost grumble there i' th' straw?
Come forth.

Enter EDGAR *as* Tom o' Bedlam.

Edgar. Away! the foul fiend follows me. Through 45
the sharp hawthorn blow the winds. Humh! go to thy cold bed, and warm thee.

Lear. Didst thou give all to thy daughters? And art thou come to this?

Edgar. Who gives anything to poor Tom? whom the foul fiend hath led through fire and through flame, through ford and whirlpool, o'er bog and quagmire; that hath laid knives under his pillow and halters 53
in his pew, set ratsbane by his porridge, made him proud of heart, to ride on a bay trotting horse over 55
four-inched bridges, to course his own shadow for 56
a traitor. Bless thy five wits, Tom's acold. O, do, de, 57
do, de, do, de. Bless thee from whirlwinds, star- 58
blasting, and taking. Do poor Tom some charity, whom the foul fiend vexes. There could I have him now — and there — and there again — and there —
                                [*Storm still.*

Lear. Have his daughters brought him to this pass? Couldst thou save nothing? Wouldst thou give 'em all?

Fool. Nay, he reserved a blanket, else we had been 64
all shamed.

Lear. Now all the plagues that in the pendulous air 66
Hang fated o'er men's faults light on thy daughters!

Kent. He hath no daughters, sir.

Lear. Death, traitor; nothing could have subdued nature
To such a lowness but his unkind daughters.
Is it the fashion that discarded fathers
Should have thus little mercy on their flesh? 72
Judicious punishment — 'twas this flesh begot
Those pelican daughters. 74

Edgar. Pillicock sat on Pillicock Hill. Alow, alow, 75
loo, loo!

Fool. This cold night will turn us all to fools and madmen.

Edgar. Take heed o' th' foul fiend; obey thy parents; keep thy words' justice; swear not; commit 80
not with man's sworn spouse; set not thy sweet heart on proud array. Tom's acold.

Lear. What hast thou been?

Edgar. A servingman, proud in heart and mind; that curled my hair, wore gloves in my cap; served 85
the lust of my mistress' heart, and did the act of darkness with her; swore as many oaths as I spake words, and broke them in the sweet face of heaven. One that slept in the contriving of lust, and waked to do it. Wine loved I deeply, dice dearly; and in

45-6. "Through . . . winds": a line from an old ballad.

53-4. "knives," "halters," "ratsbane": various means to suicide.

55-6. "ride . . . bridges": take excessive risks.

56-7. "course . . . traitor": pursue his shadow as an enemy.

57-8. "O, do . . . de": syllables indicating both poor Tom's shivering and his attempt to sing.

58-9. "star-blasting": i.e., destruction by malignant planets.
"taking": being 'taken' by evil forces.

64. "blanket": i.e., to cover his nakedness.

66. "pendulous": suspended above us.

72. "have . . . flesh": i.e., punish their own flesh.

74. "pelican": the pelican's young were supposed to feed on the parent.

75. "Pillicock": from a nursery rhyme, suggested to Tom by 'pelican' in the preceding line.

80. "commit not": i.e., adultery.

85. "gloves in my cap": it was fashionable for an Elizabethan courtier to wear his lady's glove fastened to his hat.

KING LEAR

ACT III SCENE IV

Lear has protested that for the evil daughters "Man's life is cheap as beast's." "Poor Tom" represents a life actually reduced to bestial nature; in this sense he is a powerful dramatic character in his own right, and not simply a disguise Edgar happens to adopt. His repeated line from an old ballad—"Through the sharp hawthorn blow the cold winds"—is a beautiful poetic evocation of the bleak harshness of nature. Edmund had exalted "Nature" as a goddess, and implied that the morality of the animal world was more appropriate to man than the "plague of custom." "Poor Tom" is a dramatic representation of life below the level of "custom," or civilization. He "eats the swimming frog, the toad . . . eats cow-dung for sallets, swallows the old rat and the ditch-dog, drinks the green mantle of the standing pool." The enumeration of all that is revolting is deliberate; this is what "nature" is, and beneath the "gorgeous" trappings of the new party in power, lie these realities of bestial life. This connection is made clear in the speech beginning at line 84. When he is asked what he "has been," "poor Tom" gives a picture of someone very like Edmund, "proud in heart and mind," who "swore as many oaths as I spake words, and broke them in the sweet face of heaven"; he goes on to make the animal parallel explicit: "fox in stealth, wolf in greediness, dog in madness, lion in prey." Life in the court, without moral awareness, is after all close to the animal level. It is for these apparently irrelevant but penetrating speeches that Lear turns to "poor Tom" as "the philosopher" and the "learned Theban." In his unbalanced state, Lear somehow sees that "poor Tom" represents, in his extreme state, some sort of truth about man: Lear and the rest may be "sophisticated" but he is "the thing itself." Lear has already suspected that man, without the love, duty and morality of society is "unaccommodated," as he himself has become. "Poor Tom" is an object lesson to him: "unaccommodated man is no more but such a poor, bare, forked animal as thou art." Lear feels that there is a kind of truth to be learned in this ultimate debasement, and hence his cry of "Off, off you lendings; come, unbutton here" with which he throws off his own clothes—symbol of society—and tries to reduce himself to what he imagines, at this point, man really is—the poor, bare, forked animal.

woman out-paramoured the Turk. False of heart, 90
light of ear, bloody of hand; hog in sloth, fox in 91
stealth, wolf in greediness, dog in madness, lion in
prey. Let not the creaking of shoes nor the rustling
of silks betray thy poor heart to woman. Keep thy
foot out of brothels, thy hand out of plackets, thy 95
pen from lenders' books, and defy the foul fiend.
Still through the hawthorn blows the cold wind; says
suum, mun, nonny. Dolphin my boy, boy, sessa! let 98
him trot by.   [*Storm still.*

Lear. Thou wert better in a grave than to answer 100
with thy uncovered body this extremity of the skies.
Is man no more than this? Consider him well.
Thou ow'st the worm no silk, the beast no hide, the 103
sheep no wool, the cat no perfume. Ha! here's three
on's are sophisticated. Thou art the thing itself; un- 105
accommodated man is no more but such a poor, bare,
forked animal as thou art. Off, off, you lendings! 107
Come, unbutton here.

                                    [*Begins to disrobe.*

Fool. Prithee, nuncle, be contented; 'tis a naughty
night to swim in. Now a little fire in a wild field
were like an old lecher's heart — a small spark, all
the rest on's body cold. Look, here comes a walking 112
fire.

Enter GLOUCESTER *with a torch.*

Edgar. This is the foul Flibbertigibbet. He begins 113
at curfew, and walks till the first cock. He gives the 114
web and the pin, squints the eye, and makes the hare- 115
lip; mildews the white wheat, and hurts the poor
creature of earth.

    Swithold footed thrice the 'old; 118
    He met the nightmare, and her nine fold 119
      Bid her alight
      And her troth plight, 121
    And aroint thee, witch, aroint thee! 122

Kent. How fares your Grace?

Lear. What's he? 124

Kent. Who's there? What is't you seek?

Gloucester. What are you there? Your names?

Edgar. Poor Tom, that eats the swimming frog, the
toad, the todpole, the wall-newt and the water; that 128
in the fury of his heart, when the foul fiend rages,
eats cow-dung for sallets, swallows the old rat and 130
the ditch-dog, drinks the green mantle of the stand- 131
ing pool; who is whipped from tithing to tithing, and 132
stock-punished and imprisoned; who hath had three
suits to his back, six shirts to his body.

    Horse to ride, and weapon to wear,
    But mice and rats, and such small deer, 136
    Have been Tom's food for seven long year.
Beware my follower! Peace, Smulkin, peace, thou
fiend!

Gloucester. What, hath your Grace no better company?

Edgar. The prince of darkness is a gentleman.
Modo he's called, and Mahu.

Gloucester. Our flesh and blood, my lord, is grown
so vile

90. "out-paramoured the Turk": outdid the Sultan, who had many mistresses.

91. "light of ear": listening to rumor and slander.

95. "plackets": slits cut in Elizabethan skirts.

98. "Dolphin my boy": refrain from a song.

100. "to answer": to confront, expose oneself to.

103. "ow'st": owe, have borrowed from.

105-6. "unaccommodated": bare, without the protection of civilization.

107. "lendings": borrowed covering, clothes.

112. "walking fire": a reference to Gloucester's torch, and also to Gloucester as an 'old lecher' (see I,i).

113. "Flibbertigibbet": the name of a devil; here and later Shakespeare takes the names of his devils—Smulkin, Modo, Mahu &c—from a book by Samuel Harsnett published in 1603. The names also give the effect of the devils, fiends and goblins of folk-mythology, which would come naturally to Tom o' Bedlam.

114. "curfew": 9 p.m.
"first cock": i.e., the first cockcrow before dawn.

115. "web and pin": afflictions of the eye.

118. "Swithold": St. Withold, an Anglo-Saxon saint, held to be able to exorcise devils.
" 'old": wold, upland.

119. "fold": offspring.

121. "her troth plight": give her word, i.e., not to appear again.

122. "aroint thee": begone.

124. "he": Gloucester.

128. "todpole": tadpole.
"wall newt and water": the lizard and the water newt.

130. "sallets": salads.

131. "ditch-dog": carcass of the dog left in the ditch.

132. "tithing": settlement, originally one made up of ten households.

136. "deer": originally any small game.

KING LEAR

ACT III SCENE IV

The last four lines of the scene are deliberately mysterious, in the combination of the mystery of the "dark tower" and the ominous children's rhyme about "the blood of a British man" they; carry on the strange, sometimes surrealistic quality of the whole scene. Robert Browning wrote a poem with the 'Child Rowland' line as its title, in which he imagines an obscure and terrifying quest of some sort. He could not, on being questioned, "explain" the poem, anymore than critics can explain the enigmatic line he used as a title.

That it doth hate what gets it. 143

Edgar. Poor Tom's acold.

Gloucester. Go in with me. My duty cannot suffer 145
T' obey in all your daughter's hard commands.
Though their injunction be to bar my doors
And let this tyrannous night take hold upon you,
Yet have I ventured to come seek you out
And bring you where both fire and food is ready.

Lear. First let me talk with this philosopher.
What is the cause of thunder?

Kent. Good my lord, take his offer; go into th'
house.

Lear. I'll talk a word with this same learned 154
Theban.
What is your study? 155

Edgar. How to prevent the fiend, and to kill vermin. 156

Lear. Let me ask you one word in private.

Kent. Importune him once more to go, my lord.
His wits begin t' unsettle.

Gloucester. Canst thou blame him?
[*Storm still.*
His daughters seek his death. Ah, that good Kent,
He said it would be thus, poor banished man!
Thou say'st the King grows mad — I'll tell thee,
friend,
I am almost mad myself. I had a son,
Now outlawed from my blood; he sought my life
But lately, very late. I loved him, friend,
No father his son dearer. True to tell thee,
The grief hath crazed my wits. What a night 's this!
I do beseech your Grace —

Lear. O, cry you mercy, sir. 168
Noble philosopher, your company.

Edgar. Tom's acold.

Gloucester. In, fellow, there, into th' hovel; keep
thee warm.

Lear. Come, let's in all.

Kent. This way, my lord.

Lear. With him!
I will keep still with my philosopher.

Kent. Good my lord, soothe him; let him take the 174
fellow.

Gloucester. Take him you on.

Kent. Sirrah, come on; go along with us.

Lear. Come, good Athenian.

Gloucester. No words, no words! Hush.

Edgar. Child Rowland to the dark tower came; 179
His word was still, 'Fie, foh, and fum, 180
I smell the blood of a British man.'
[*Exeunt.*

143. "gets": begets; the reference is to Lear's and Gloucester's children.

145. "suffer": allow.

154. "Theban": the association of the Greek city Thebes, as with Athens at I,177, is with philosophical enquiry.
155. "study": philosophical specialty.
156. "prevent . . . vermin": i.e., to provide security and health for the mind (against 'the fiend') and the body (against 'vermin').

168. "cry you mercy": excuse me; Lear puts Gloucester aside and turns back to Tom.

174. "soothe": calm.

179. "Child Rowland": the term 'Child' indicated an aspirant to knighthood; Child Rowland occurred in the French legendary romances, and this line is possibly from an old ballad.

180-1. "His word . . . man": the Giant's speech in the child's story of Jack the Giant Killer; it is a deliberate descent from the heroic association of Child Rowland.

KING LEAR

ACT III SCENE V

Because of the intensity of the two scenes of Lear's madness we need some change or respite between them. Shakespeare provides it with this short scene further delineating Edmund's villainy as he betrays his father to Cornwall. We may compare the careful, cold-blooded use of language with the poetry of the "heart-struck injuries" of the preceding and following scenes. The actor who plays Edmund must underline the various ironies that Shakespeare gives him, which mean one thing to Cornwall, and another to Edmund and the audience. For example, "I will persevere, in my course of loyalty, though the conflict be sore between that and my blood" seems to say that Edmund is torn between loyalty to the state (or Cornwall), and his "blood" (or Gloucester); that is the surface meaning, and what Edmund really means is that he will certainly "persevere" in the course of his "loyalty," but that that loyalty is neither to the state, nor Cornwall. It is to himself, and there is, therefore, no conflict between his "loyalty" and his "blood," since the only blood that concerns him is his own.

ACT III SCENE VI

The farmhouse adjoining his castle is all that is left for Gloucester to command. When we reflect on it, we are surprised at the rapidity with which the evil party have assumed complete power, so that Lear, Kent, Gloucester and Edgar find themselves expelled and under sentence of death, and all this with a minimum of explicit dramatic action. Shakespeare does not bother with the details of plot, having shown us clearly enough the way in which Edmund, Goneril, Regan and Cornwall work. We have also ceased to expect succour or release for the sufferers. Increasingly toward the end of the play we see good suffer and evil triumph and prayers and calls for help, such as Lear's, seem always to be answered with added torment. Now when Gloucester goes for aid, and Kent says "The gods reward your kindness," we feel it as an ominous sign, given the kind of world that this play represents. Gloucester's kindness brings a terrible punishment upon him in the next scene.

Scene five.

(A ROOM IN GLOUCESTER'S CASTLE.)

Enter CORNWALL, *and* EDMUND.

Cornwall. I will have my revenge ere I depart his house.

Edmund. How, my lord, I may be censured, that nature thus gives way to loyalty, sometimes fears me to think of. — 3 / 4

Cornwall. I now perceive it was not altogether your brother's evil disposition made him seek his death; but a provoking merit, set awork by a reproveable badness in himself. — 8

Edmund. How malicious is my fortune that I must repent to be just! This is the letter which he spoke of, which approves him an intelligent party to the advantages of France. O heavens, that this treason were not! or not I the detector! — 12

Cornwall. Go with me to the Duchess.

Edmund. If the matter of this paper be certain, you have mighty business in hand.

Cornwall. True or false, it hath made thee Earl of Gloucester. Seek out where thy father is, that he may be ready for our apprehension.

Edmund. [*aside*] If I find him comforting the King, it will stuff his suspicion more fully.—I will persevere in my course of loyalty, though the conflict be sore between that and my blood. — 22

Cornwall. I will lay trust upon thee, and thou shalt find a dearer father in my love. [*Exeunt.*

3-4. "nature": filial nature.

4. "loyalty": i.e., loyalty to Cornwall, to whom Edmund is betraying his father.
"something fears me": makes me a little afraid.

8-9. "provoking merit . . . himself": i.e., Edgar's evil was incited by Gloucester's.

12. "approves": proves.
"intelligent party": spy.

22. "stuff": increase.

Scene six.

(A FARMHOUSE ADJOINING THE CASTLE.)

Enter KENT *and* GLOUCESTER.

Gloucester. Here is better than the open air; take it thankfully. I will piece out the comfort with what addition I can. I will not be long from you.

Kent. All the power of his wits have given way to his impatience. The gods reward your kindness. — 5
[*Exit* GLOUCESTER.

Enter LEAR, EDGAR, *and* Fool.

Edgar. Fraretto calls me, and tells me Nero is an angler in the lake of darkness. Pray, innocent, and beware the foul fiend. — 6 / 7

Fool. Prithee, nuncle, tell me whether a madman be a gentleman or a yeoman. — 10

Lear. A king, a king.

Fool. No, he's a yeoman that has a gentleman to his son; for he's a mad yeoman that sees his son a gentleman before him. — 13

Lear. To have a thousand with red burning spits Come hizzing in upon 'em —

5. "impatience": rage; the word was far stronger for the Elizabethans.

6. "Fraretto": another of Harsnett's devils.
"Nero": tradition had Nero a fiddler in hell, but Shakespeare makes him a fisherman.

7. "innocent": innocent victim.

10. "yeoman": a property owner, but beneath a gentleman in social rank.

13. "sees": i.e., arranges for his son to be.

55

KING LEAR

ACT III SCENE VI

Coleridge has said of this scene, "O, what a world's convention of agonies is here! All external nature in a storm, all moral nature convulsed—the real madness of Lear, the feigned madness of Edgar, the babbling of the Fool, the desperate fidelity of Kent—surely such a picture was never conceived before or since!" The scenes of Lear's madness have a nightmarish quality because of the wild power of his language; we see reality through his eyes, and in his fragmented, incoherent way. Lear, "poor Tom," and the Fool form a demented trio, and their dialogue in this scene is a crescendo of irrationality. Yet Lear's mock trial is meaningful just because it is his attempt to impose some kind of order. He is obsessed here and later (IV,vi,151) with the idea of justice, and the obsession takes two forms. We see the first in his ungovernable (and understandable) anger against his daughters: "To have a thousand with red burning spits/Come hizzing in upon 'em—." This is the Lear of earlier in the play, the irascible old man driven beyond endurance. The second form of his obsession is concerned with the idea of justice in general, and is caused by the upset of order (in the individual, the family, and society in general) throughout the play. Lear has, as we have seen, assumed that human association was somehow founded on mutual love and obligation (although he himself misunderstood the nature of the "bond" of love in I,i) which decreed certain forms of order, reverence and obedience —Edmund's hated "plagues of custom." These forms have been destroyed by Goneril and Regan, who substitute for them the "natural" law of force. Having been subjected to the Goneril-Regan view of what society and human obligations are, Lear feels, in an imprecise but anguished way, that justice has been destroyed. Justice, law, and order are all founded on the notion of society as an ethical organism, transcending the individual. In a society based simply on the individual's drive for power (e.e. Edmund), law, and therefore justice, vanish. Thus it is at this point in the play, when disorder reigns both in the outside world and in Lear's mind, that Lear tries to establish justice. It is, of course, a demented and pathetic attempt, adding to our sense of Lear's tragedy. He sets up his court by calling two judges—"Thou, robed man of justice, take thy place/And thou, his yokefellow in equity"—a madman and a professional fool. Lear's dream of justice is a grotesque parody.

Edgar. The foul fiend bites my back.

Fool. He's mad that trusts in the tameness of a wolf, a horse's health, a boy's love, or a whore's oath.

Lear. It shall be done; I will arraign them straight. 20
[*To Edgar*] Come, sit thou here, most learned justice.
[*To the Fool*] Thou, sapient sir, sit here. Now, you shefoxes—

Edgar. Look, where he stands and glares. Want'st 23
thou eyes at trial, madam? 24
        Come o'er the bourn, Bessy, to me. 25

Fool.   Her boat hath a leak,
        And she must not speak
Why she dares not come over to thee.

Edgar. The foul fiend haunts poor Tom in the voice of a nightingale. Hoppedance cries in Tom's belly 30 for two white herring. Croak not, black angel; I have no food for thee.

Kent. How do you, sir? Stand you not so amazed. Will you lie down and rest upon the cushions?

Lear. I'll see their trial first. Bring in their evidence.
[*To Edgar*] Thou, robed man of justice, take thy place.
[*To the Fool*] And thou, his yokefellow of equity, 37
Bench by his side. [*to Kent*] You are o' th' commission;
Sit you too.

Edgar. Let us deal justly.
      Sleepest or wakest thou, jolly shepherd?
        Thy sheep be in the corn;
      And for one blast of thy minikin mouth. 43
        Thy sheep shall take no harm
Purr, the cat is gray. 45

Lear. Arraign her first. 'Tis Goneril, I here take my oath before this honourable assembly, kicked the poor King her father.

Fool. Come hither, mistress. Is your name Goneril?

Lear. She cannot deny it.

Fool. Cry you mercy, I took you for a joint-stool. 51

Lear. And here's another, whose warped looks proclaim
What store her heart is made on. Stop her there! 53
Arms, arms, sword, fire! Corruption in the place! 54
False justicer, why hast thou let her 'scape?

Edgar. Bless thy five wits!

Kent. O pity! Sir, where is the patience now
That you so oft have boasted to retain?

Edgar. [*aside*] My tears begin to take his part so 59
much
They mar my counterfeiting. 60

Lear. The little dogs and all,
Tray, Blanch, and Sweetheart—see, they bark at me.

Edgar. Tom will throw his head at them. Avant,
   you curs.
      Be thy mouth or black or white,
      Tooth that poisons if it bite;
      Mastiff, greyhound, mongrel grim,
      Hound or spaniel, brach or lym, 67
      Or bobtail tike, or trundle-tail —
      Tom will make him weep and wail;
      For, with throwing thus my head,

20. "arraign": bring to justice. Lear now stages a mock trial, and we are to imagine a bench of several judges. This attempt to establish 'justice,' or order, comes at the moment of Lear's greatest mental chaos. See commentary.

23. "he": the 'foul fiend,' or possibly Lear.

24. "eyes": observers, an audience. "madam": Goneril or Regan.

25. "bourn": brook; this is a line from a popular song, to which the Fool adds an indecent variation.

30. "nightingale": sardonic reference to the Fool's voice.
"Hoppedance": another of Harsnett's devils.

37. "yokefellow of equity": partner in justice.

43. "minikin": little; again Tom repeats a snatch from a song.

45. "cat is gray": a gray cat was one of the forms supposedly taken by the devil; on another interpretation, Tom's phrase suggests that no justice can be done—'all cats are gray in the dark.'

51. "joint-stool": joined, carpentered stool; Lear takes the stools to stand for his daughters.

53. "store": stuff.

54. "Corruption": bribery, dishonesty (in letting the accused escape).

59. "take his part": i.e., weep in sympathy.

60. "counterfeiting": the disguise of poor Tom.

67. "brach": hound bitch.
"lym": bloodhound.

KING LEAR

ACT III SCENE VI

Lear's sudden question at 74—"let them anatomize Regan . . . Is there any cause in nature that makes these hard hearts?"—raises a central problem of the play. In a sense, the whole play might be said to be the answer to this question. The "Nature" that Edmund deifies—pure biological and mechanical cause and effect—cannot produce a "hard" heart because in it there is no such thing as "hard" or "soft," inhuman or human. There is simply the natural drive to power and self-satisfaction. Thus for Edmund and the evil sisters neither good nor evil exists, and the answer to Lear's question is no. But from the point of view of tragedy man is more than a "naturally" conditioned mechanism. He stands above his own natural causes, and exercises free will and responsibility. The cause of "hard hearts," i.e., of deliberate evil-doing, is not in "nature" but in the way man, as a free agent, distorts or perverts his nature. The answer to Lear's question is again no, but for an entirely different reason. Put another way, in the world of the evil sisters there is not, from their point of view, any "evil," and therefore no tragedy: only a stupid old man going to his deserved destruction ("Age is unnecessary," and "The younger rises when the old doth fall"). But in the world of the play (and of Shakespeare) evil does exist; it lies in man's will, and above any "natural" cause.

Dogs leaped the hatch, and all are fled.
Do, de, de, de. Sessa! Come, march to wakes and
fairs and market towns. Poor Tom, thy horn is dry. 73
Lear. Then let them anatomize Regan. See what
breeds about her heart. Is there any cause in nature
that makes these hard hearts? [*to Edgar*] You, sir,
I entertain for one of my hundred; only I do not like
the fashion of your garments. You will say they are
Persian; but let them be changed. 79
Kent. Now, good my lord, lie here and rest awhile.
Lear. Make no noise, make no noise; draw the 81
curtains.
So, so. We'll go to supper i' th' morning.
Fool. And I'll go to bed at noon. 83

Enter GLOUCESTER.

Gloucester. Come hither, friend. Where is the King
my master?
Kent. Here, sir, but trouble him not; his wits are
gone.
Gloucester. Good friend, I prithee take him in thy
arms.
I have o'erheard a plot of death upon him.
There is a litter ready; lay him in't
And drive toward Dover, friend, where thou shalt
meet
Both welcome and protection. Take up thy master.
If thou shouldst dally half an hour, his life,
With thine and all that offer to defend him,
Stand in assured loss. Take up, take up,
And follow me, that will to some provision 94
Give thee quick conduct.
Kent.   Oppressed nature sleeps
This rest might yet have balmed thy broken sinews, 96
Which, if convenience will not allow, 97
Stand in hard cure. [*to the Fool*] Come, help to bear 98
thy master.
Thou must not stay behind.
Gloucester.   Come, come, away!
[*Exeunt all but* EDGAR.
Edgar. When we our betters see bearing our woes, 100
We scarcely think our miseries our foes.
Who alone suffers suffers most i' th' mind,
Leaving free things and happy shows behind; 103
But then the mind much sufferance doth o'erskip 104
When grief hath mates, and bearing fellowship.
How light and portable my pain seems now, 106
When that which makes me bend makes the King
bow.
He childed as I fathered. Tom, away.
Mark the high noises, and thyself bewray 109
When false opinion, whose wrong thoughts defile 110
thee,
In thy just proof repeals and reconciles thee. 111
What will hap more to-night, safe 'scape the King! 112
Lurk, lurk. [*Exit.* 113

73. "horn": the horn held out by Tom o' Bedlams in begging money.

79. "Persian": i.e., very grand, ornate.

81. "curtains": i.e., of a bed; Lear is about to sleep.

83. "And I'll . . . noon": this line answers the lunacy of Lear's 'supper in the morning,' but it is also the Fool's last line; most actors play the end of this scene so as to convey the notion that the Fool, broken and exhausted, is in fact dying.

94. "provision": supplies.

96. "broken sinews": racked nerves.

97. "convenience": circumstances.

98. "hard cure": difficult to cure.

100. "our woes": woes like ours.

103. "happy shows": pleasant scenes.

104. "sufferance": suffering.

106. "portable": bearable.

109. "bewray": reveal.

110. "wrong thoughts": misconceptions (of Tom's identity).

111. "In thy . . . thee": i.e., when you are reinstated (as Edgar) and recalled.

112. "What . . . more": whatever else happens.

113. "Lurk": keep out of sight, hidden.

KING LEAR

ACT III SCENE VII

This scene brings the sub-plot to its crisis in the blinding of Gloucester. Gloucester's faults, his sensuality and self-deception (I,i) may seem minor in contrast to the punishment inflicted on him, and the same may be said of Lear. In both cases Shakespeare seems to apply a kind of inverted poetic justice; the intensity of the punishments are out of all proportion to their causes. However in KING LEAR Shakespeare's concern is with the dramatization of suffering, not with justice. In the world he presents in the play one of the elements of suffering lies in just this arbitrary and senseless infliction of punishment.

When Gloucester is apprehended his sense of shock manifests itself first in his feeling that some standard of social decorum has been violated. "Consider," he says to Cornwall and Regan, "you are my guests," and later, "I am your host./With robber's hands my hospitable favours/You should not ruffle thus." This appeal has far more force for an Elizabethan audience than for us. What Gloucester has in mind is not simply good manners, but the whole conception on which the idea of hospitality rests. It is, like Cordelia's "bond," one of the forms of ethical obligation between human beings—we may compare Macbeth's intense guilt at the thought of Duncan being in his "trust" while his murder is contemplated. It is another variation of the general conception of society as imposing the obligation of mutual trust and support on its mmbers, as opposed to the "natural" amorality the evil party.

The actual blinding of Gloucester on stage has occasioned much criticism, from the 17th cen-

---

Scene seven.

(A ROOM IN GLOUCESTER'S CASTLE.)

Enter CORNWALL, REGAN, GONERIL, EDMUND *and* Servants.

Cornwall. [*to Goneril*] Post speedily to my lord your husband; show him this letter. The army of France is landed. [*to Servants*] Seek out the traitor Gloucester.   [*Exeunt some* Servants.

Regan. Hang him instantly.

Goneril. Pluck out his eyes.

Cornwall. Leave him to my displeasure. Edmund, keep you our sister company. The revenges we are bound to take upon your traitorous father are not fit for your beholding. Advise the Duke where you are going, to a most festinate preparation. We are bound 11
to the like. Our posts shall be swift and intelligent 12
betwixt us. Farewell, dear sister; farewell, my Lord 13
of Gloucester.

Enter OSWALD.

How now? Where's the King?

Oswald. My Lord of Gloucester hath conveyed him
    hence.
Some five or six and thirty of his knights,
Hot questrists after him, met him at gate; 18
Who, with some other of the lord's dependants,
Are gone with him toward Dover, where they boast
To have well-armed friends.

Cornwall.   Get horses for your mistress.
                    [*Exit* OSWALD.

Goneril. Farewell, sweet lord, and sister.

Cornwall. Edmund, farewell.
                    [*Exeunt* GONERIL *and* EDMUND.
                    Go seek the traitor Gloucester,
Pinion him like a thief, bring him before us.
                    [*Exeunt other* Servants.
Though well we may not pass upon his life 25
Without the form of justice, yet our power
Shall do a court'sy to our wrath, which men 27
May blame, but not control.

Enter GLOUCESTER *and* Servants.

                    Who's there, the traitor?

Regan. Ingrateful fox, 'tis he.

Cornwall. Bind fast his corky arms. 30

Gloucester. What means your Graces? Good my
    friends, consider
You are my guests. Do me no foul play, friends.

Cornwall. Bind him, I say.   [*Servants bind him.*

Regan.   Hard, hard! O filthy traitor.

Gloucester. Unmerciful lady as you are, I'm none.

Cornwall. To this chair bind him. Villain, thou shalt
    find —
                    [*Regan plucks his beard.* s.d.

Gloucester. By the kind gods, 'tis most ignobly done
To pluck me by the beard.

Regan. So white, and such a traitor?

Gloucester.   Naughty lady, 38

---

11. "festinate": speedy.

12. "intelligent": giving much intelligence, informative.

13-14. "Lord of Gloucester": Edmund's new title.

18. "questrists": hunters.

25. "pass upon": sentence, pass judgment on.

27. "do a court'sy": step aside for.

30. "corky": dry with age.

Stage Direction "plucks his beard": throughout Elizabethan drama this act is used to signify the inflicting of extreme humiliation, as spitting in the face would do on our stage.

38. "Naughty": evil; the word was much stronger for the Elizabethans.

KING LEAR

ACT III SCENE VII

tury to our day. The practice in classical drama was to keep such acts of violence off stage and have them reported to the audience by a messenger, and academic critics in particular have felt that Shakespeare has here gone too far in staging so repulsive a scene before our eyes. Many have felt, with Robert Bridges, that in such scenes as these Shakespeare the popular playwright was catering to what Bridges called the "depraved taste" for violence and bloodshed of the Elizabethan audience. On the other hand it ought to be said that i) Shakespeare was not obliged to follow the classical rule, or indeed any rule, in this matter, and ii) that he has Gloucester blinded on stage because he wants the audience to feel the full brutality of Cornwall and Regan, and, by implication, of the whole evil party. Physical brutality, after all, occur.

Dramatically, one of the reasons for the blinding lies in the nature of main plot. Lear's suffering is intense and prolonged; but it is primarily mental and verbal and, though not the less impressive for that, the extent of the inhumanity of the evil party needs some shocking, visible presentation. This is amply supplied by the blinding scene which gives us, unlike Lear's torments, a concentrated physical example of man's inhumanity to man.

The blinding of Gloucester also has its symbolic aspect. There are references to "sight" and "seeing" throughout the play, usually in relation to intelligence. Thus when Kent accuses Lear of blindness in dealing with his daughters Lear orders him out of his "sight," to which Kent replies, "See better, Lear." "Sight" and "blindness" are often used in drama to represent intelligence, or the lack of it, and sometimes in a paradoxical way, so that physical sight may mean moral blindness, while physical blindness may stand for penetrating insight into spiritual problems. In the great Greek tragedy OEDIPUS REX, for example, the blind prophet Tiresias can 'see' (i.e., understand) Oedipus' situation, while Oedipus, who can see, cannot understand it. When Oedipus does discover his own tragic position he blinds himself. His new spiritual insight is accompanied by physical blindness. In the same way Gloucester gains an insight into his real position in what is literally a blinding flash: "O my follies! Then Edgar was abused./Kind gods, forgive me that, and prosper him." It has taken the violence of the blinding to bring Gloucester to this new kind of vision. As he says later: "I . . . want no eyes; I stumbled when I saw."

These hairs which thou dost ravish from my chin
Will quicken and accuse thee. I am your host. 40
With robber's hands my hospitable favours 41
You should not ruffle thus. What will you do? 42
   Cornwall. Come, sir, what letters had you late from France?
   Regan. Be simple-answered, for we know the truth.
   Cornwall. And what confederacy have you with the traitors
Late footed in the kingdom?
   Regan. To whose hands you have sent the lunatic King.
Speak.
   Gloucester. I have a letter guessingly set down, 49
Which came from one that's of a neutral heart,
And not from one opposed.
   Cornwall.   Cunning.
   Regan.   And false.
   Cornwall. Where has thou sent the King?
   Gloucester. To Dover.
   Regan. Wherefore to Dover? Wast thou not charged 54
   at peril —
   Cornwall. Wherefore to Dover? Let him answer that.
   Gloucester. I am tied to th' stake, and I must stand the course. 56
   Regan. Wherefore to Dover?
   Gloucester. Because I would not see thy cruel nails
Pluck out his poor old eyes; nor thy fierce sister
In his anointed flesh stick boarish fangs. 60
The sea, with such a storm as his bare head
In hell-black night endured, would have buoyed up 62
And quenched the stelled fires. 63
Yet, poor old heart, he holp the heavens to rain 64
If wolves had at thy gate howled that stern time,
Thou should'st have said, 'Good porter, turn the key'. 66
All cruels else subscribe. But I shall see 67
The winged vengeance overtake such children.
   Cornwall. See't shalt thou never. Fellows, hold the chair.
Upon these eyes of thine I'll set my foot.
   Gloucester. He that will think to live till he be old,
Give me some help. — O cruel! O ye gods!
   Regan. One side will mock another. Th' other too.
   Cornwall. If you see vengeance —
   1. Servant.   Hold your hand, my lord!
I have served you ever since I was a child;
But better service have I never done you
Than now to bid you hold.
   Regan.   How now, you dog?
   1. Servant. If you did wear a beard upon your chin,
I'd shake it on this quarrel. What do you mean! 79
   Cornwall. My villain!   *[Draw and fight.*
   1. Servant. Nay, then, come on, and take the chance of anger.
   Regan. Give me thy sword. A peasant stand up thus?
      [She takes a sword and runs at him behind,
                      kills him.
   1. Servant. O, I am slain! My lord, you have one eye left

40. "quicken": come alive.
41. "favours": features.
42. "ruffle": tear at.

49. "guessingly": tentative, not certain.

54. "charged at peril": ordered on peril of death.

56. "course": of being baited, as a bear tied to a stake.

60. "anointed": as a king.

62. "bouyed": surged.

63. "stelled fires": fire of the stars.

64. "holp": helped.

66. "turn the key": i.e., let them come in.

67. "All cruels . . . subscribe": i.e., at such times other cruel creatures renounce their cruelty.

79. "shake it": see note at SD, l. 35.

KING LEAR

ACT III SCENE VII

The scene carries a deep sense of shock; certainly here Shakespeare extends his dramatization of man's evil potential as far as it can go on the stage. Shakespeare sets up a moving contrast between the blundering bleeding Gloucester and the comments of the torturers around him: "Go thrust him out at gates, and let him smell/His way to Dover," and "Turn out that eyeless villain. Throw this slave/Upon the dunghill." These lines are, in their compressed, efficient brutality, as shocking as any in the drama.

To see some mischief on him. O!   [*Dies.* 84
   Cornwall. Lest it see more, prevent it.   Out, vile
    jelly.
Where is thy lustre now?

                 [GLOUCESTER'S *other eye put out.*
   Gloucester. All dark and comfortless. Where's my
    son Edmund?
Edmund, enkindle all the sparks of nature   88
To quit this horrid act.   89
   Regan.   Out, treacherous villain;
Thou call'st on him that hates thee. It was he
That made the overture of thy treasons to us;   91
Who is too good to pity thee.
   Gloucester. O my follies! Then Edgar was abused   93
Kind gods, forgive me that, and prosper him.
   Regan. Go thrust him out at gates, and let him
    smell
His way to Dover.   [*Exit one with* GLOUCESTER.
            How is't, my lord? How look you? 96
   Cornwall. I have received a hurt. Follow me, lady.
Turn out that eyeless villain. Throw this slave
Upon the dunghill. Regan, I bleed apace.
Untimely comes this hurt. Give me your arm.
                      [*Exeunt.*
   2. Servant. I'll never care what wickedness I do,
If this man come to good.
   3. Servant.   If she live long,
And in the end meet the old course of death,   103
Women will all turn monsters.
   2. Servant. Let's follow the old Earl, and get the
    bedlam
To lead him where he would. His roguish madness 106
Allows itself to anything.   [*Exit.*
   3. Servant. Go thou. I'll fetch some flax and whites
    of eggs
To apply to his bleeding face. Now heaven help him.
                      [*Exit.*

84. "mischief": injury.

88. "nature": natural feeling.
89. "quit": revenge.

91. "overture": disclosure.

93. "abused": wronged.

96. "How look you": i.e., how are you?

103. "old course of death": natural death.

106-7. "His roguish . . . anything": in his lunacy he will do anything.

60

KING LEAR

ACT IV SCENE I

Edgar enters and ponders the nature of misfortune, concluding that "The worst returns to laughter." This is an expression of qualified optimism, but it is just at this point, having reached some acceptance of the misery around him, that he sees his blinded father. This makes nonsense of his earlier philosophizing. It seems to be a deliberate strategy on Shakespeare's part to follow any bettering of the situation, or any expression of hope, with a new misfortune. Edgar (and he is the optimist of the play) is forced, at the sight of his father, to the conclusion that "Who is't can say 'I am at the worst'?/I am worse than e'er I was." The effect of this device seems to be to keep us aware of the apparently limitless possibilities for suffering.

Gloucester follows these reflections on Edgar's part with two lines that have seemed to many to sum up the dark pessimism of the whole play: "As flies to wanton boys are we to th' gods;/They kill us for their sport." For the Elizabethan audience the lines would have a more special, though equally pessimistic, association. They represent the sort of stoic point of view that we frequently find in Elizabethan tragedies. Very roughly this view, which is taken in

---

ACT FOUR, scene one.

(THE HEATH.)
Enter EDGAR.

Edgar. Yet better thus, and known to be contemned, 1
Than still contemned and flattered. To be worst,
The lowest and most dejected thing of fortune,
Stands still in esperance, lives not in fear. 4
The lamentable change is from the best;
The worse returns to laughter. Welcome then, 6
Thou unsubstantial air that I embrace:
The wretch that thou hast blown unto the worst
Owes nothing to thy blasts. 9
    Enter GLOUCESTER *and an* Old Man.
                  But who comes here?
My father, poorly led? World, world, O world!
But that thy strange mutations make us hate thee, 11
Life would not yield to age.
   Old Man.   O my good lord,
I have been your tenant, and your father's tenant,
These fourscore years.
   Gloucester. Away, get thee away. Good friend, be
      gone.
Thy comforts can do me no good at all;
Thee they may hurt.
   Old Man.   You cannot see your way.
   Gloucester. I have no way, and therefore want no
      eyes;
I stumbled when I saw. Full oft 'tis seen
Our means secure us, and our mere defects 20
Prove our commodities. O dear son Edgar,
The food of thy abused father's wrath, 22
Might I but live to see thee in my touch
I'd say I had eyes again!
   Old Man.   How now? Who's there?
   Edgar. [*aside*] O gods! who is't can say 'I am at
      the worst'?
I am worse than e'er I was.
   Old Man.   'Tis poor mad Tom.
   Edgar. [*aside*] And worse I may be yet. The worst 27
      is not
So long as we can say 'This is the worst.'
   Old Man. Fellow, where goest?
   Gloucester.   Is it a beggerman?
   Old Man. Madman and beggar too.
   Gloucester. He has some reason, else he could not 31
      beg.
I' th' last night's storm I such a fellow saw,
Which made me think a man a worm. My son
Came then into my mind, and yet my mind
Was then scarce friends with him. I have heard more
      since.
As flies to wanton boys are we to th' gods;
They kill us for their sport.
   Edgar.   [*aside*] How should this be?
Bad is the trade that must play fool to sorrow,
Ang'ring itself and others. — Bless thee, master. 39

61

---

1. "contemned": despised.

4. "esperance": hope.

6. "worse . . . laughter": i.e., at the worst we can only get better.

9. "Owes nothing": has no debt to, is free of.

11-12. "But that . . . age": i.e., if the irrational changes in fortune did not make us indifferent (to the world) we would never be reconciled to age and death.

20-1. "Our means . . . commodities": i.e., what we have is what we are, and even our losses may prove to be gains.

22. "food": i.e., what is fed on. "abused": deceived, confused.

27-8. "The worst . . . worst": i.e., since to say that we are at the worst is a kind of comfort, at the very worst we shall not be able to say it.

31. "reason": ability to reason.

39. "Ang'ring itself": offensive to itself.

KING LEAR

ACT IV SCENE I

part from the Roman Stoic philosophers, and in part from the Roman dramatist Seneca, holds that the universe is mindless and without direction; that man has no control over his fortune; and that therefore virtue lies in accepting, and enduring, what happens to him: "Pour on, I will endure!" as Lears says (III,iv,18). There are many such utterances in the play, but we must not identify what the characters say with 'the play's meaning."

Another obvious parallel between Lear and Gloucester is revealed in this scene. Both, in their suffering, come to realize the universality of suffering. As Lear felt for, and blessed, the "poor naked wretches," so Gloucester feels that "distribution should undo excess/ And each man have enough." Notice that it is also, in both cases, "poor Tom" who brings them to this realization. Edgar is not, in himself, a complicated or even very interesting character; instead he plays an important role throughout, in his various disguises; as "poor Tom" he is an enlightening spirit to both Lear and Gloucester in their pugatorial struggle.

The question that always arises when KING LEAR is looked at from the point of view of the modern, plausible, naturalistic theater is 'Why does Edgar not reveal himself to his blinded father at this point?' The answer is a difficult one (see, e.g., V.iii.193), and it lies in the nature of the play itself. Among other things, the play is a study of the course of suffering, and the understanding that arises from it. Like Lear, Gloucester must undergo a period of suffering that requires him to reach the point of absolute despair, attempting to kill himself (on the "cliff, whose high and bending head/Looks fearfully in the confined deep"), being saved, and "enduring" all these things. Edgar's revelation of his identity would naturally deflect Gloucester from this course, so it is "poor Tom" who must lead him through it.

ACT IV SCENE II

The opening of the scene reveals a liaison between Goneril and Edmund. It has apparently developed on their journey ("Our wishes on the way/May prove effects") but the facts are unimportant and neither Shakespeare nor the audi-

---

Gloucester. Is that the naked fellow?
Old Man.   Ay, my lord.
Gloucester. Get thee away. If for my sake
Thou wilt o'ertake us hence a mile or twain
I' th' way toward Dover, do it for ancient love;   43
And bring some covering for this naked soul,
Which I'll entreat to lead me.
Old Man.   Alack, sir, he is mad.
Gloucester. 'Tis the time's plague when madmen   46
   lead the blind.
Do as I bid thee, or rather do thy pleasure.
Above the rest, be gone.
Old Man. I'll bring him the best 'parel that I have,   49
Come on't what will.   [*Exit.*
Gloucester. Sirrah naked fellow —
Edgar. Poor Tom's acold. [*aside*] I cannot daub   52
   it further.
Gloucester. Come hither, fellow.
Edgar. [*aside*] And yet I must. — Bless thy sweet
   eyes, they bleed.
Gloucester. Know'st thou the way to Dover?
Edgar. Both stile and gate, horseway and footpath.
Poor Tom hath been scared out of his good wits.
Bless thee, good man's son, from the foul fiend. Five
fiends have been in poor Tom at once: of lust, as
Obidicut; Hobbididence, prince of dumbness; Mahu,   60
of stealing; Modo, of murder; Flibbertigibbet, of
mopping and mowing, who since possesses chamber-   62
maids and waiting women. So, bless thee, master.
Gloucester. Here, take this purse, thou whom the
   heavens' plagues
Have humbled to all strokes. That I am wretched   65
Makes thee the happier. Heavens, deal so still!   66
Let the superfluous and lust-dieted man,   67
The slaves your ordinance, that will not see   68
Because he does not feel, feel your pow'r quickly;
So distribution should undo excess,
And each man have enough. Dost thou know Dover?
Edgar. Ay, master.
Gloucester. There is a cliff, whose high and bend-   73
   ing head
Looks fearfully in the confined deep.   74
Bring me but to the very brim of it,
And I'll repair the misery thou dost bear
With something rich about me. From that place   77
I shall no leading need.
Edgar.   Give me thy arm.
Poor Tom shall lead thee.   [*Exeunt.*

Scene two.

(*Before* THE DUKE OF ALBANY'S PALACE.)
Enter GONERIL, EDMUND, *and* OSWALD.

Goneril. Welcome, my lord. I marvel our mild
   husband
Not met us on the way. [*to Oswald*] Now, where's   2
   your master?

---

43. "ancient love": i.e., the sort of love that used to exist between men.

46. "time's plague": disease characteristic of the time.

49. "'parel": apparel.

52. "daub": disguise (in the sense of 'paint').

60. "Obidicut &c": more of Harsnett's devils.

62. "mopping and mowing": grimacing.

65. "all strokes": any injury.

66. "happier": less wretched by comparison.

67. "superfluous": having superfluous or excessive riches.
"lust-dieted": whose lusts are satisfied.

68. "slaves your ordinance": suppresses your command (to share).

73. "bending": overhanging.

74. "confined deep": bounded (by the cliff).

77. "something rich": i.e., a gift.

2. "Not met": has not met.

62

KING LEAR

ACT IV SCENE II

ence bother about them. What is dramatically important is the inevitability of the union. Both Edmund and Goneril are outside any moral law, and both believe in the supremacy of power and appetite as the basis of human action. Therefore it is not surprising that for them love is both a matter of sexual appetite, and an alliance for power. Adultery produced Edmund, and it holds no fears for Goneril; the marital tie is simply another example of the "plague of custom." Goneril is without any tremor of conscience, and logically so, since she breaks no commandment that she holds sacred. Granville-Barker remarks on "the regal impudence of the woman" and "the falsely chivalrous flourish of the man's reply." Edmund's reply—"Yours in the ranks of death"—is actually a piece of dramatic irony. He speaks truer than he knows, since it will be "in the ranks of death" that he, Goneril and Regan "marry in an instant" (V,iii,230).

Oswald's opening announcement, and the subsequent dialogue between Goneril and her husband, reveal that Albany has realized Goneril's evil, and the extent of the evil around him. As a character Albany is not developed in the play, and there is no need to speculate on his change of heart, or to try to account for his previous blindness to the viciousness of his wife. His function here is to comment, as a chorus might, on the evils of Goneril. He makes the bestial reference that recurs so frequently in the imagery of the play: Regan and Goneril are "Tigers, not daughters." Albany ends with three lines which have many echoes in Shakespeare's plays and Elizabethan literature generally. If these "vile offences" are not punished, Albany says, "It will come, /Humanity must perforce prey on itself/Like monsters of the deep." The Elizabethan thought of the universe, society, family and self as divinely ordered, harmonious organisms. But he was also aware of the way in which this divine order could be upset—in the individual, by the dominance of passion over reason, in society, by the dominance of the destructive and amoral over the "bond" of human intercourse. In Shakespeare's TROILUS AND CRESSIDA Ulysses is given a long speech in which this notion of order, and its destructive opposite, disorder, is outlined. The speech ends with an image very like the one Albany uses here: if order is taken away, then "Appetite, an universal wolf . . . Must make perforce an universal prey,/And last eat up himself." In back of all Elizabethan assumptions about "order" and "ceremony" and the obligations of the individual in

Oswald. Madam, within, but never man so changed.
I told him of the army that was landed:
He smiled at it. I told him you were coming:
His answer was, 'The worse.' Of Gloucester's
    treachery
And of the loyal service of his son
When I informed him, then he called me sot
And told me I had turned the wrong side out.
What most he should dislike seems pleasant to him;
What like, offensive.   11
Goneril.   [*to Edmund*] Then shall you go no
    further.
It is the cowish terror of his spirit,
That dares not undertake. He'll not feel wrongs   13
Which tie him to an answer. Our wishes on the way 14
May prove effects. Back, Edmund, to my brother.   15
Hasten his musters and conduct his pow'rs.   16
I must change names at home, and give the distaff 17
Into my husband's hands. This trusty servant
Shall pass between us. Ere long you are like to hear
(If you dare venture in your own behalf)
A mistress's command. Wear this. Spare speech   21
                              [*Gives a favour.*
Decline your head. This kiss, if it durst speak,
Would stretch thy spirits up into the air.
Conceive, and fare thee well.   24
Edmund. Yours in the ranks of death.   [*Exit.*
Goneril.   My most dear Gloucester.
O, the difference of man and man:
To thee a woman's services are due;
My fool usurps my body.   28
Oswald.   Madam, here comes my lord.
                                            [*Exit.*

Enter ALBANY.

Goneril. I have been worth the whistle.   29
Albany.   O Goneril,
You are not worth the dust which the rude wind
Blows in your face. I fear your disposition: 31
That nature which contemns its origin
Cannot be bordered certain in itself.   33
She that herself will sliver and disbranch   34
From her material sap, perforce must wither   35
And come to deadly use.
Goneril. No more; the text is foolish.   37
Albany. Wisdom and goodness to the vile seem vile;
Filths savour but themselves. What have you done?   39
Tigers not daughters, what have you performed?
A father, and a gracious aged man,
Whose reverence even the head-lugged bear would   42
    lick,
Most barbarous, most degenerate, have you madded.
Could my good brother suffer you to do it?
A man, a prince, by him so benefited!   45
If that the heavens do not their visible spirits   46
Send quickly down to tame these vile offences,
It will come,   48
Humanity must perforce prey on itself,
Like monsters of the deep.
Goneril.   Milk-livered man,
That bear'st a cheek for blows, a head for wrongs;

11. "What like": what he should like.

13. "undertake": commit himself.

14. "Our wishes": i.e., that Edmund might supplant Albany.

15. "prove effects": come true.

16. "musters": recruitments.
    "conduct his pow'rs": lead his army.

17. "change names": i.e., change roles, from wife to husband.
    "distaff": the spinning staff, and hence symbol of the woman.

21. "mistress's": i.e., Edmund's wife's.

24. "Conceive": understand.

28. "My fool usurps": i.e., my husband wrongfully commands.

29. "worth the whistle": worth being welcomed home.

31. "fear your disposition": distrust your nature.

33. "bordered certain": safely confined, predictable.

34. "sliver and disbranch": cut off.

35. "material sap": nourishing trunk (of the tree 'disbranched' in the preceding line).

37. "text": subject of your sermon.

39. "savour": understand and appreciate.

42. "head-lugged": chained by the head, hence fierce.

45. "him": Lear.

46. "visible": made visible (as avengers).

48. "It": chaos, final and complete disorder.

KING LEAR

ACT IV SCENE II

society, there was also the fear of anarchy and disorder. Edmund's "Nature" would lead to just such anarchic chaos. Edmund exalts the vital, animal quality of "Nature" over the dead hand of custom; but the rest of the play, and Albany's lines here, exhibit the self destructive qualities of nature when it is uncontrolled by reverence for law and morality.

Who hast not in thy brows an eye discerning   52
Thine honour from thy suffering; that not know'st
Fools do those villains pity who are punished   54
Ere they have done their mischief. Where's thy
    drum?   55
France spreads his banners in our noiseless land,   56
With plumed helm thy state begins to threat,
Whilst thou, a moral fool, sits still and cries
'Alack, why does he so?'
   Albany.   See thyself, devil:
Proper deformity seems not in the fiend   60
So horrid as in woman.
   Goneril.   O vain fool!
   Albany. Thou changed and self-covered thing, for
    shame
Bemonster not thy feature. Were't my fitness
To let these hands obey my blood,
They are apt enough to dislocate and tear
Thy flesh and bones. Howe'er thou art a fiend,   66
A woman's shape doth shield thee.
   Goneril. Marry, your manhood — mew!   68

         Enter a Messenger.

   Albany. What news?
   Messenger. O, my good lord, the Duke of Corn-
    wall's dead,
Slain by his servant, going to put out
The other eye of Gloucester.
   Albany.   Gloucester's eyes?
   Messenger. A servant that he bred, thrilled with re-   73
    morse,
Opposed against the act, bending his sword
To his great master; who, thereat enraged,
Flew on him, and amongst them felled him dead;
But not without that harmful stroke which since
Hath plucked him after.
   Albany.   This shows you are above,
You justicers, that these our nether crimes   79
So speedily can venge. But, O poor Gloucester,
Lost he his other eye?
   Messenger.   Both, both, my lord.
This letter, madam, craves a speedy answer.
'Tis from your sister.
   Goneril.   [*aside*] One way I like this well;
But being widow, and my Gloucester with her,
May all the building in my fancy pluck   85
Upon my hateful life. Another way   86
The news is not so tart. — I'll read, and answer.   87
                          [*Exit.*
   Albany. Where was his son when they did take his
    eyes?
   Messenger. Come with my lady hither.
   Albany.   He is not here.
   Messenger. No, my good lord; I met him back
    again.
   Albany. Knows he the wickedness?
   Messenger. Ay, my good lord. 'Twas he informed
    against him,
And quit the house on purpose, that their punish-
    ment
Might have the freer course.

52. "discerning": which can distinguish between.

54. "Fools . . . villains": i.e., the Fool and Lear.

55. "drum": i.e., to call together his troops.

56. "noiseless": making no noise of military preparation.

60. "Proper deformity": deformity of self.

66. "Howe'er": although.

68. "Marry": by Mary.
    "mew": an expression of disgust.

73. "thrilled": moved, excited by.

79. "justicers": those who dispense justice.
    "nether crimes": crimes here below.

85-6. "May all . . . life": i.e., may make my life hateful by destroying all my imagined plans.

86. "Another way": i.e., if Cornwall is looked on as barring Edmund's way to sole command.

87. "tart": sharp, unpleasant.

ACT IV SCENE III

This brief scene prepares us for the reunion of Lear and Cordelia. The King of France is returned to France by Shakespeare for two reasons, i) it would be impolitic to show a French king invading English soil on the Elizabethan stage, and ii) from a dramatic point of view, the presence of Cordelia's husband would complicate her appearances on stage and her relation with Lear. Cordelia is an important character in the play, but she is also a simple one, and must remain so. To provide her at this point with a husband and consequent additional dialogue would give her character more detail and complications, which is not the effect that Shakespeare wants at this point. The way in which he does want to convey Cordelia to us in this scene is made clear by the Gentleman's description. In contrast to the evil sisters, and to the evil which pervades the play, Cordelia represents a model of goodness, forgiveness and charity. Absolute goodness is immensely difficult to represent on the stage, which is one of the reasons that Cordelia appears so infrequently in the play. When she is described, as here, it is in terms which are not meant to be realistic or descriptive, but to suggest some ideal figure. Hence the imagery of "pearls and diamonds," for tears and eyes, and the deliberately religious association of "The holy water from her heavenly eyes . . ."

Albany.   Gloucester, I live
To thank thee for the love thou showed'st the King,
And to revenge thine eyes. Come hither, friend.
Tell me what more thou know'st.   [*Exeunt.*

Scene three.

(THE FRENCH CAMP NEAR DOVER.)

Enter KENT *and a* Gentleman.

Kent. Why the King of France is so suddenly gone back know you no reason?

Gentleman. Something he left imperfect in the state, which since his coming forth is thought of, which imports to the kingdom so much fear and danger that his personal return was most required and necessary.   3

Kent. Who hath he left behind him general?

Gentleman. The Marshal of France, Monsieur La Far.

Kent. Did your letters pierce the Queen to any demonstration of grief?

Gentleman. Ay, sir. She took them, read them in my presence,
And now and then an ample tear trilled down
Her delicate cheek. It seemed she was a queen
Over her passion, who, most rebel-like   15
Sought to be king o'er her.

Kent.   O, then it moved her?

Gentleman. Not to a rage. Patience and sorrow strove
Who should express her goodliest. You have seen   18
Sunshine and rain at once — her smiles and tears
Were like a better way: those happy smilets   20
That played on her ripe lip seem not to know
What guests were in her eyes, which parted thence
As pearls from diamonds dropped. In brief,
Sorrow would be a rarity most beloved,
If all could so become it.   25

Kent.   Made she no verbal question?

Gentleman. Faith, once or twice she heaved the name of father
Pantingly forth, as if it pressed her heart;
Cried 'Sisters, sisters, shame of ladies, sisters!
Kent, father, sisters? What, i' th' storm i' th' night?
Let pity not be believed!' There she shook
The holy water from her heavenly eyes,
And clamour moistened; then away she started   32
To deal with grief alone.

Kent.   It is the stars,
The stars above us govern our conditions;
Else one self mate and make could not beget   35
Such different issues. You spoke not with her since?

Gentleman. No.

Kent. Was this before the King returned?

Gentleman.   No, since.

Kent. Well, sir, the poor distressed Lear's i' th' town;

3. "imperfect": undone.

15. "who": which.

18. "goodliest": most fittingly.

20. "smilets": little smiles.

25. "become": assume.

32. "clamour moistened": i.e., subdued her laments with her tears.

35. "one self . . . make": the same husband and wife.

65

KING LEAR

ACT IV SCENE III

We learn from Kent of Lear who is "sometime" in "better tune," and of his "sovereign shame" concerning Cordelia. In fact, when we next see Lear, he is mad. However the possibility of his sanity must be kept in our minds, together with the notion of Cordelia healing and restoring him.

ACT IV SCENE IV

Again we see Shakespeare compensating for the simplicity of Elizabethan staging with language. As in the preceding scene the Gentleman had described Cordelia for us, now Cordelia describes Lear. He is "mad as the vexed sea," and the completeness of his collapse is underlined by the symbolic crown of "rank fumiter and furrow weeds" which has replaced his real crown. The symbolism of nature is carried on through the dialogue between Cordelia and the doctor. Lear's disordered state may be represented by the crown of rank weeds, but nature is also a healer, in the herbs or "simples" and all those "virtues of the earth" which, Cordelia says, will "Spring with my tears." Cordelia is herself a healing power; she may be thought of as associated with that in nature which is "aidant and remediate" rather than destructive. Cordelia's association with love is also made clear at the end of the scene. It is hatred that has undone Lear, and therefore love that must cure him. Cordelia's invasion, then, is the opposite of the attack arising from "blown ambition;" it springs from "love" and "right."

Who sometime, in his better tune, remembers   40
What we are come about, and by no means
Will yield to see his daughter.
   Gentleman.   Why, good sir?
   Kent. A sovereign shame so elbows him; his own   43
     unkindness,
That stripped her from his benediction, turned her
To foreign casualties, gave her dear rights   45
To his dog-hearted daughters — these things sting
His mind so venomously that burning shame
Detains him from Cordelia.
   Gentleman.   Alack, poor gentleman.
   Kent. Of Albany's and Cornwall's powers you
     heard not?
   Gentleman. 'Tis so; they are afoot.   50
   Kent. Well, sir, I'll bring you to our master Lear
And leave you to attend him. Some dear cause   52
Will in concealment wrap me up awhile.
When I am known aright, you shall not grieve
Lending me this acquaintance. I pray you go
Along with me.   [*Exeunt.*

Scene four.

(THE SAME.)

Enter, with Drum and Colors, CORDELIA, *Doctor,*
and Soldiers.

   Cordelia. Alack, 'tis he! Why, he was met even
     now
As mad as the vexed sea, singing aloud,
Crowned with rank fumiter and furrow weeds,   3
With hardocks, hemlock, nettles, cuckoo flow'rs,
Darnel, and all the idle weeds that grow
In our sustaining corn. A century send forth!   6
Search every acre in the high-grown field
And bring him to our eye. [*Exit an Officer.*] What
     can man's wisdom   8
In the restoring his bereaved sense?
He that helps him take all my outward worth.
   Doctor. There is means, madam.
Our foster nurse of nature is repose,
The which he lacks. That to provoke in him
Are many simples operative, whose power   14
Will close the eye of anguish.
   Cordelia.   All blest secrets,
All you unpublished virtues of the earth,   16
Spring with my tears; be aidant and remediate   17
In the good man's distress. Seek, seek for him,
Lest his ungoverned rage dissolve the life
That wants the means to lead it.   20
         Enter Messenger.
   Messenger.   News, madam.
The British pow'rs are marching hitherward.
   Cordelia. 'Tis known before. Our preparation
     stands
In expectation of them. O dear father,

---

40. "better tune": more harmonious, or rational state.

43. "sovereign": overpowering.

45. "casualties": chances.

50. "'Tis so": i.e., it is this way.

52. "dear cause": important reason.

3. "fumiter, furrow &c": various 'idle weeds.'

6. "sustaining corn": the wheat that supports us.
"century": a unit of a hundred men.

8. "can": i.e., is able to perform.

14. "simples operative": healing herbs.

16. "unpublished virtues": unknown healing powers.

17. "aidant and remediate": helpful and remedial.

20. "wants": lacks.
"means": i.e., the reason.

KING LEAR

ACT IV SCENE IV

ACT IV SCENE V

The scenes in which we witness the trials and sufferings of Lear and Gloucester are interspersed with brief scenes, such as this one, exhibiting the struggle for power within the evil party, and the machinations of the two sisters and Edmund. What we know already of Regan and Goneril makes further elaboration on their characters unnecessary; Lear, Gloucester and Albany have already said enough. All that is needed is to see them in action.

Here, in the opening seven lines of dialogue, Regan raps out her questions with the machine-like efficiency of the practiced interrogator. Devious and dishonest in her own actions, she takes dishonesty as a matter of natural policy and suspects it in everyone. She is also (as are Edmund and Goneril) sharply aware of the tactics of their situation. Failing to kill Gloucester, for example, was "great ignorance . . . Where he arrives he moves/All hearts against us."

Perhaps the main significance in the scene lies in the conflict between Regan and her sister over Edmund. In the society of Lear, Cordelia, Kent and Edgar love is a bond," a force for coherence. The reverse is true in the "natural" world of Regan and Goneril. There, love is appetite—a matter of self-satisfaction and self-interest. It is therefore the reverse of a "bond," it is a division, producing competitive strife. The division here, as it happens, will bring about the death of the two competitors. Given the "dog-hearted daughters" and their desires "Humanity must perforce prey on itself," and they will end by destroying each other.

It is thy business that I go about.
Therefore great France
My mourning, and importuned tears hath pitied.   26
No blown ambition doth our arms incite,   27
But love, dear love, and our aged father's right.
Soon may I hear and see him!   [*Exeunt.*

Scene five.

(GLOUCESTER'S CASTLE.)
Enter REGAN *and* OSWALD.

Regan. But are my brother's pow'rs set forth?
Oswald.   Ay, madam.
Regan. Himself in person there?
Oswald.   Madam, with much ado.   2
Your sister is the better soldier.
Regan. Lord Edmund spake not with your lord at
    home?
Oswald. No, madam.
Regan. What might import my sister's letter to
    him?
Oswald. I know not, lady.
Regan. Faith, he is posted hence on serious matter.   8
It was great ignorance, Gloucester's eyes being out,
To let him live. Where he arrives he moves
All hearts against us. Edmund, I think, is gone,
In pity of his misery, to dispatch
His nighted life; moreover, to descry   13
The strength o' th' enemy.
Oswald. I must needs after him, madam, with my
    letter.
Regan. Our troops set forth to-morrow. Stay with
    us.
The ways are dangerous.
Oswald.   I may not, madam.
My lady charged my duty in this business.   18
Regan. Why should she write to Edmund? Might
    not you
Transport her purposes by word? Belike,   20
Some things — I know not what. I'll love thee much,
Let me unseal the letter.
Oswald.   Madam, I had rather —
Regan. I know your lady does not love her husband
I am sure of that; and at her late being here
She gave strang eliads and most speaking looks   25
To noble Edmund. I know you are of her bosom.   26
Oswald. I, madam?
Regan. I speak in understanding—y'are, I know't—
Therefore I do advise you take this note: 29
My lord is dead; Edmund and I have talked,
And more convenient is he for my hand   31
Than for your lady's. You may gather more.   32
If you do find him, pray you give him this;   33
And when your mistress hears thus much from you,
I pray desire her call her wisdom to her.
So fare you well.
If you do chance to hear of that blind traitor,

26. "importuned": importunate.
27. "blown": puffed up.

2. "much ado": much trouble.

8. "posted": gone.

13. "nighted": benighted, dark.

18. "charged": ordered my obedience.

20. "Belike": probably.

25. "eliads": from the French OEIL-LADES, amorous glances.

26. "of her bosom": in her confidence.

29. "take this note": note well.

31. "convenient": proper.

32. "gather more": add what meaning you like.

33. "this": a token or letter.

67

KING LEAR

ACT IV SCENE V

ACT IV SCENE VI

This long scene falls into three parts, which can be best discussed separately. The parts are i) Gloucester's imagined suicide and recovery (1-80); ii) Lear's dialogue with Gloucester and Lear's escape (80-203; and iii) the continuation of the plot (203-286).

i) Gloucester's imagined suicide is one of the central actions of the play, and might well make an individual scene. It is also one of the most difficult things in the play to make effective on the modern stage. For the Elizabethan audience, who were ready to accept the imagined situations the playwright offered, there was no difficulty. For a modern audience who want as realistic and detailed a staging as possible, it is difficult to believe in Gloucester's acceptance of the flat stage across which he walks as the "cliff" of IV,i,73, and of his "leap" as a fall "ten masts" high. The fault here is with the modern audience's excessive desire for total plausibility. There is no real imaginative difficulty. The blinded, grouping, bemused Gloucester is an apt listener for Edgar's hypnotically persuasive descriptions. Here again we see Shakespeare overcoming the limitations of the Elizabethan stage. No actual cliff would be possible on any stage (Gloucester could hardly be expected to vault down from the Elizabethan upper stage), and in any case it is better to have Edgar's verbally created cliff: it gives us both the sense of height, and the imaginative reaction to it. Not only do we see the sampire gatherer who "hangs" half-way down, and "the fishermen that walk upon the beach" like mice; we are also made to feel "How fearful/And dizzy 'tis to cast one's eyes so low!," and we know the combination of fascination and fear Edgar speaks of when he recoils: "I'll look no more, /Lest my brain turn . . ."

We have already noticed the difficulty that critics have raised concerning Edgar's continued disguise. Why, in this crisis, has he not revealed himself to his father? He gives the answer himself: "Why I do trifle thus with his despair/Is done to cure it." Edgar's assertion may be understood at two levels. In the first place

---

Preferment falls on him that cuts him off. 38

Oswald. Would I could meet him, madam! I should show
What party I do follow.

Regan. Fare thee well. [*Exeunt.*

```
┌─────────────────────────────────┐
│                                 │
│          Scene six.             │
│                                 │
└─────────────────────────────────┘
```

(THE COUNTRY NEAR DOVER.)

Enter GLOUCESTER *and* EDGAR.

Gloucester. When shall I come to th' top of that same hill? 1

Edgar. You do climb up it now. Look how we labour.

Gloucester. Methinks the ground is even.

Edgar. Horrible steep.
Hark, do you hear the sea?

Gloucester. No, truly.

Edgar. Why, then, your other senses grow imperfect
By your eyes' anguish.

Gloucester. So may it be indeed.
Methinks thy voice is altered, and thou speak'st
In better phrase and matter than thou didst.

Edgar. Y'are much deceived. In nothing am I changed
But in my garments.

Gloucester. Methinks y'are better spoken.

Edgar. Come on, sir; here's the place. Stand still.
How fearful
And dizzy 'tis to cast one's eyes so low!
The crows and choughs that wing the midway air 13
Show scarce so gross as beetles. Halfway down 14
Hangs one that gathers sampire — dreadful trade; 15
Methinks he seems no bigger than his head.
The fishermen that walk upon the beach
Appear like mice; and yond tall anchoring bark,
Diminished to her cock; her cock, a buoy 19
Almost too small for sight. The murmuring surge
That on th' unnumb'red idle pebble chafes
Cannot be heard so high. I'll look no more,
Lest my brain turn, and the deficient sight 23
Topple down headlong.

Gloucester. Set me where you stand.

Edgar. Give me your hand. You are now within a foot
Of th' extreme verge. For all beneath the moon
Would I not leap upright. 27

Gloucester. Let go my hand.
Here friend, 's another purse; in it a jewel
Well worth a poor man's taking. Fairies and gods
Prosper it with thee. Go thou further off; 30
Bid me farewell, and let me hear thee going.

Edgar. Now fare ye well, good sir.

Gloucester. With all my heart.

Edgar. [*aside*] Why I do trifle thus with his despair 33
Is done to cure it.

1. "that same hill": see IV,i,73.

13. "choughs": jackdaws.

14. "gross": big.

15. "sampire": a herb used in cooking. "dreadful": i.e., inducing fear through height.

19. "cock": cockboat.

23. "deficient": i.e., through dizziness.

27. "leap upright": stand straight up.

30. "Prosper . . . thee": may it bring you luck.

33. "Why I": the reason why I.

KING LEAR

ACT IV SCENE VI

Edgar's "cure" involves the shock of the supposed suicide. This would be immediately comprehensible to the Elizabethan audience. While their psychological theory was erratic and primitive, they had arrived at the practice of what we should call 'shock therapy,' the attempt to cure abnormal mental states by some sort of powerful disturbance. This sometimes took the form of frightening the patient, and Edgar fears that his father may succumb to the severity of the shock: "and yet I know not how conceit may rob/The treasury of life." Secondly, and more important for the general meaning of the play, the "cure" of the supposed suicide is a part of Gloucester's suffering, and in fact completes the process that Regan and Cornwall began. Gloucester has been brought to the point where he sees life as cruel, arbitrary, and senseless, where whatever powers there are "kill us for their sport." Edgar will now bring him, through this final crisis and his survival of it, to the point where it can be said that Gloucester's life "is a miracle," and, instead of the gods like "wanton boys," Edgar can speak of "the clearest gods" who have saved his father. One commentator has put the matter of Gloucester's attempted suicide in this way: "Gloucester must psychologically and symbolically go through despair and death, not circumvent it. Before one can take on the burden of life, he must shoulder the burden of death. This Gloucester does symbolically, he 'dies;' more accurately, his despair dies. Each man must murder his own despair. The deception is necessary so that he does not murder himself in the process."

Edgar's further change of disguise is necessary to the deception. In his assumption of various guises Edgar directs and illuminates the other outcasts. He has been Lear's "philosopher," and now he is in turn the "fiend" who is with Gloucester at the cliff top (72), and the peasant who discovers him still alive at the bottom. Edgar's description of the fiend may seem at first to be a kind of extravagant surrealism ("methought his eyes/Were two full moons; he had a thousand noses, /Horns whelked and waved like the enridged sea"), yet it is necessary. It is in accord with Gloucester's wild and despairing state—he has indeed been the victim of "some fiend," if not in a literal sense. Edgar describes it in order that Gloucester may see his earlier state as a kind of evil hallucination, and pass on from it to "free and patient thoughts."

Gloucester.   O you mighty gods!
                         [*He kneels.*
This world I do renounce, and in your sights
Shake patiently my great affliction off.
If I could bear it longer and not fall   37
To quarrel with your great opposeless wills,   38
My snuff and loathed part of nature should   39
Burn itself out. If Edgar live, O bless him!
Now, fellow, fare thee well.
                         [*He falls forward and swoons.*
Edgar.   Gone, sir — farewell.
And yet I know not how conceit may rob   42
The treasury of life when life itself
Yields to the theft. Had he been where he thought,
By this had thought been past. Alive or dead?   45
Ho you, sir! Friend! Hear you, sir? Speak!   46
Thus might he pass indeed. Yet he revives.
What are you, sir?
Gloucester.   Away, and let me die.
Edgar. Hadst thou been aught but gossamer, feath-
    ers, air,
So many fathom down precipitating,   50
Thou'dst shivered like an egg; but thou dost breathe,
Hast heavy substance, bleed'st not, speak'st, art
    sound.
Ten masts at each make not the altitude   53
Which thou hast perpendicularly fell.
Thy life 's a miracle. Speak yet again.
Gloucester. But have I fall'n, or no?
Edgar. From the dread summit of this chalky bourn.   57
Look up a-height. The shrill-gorged lark so far   58
Cannot be seen or heard. Do but look up.
Gloucester. Alack, I have no eyes.
Is wretchedness deprived that benefit
To end itself by death? 'Twas yet some comfort
When misery could beguile the tyrant's rage   63
And frustrate his proud will.
Edgar.   Give me your arm.
Up — so. How is't? Feel you your legs? you stand.
Gloucester. Too well, too well.
Edgar.   This is above all strangeness
Upon the crown o' th' cliff what thing was that
Which parted from you?
Gloucester.   A poor unfortunate beggar.
Edgar. As I stood here below, methought his eyes
were two full moons; he had a thousand noses,
Horns whelked and waved like the enridged sea.   71
It was some fiend. Therefore, thou happy father,   72
Think that the clearest gods, Who make them honours   73
Of men's impossibilities, have preserved thee.
Gloucester. I do remember now. Henceforth I'll bear
Affliction till it do cry out itself
'Enough, enough, and die.' That thing you speak of,
I took it for a man. Often 'twould say
'The fiend, the fiend'—he led me to that place.
Edgar. Bear free and patient thoughts.   80
              Enter LEAR *mad, fantastically dressed with flowers.*
                         But who comes here?
The safer sense will ne'er accommodate   81
His master thus.

37-8. "fall . . . with": oppose.

38. "opposeless": not to be opposed.

39. "snuff": guttering, as in a spent candle.

42. "conceit . . . of life": imagination may kill him.

45. "By this": i.e., by this time.

46. "Ho you": Edgar now pretends that they are at the bottom of the 'cliff.'

50. "precipitating": falling.

53. "at each": on top of one another.

57. "bourn": boundary, cliff.

58. "gorged": throated.

63. "beguile": outwit by suicide.

71. "whelked": gnarled.
    "enridged": furrowed.

72. "happy father": lucky old man.

73-4. "Who make . . . impossibilities": whose virtue it is to do for man what he cannot do for himself.

80. "free": of despair.

81-2. "The safer . . . thus": i.e., the man in his right mind would never dress thus.

69

KING LEAR

ACT IV SCENE VI

ii) Lear enters, garlanded with wild flowers (some editors read "weeds" in the stage direction, on the basis of IV,iv,3ff). We have seen earlier the way in which Shakespeare can give sense and dramatic point to what may at first sight seem to be lunatic ramblings. Even Lear's opening line about the practice of "coining" or counterfeiting money has a bitter application. The evil party have counterfeited his power in wrongly assuming it. Here is another interpretation, of 83-93 by a recent editor: "Lear's remarks are not in full logical connection, but neither are they sheer nonsense. First he reverts to the idea of a trial, and assorts his acquittal on a charge of forgery. 'Coining' suggests (press-)money. Next he imagines he has the recruits in front of him and criticizes their archery. After the mouse interlude (an imagined enemy?) we return to war, halberdiers, archery, and a password." The request for the "word," or password, elicits Edgar's reply ("marjoram") underlining the fact of Lear's insanity. But Lear, in his madness, sees the truth. His ramblings from 97 to 106 are, indeed, a summary of his progress through the play. As king he was guilty of ignorance and—the traditional fault of the man in power—susceptibility to the dishonesty around him—"They flattered me like a dog . . . To say 'ay' and 'no' to everything that I said." But the storm acted as a revelation of these evils—"When the rain came to wet me . . . there I found 'em, there I smelt 'em out." In fact Lear's madness here suggests a kind of higher, intuitive understanding that reason would never have given him. In his humiliation he sees himself more clearly: "They told me I was everything. 'Tis a lie—I am not ague-proof."

At 108 Lear returns to his obsession with justice and the perversions of justice (see commentary at III,vi). What is significant is that Lear sees the evil and disorder in the world ruled by Goneril and Regan far more clearly in his madness than he ever did when he was sane. In the normal world, where there is some conception of ethical law, there can be sin. But without this conception, and the moral order based on it, here is neither sin, or guilt. Lear takes St. Paul's phrase "All have offended" and perverts it to "None does offend, none, I say none!" The normal bonds of human society do not hold, and no one is guilty: "Thou shalt not die. Die for adultery? No," and the reason for this 'freedom' from justice, this return to the primitive, lawless world follows at once in another reccurrence of animal imagery. "The wren goes to

Lear. No, they cannot touch me for coining; 83
I am the King himself.

Edgar. O thou side-piercing sight!

Lear. Nature's above art in that respect. There's 87
your press money. That fellow handles his bow like
a crow-keeper. Draw me a clothier's yard. Look, look, 88
a mouse! Peace, peace; this piece of toasted cheese
will do't. There's my gauntlet; I'll prove it on a 90
giant. Bring up the brown bills. 91
O, well flown, bird. I' th' clout, i' th' clout—hewgh! 92
Give the word. 93

Edgar. Sweet marjoram. 94

Lear. Pass.

Gloucester. I know that voice.

Lear. Ha! Goneril with a white beard? They flattered me like a dog, and told me I had the white 98
hairs in my beard ere the black ones were there.
To say 'ay' and 'no' to everything that I said! 'Ay'
and 'no' was no good divinity. When the rain came 101
to wet me once, and the wind to make me chatter; when the thunder would not peace at my bidding; there I found 'em, there I smelt 'em out. Go
to, they are not men o' their words. They told me I
was everything. 'Tis a lie — I am not ague-proof. 106

Gloucester. The trick of that voice I do well re- 107
member.
Is't not the King?

Lear.   Ay, every inch a king.
When I do stare, see how the subject quakes.
I pardon that man's life. What was thy cause? 110
Adultery?
Thou shalt not die. Die for adultery? No.
The wren goes to't, and the small gilded fly
Does lecher in my sight. 114
Let copulation thrive; for Gloucester's bastard son
Was kinder to his father than my daughters
Got 'tween the lawful sheets.
To't, luxury, pell-mell, for I lack soldiers. 118
Behold yond simp'ring dame,
Whose face between her forks presages snow, 120
That minces virtue, and does shake the head 121
To hear of pleasure's name.
The fitchew nor the soiled horse goes to't 123
With a more riotous appetite.
Down from the waist they are Centaurs, 125
Though women all above.
But to the girdle do the gods inherit, 127
Beneath is all the fiend's.
There's hell, there's darkness, there is the sulphurous pit; burning, scalding, stench, consumption. Fie,
fie, fie! pah, pah! Give me an ounce of civet; good 131
apothecary, sweeten my imagination! There's money 132
for thee.

Gloucester. O, let me kiss that hand.

Lear. Let me wipe it first; it smells of mortality. 135

Gloucester. O ruined piece of nature; this great 136
world
Shall so wear out to naught. Dost thou know me?

Lear. I remember thine eyes well enough. Dost thou

83. "touch me for coining": arrest me for counterfeiting the king's image on a coin.

87. "press money": money for being impressed into service.

88. "crow-keeper": farmer warding off crows.
"clothier's yard": i.e., an arrow (usually a yard long).

90. "gauntlet": armored glove flung down as a challenge.
"prove it on": support the challenge against.

91. "brown bills": halberds, i.e., the soldiers carrying this weapon.

92. "well flown": a hawking cry.
"clout": bull's-eye in archery.
"hewgh": imitation of the sound of a whistling arrow.

93. "word": password.

94. "Sweet marjoram": a herb associated with the treatment of madness.

98. "like a dog": as a dog would flatter, or fawn.
"white hairs": standing for wisdom.

101. "no good divinity": apparently a reference to 2 Corinthians 1:18 'as God is true our word to you was not yea and nay.'

106. "ague-proof": proof against fever.

107. "trick": particular character.

110. "cause": case.

114. "lecher": lust.

118. "luxury": lechery.
"lack soldiers": and therefore need more births.

120. "forks": legs.
"presages snow": suggests frigidity.

121. "minces": mincingly affects.

123. "fitchew": polecat.
"soiled": pastured.

125. "Centaurs": mythological creatures, half-human and half-beast, usually representing appetite.

127. "girdle": waist.
"inherit": possess, control.

131. "civet": perfume.

132. "apothecary": seller of drugs.

135. "mortality": death.

136-7. "this great . . . naught": the world will itself decay, like this man.

KING LEAR

ACT IV SCENE VI

't, and the small gilded fly/Does lecher in my sight./Let copulation thrive." We are reminded again that morally, as well as materially, in the world of Edmund's "Nature," "man's life's as cheap as beast's." This passage is followed by a savage attack on women and sexuality ("Behold yon simpering dame . . .") in which humans are again reduced to animals (the "fitchew" and the "soiled horse") and the passage ends with uncontrolled disgust and hatred on Lear's part ("There's hell, there's darkness, there is the sulphurous pit . . ."). The violence of the attack on sex here has been compared to that which occurs in HAMLET and in TROILUS AND CRESSIDA, and in all three plays it occurs for the same reason. This may be briefly summarized in this way: i) in a normal, ordered world love is the most valuable relationship between individuals. But ii), when some evil force poisons and disorders society (as in HAMLET, TROILUS AND CRESSIDA, and KING LEAR) love is corrupted (as are all human relationships), and iii) this corruption, or poisoning is represented by treating love as lust, or debased, carnal appetite. This is why Lear here, for no immediately apparent reason, launches into an hysterical denunciation of sexuality. The world of unregenerate "nature" is a world without love, or one where love is reduced to pure carnality.

The confrontation between the blinded Gloucester and the demented Lear is especially dramatic, bringing together the two wounded victim-heroes of the two plots. Gloucester's sensuality has cost him a terrible price in the damage to his senses (see Edgar at V.iii.171: "The gods are just, and of our pleasant vices/Make instruments to plague us./The dark and vicious place where thee he got/Cost him his eyes"): Lear's pride and stupidity have brought about the destruction of his reason. It is little wonder that the exchanges between the two reflect a pessimism apparently beyond cure or explanation. In the ultimate stage of his desperation, Lear hits upon an image that most might take as suggestive of fertility, growth and hope: the newborn child. But for Lear birth itself suggests tragedy, and the child's tears are like his own: "the first time that we smell the air/We wawl and cry . . . When we are born, we cry that we are come/To this great stage of fools." At 203 Lear makes his exit, running, with cries taken from the hunt. He sees himslf as the hunted quarry and those around him, who are in fact trying to help him, as seeking his life.

---

squiny at me? No, do thy worst, blind Cupid; I'll 139
not love.
Read thou this challenge; mark but the penning of it.
Gloucester. Were all thy letters suns, I could
  not see.
Edgar. [*aside*] I would not take this from report — it is,
And my heart breaks at it.
Lear. Read.
Gloucester. What, with the case of eyes? 145
Lear. O, ho, are you there with me? No eyes in your 146
head, nor no money in your purse? Your eyes are in
a heavy case, your purse in a light; yet you see how 148
this world goes.
Gloucester. I see it feelingly.
Lear. What, art mad? A man may see how this world
goes with no eyes. Look with thine ears. See how yond
justice rails upon yond simple thief. Hark in thine
ear. Change places and, handy-dandy, which is the 154
justice, which is the thief? Thou hast seen a farmer's dog bark at a beggar?
Gloucester. Ay, sir.
Lear. And the creature run from the cur. There
thou mightst behold the great image of authority—
a dog's obeyed in office. 160
Thou rascal beadle, hold thy bloody hand! 161
Why dost thou lash that whore? Strip thy own back.
Thou hotly lusts to use her in that kind 163
For which thou whip'st her. The usurer hangs the 164
  cozener.
Through tattered clothes small vices do appear;
Robes and furred gowns hide all. Plate sin with 166
  gold,
And the strong lance of justice hurtless breaks;
Arm it in rags, a pygmy's straw does pierce it.
None does offend, none — I say none! I'll able 'em. 169
Take that of me, my friend, who have the power 170
To seal th' accuser's lips. Get thee glass eyes 171
And, like a scurvy politician, seem 172
To see the things thou dost not. Now, now, now,
  now!
Pull off my boots. Harder, harder! So.
Edgar. O, matter and impertinency mixed; 175
Reason in madness.
Lear. If thou wilt weep my fortunes, take my eyes.
I know thee well enough; thy name is Gloucester.
Thou must be patient. We came crying hither;
Thou know'st, the first time that we smell the air
We wawl and cry. I will preach to thee. Mark.
Gloucester. Alack, alack the day.
Lear. When we are born, we cry that we are come
To this great stage of fools. — This' a good block. 184
It were a delicate stratagem to shoe
A troop of horse with felt. I'll put't in proof, 186
And when I have stol'n upon these son-in-laws,
Then kill, kill, kill, kill, kill!

Enter a Gentleman *with* Attendants.

Gentleman. O, here he is! Lay hand upon him. —
  Sir,
Your most dear daughter —

---

139. "squiny": squint.
"blind Cupid": reference to Gloucester's blindness; 'blind Cupid' was also often used of brothels, hence Lear's next phrase.

145. "case": empty sockets.

146. "with me": in my situation?

148. "case": situation.

150. "feelingly": i) by touch, ii) by feeling pain.

154. "handy-dandy": i.e., which is which? From the child's game of choosing which closed hand holds an object.

160. "in office": in a position of authority.

161. "beadle": local constable.

163. "in that kind": in that way.

164. "The usurer . . . cozener": i.e., the great thief hangs the little thief.

166. "Plate": plate with armor.

169. "able": enable (to offend).

170. "that": i.e., immunity from the law.

171 "glass": false.

172. "scurvy politician": vile opportunist (the word 'politician' was always used in this pejorative sense by the Elizabethan).

175. "matter and impertinency": good sense and nonsense.

184. "block": for a felt hat; the idea of 'felt' then suggests l. 186.

186. "in proof": to the test.

KING LEAR

ACT IV SCENE VI

iii) Edgar describes himself to Gloucester as "A most poor man, made tame to fortune's blows." The implication is that, having suffered himself, he is able to lead Gloucester through his sufferings. Edgar again appears as a guiding spirit and protector. His protection of Gloucester against Oswald is done in the guise of a peasant, as the dialogue indicates. This has baffled a good many of the play's directors. Theatrically, however, the meaning should be clear. Oswald has been presented throughout as the "superserviceable, finical rogue." Obviously he appears here on the stage with the glamorous dress and fashionable gestures of the courtier; yet it is Goneril's court, not the King's which he serves—he is an example of false courtliness. Edgar therefor appears as his opposite in

Lear. No rescue? What, a prisoner? I am even
The natural fool of fortune. Use me well;   192
You shall have ransom. Let me have surgeons;
I am cut to th' brains.
Gentleman.   You shall have anything.
Lear. No seconds? All myself?   195
Why, this would make a man a man of salt,   196
To use his eyes for garden waterpots,
Ay, and laying autumn's dust. I will die bravely,
Like a smug bridegroom. What, I will be jovial!   199
Come, come, I am a king; masters, know you that?
Gentleman. You are a royal one, and we obey you.
Lear. Then there's life in't. Come, an you get it,   202
you shall get it by running. Sa, sa, sa, sa!   203
               [*Exit running, followd by* Attendants.
Gentleman. A sight most pitiful in the meanest
    wretch,
Past speaking of in a king. Thou hast one daughter
Who redeems nature from the general curse
Which twain have brought her to.   207
Edgar. Hail, gentle sir.
Gentleman.   Sir, speed you. What's your will?
Edgar. Do you hear aught, sir, of a battle toward?
Gentleman. Most sure and vulgar. Every one hears 210
    that
Which can distinguish sound.
Edgar.   But, by your favour,
How near's the other army?
Gentleman. Near and on speedy foot. The main   213
    descry
Stands on the hourly thought.
Edgar.   I thank you, sir. That's all.
Gentleman. Though that the Queen on special cause
    is here,
Her army is moved on.
Edgar.   I thank you, sir.   [*Exit* Gentleman.
Gloucester. You ever-gentle gods, take my breath
    from me;
Let not my worser spirit tempt me again
To die before you please.
Edgar   Well pray you, father.
Gloucester. Now, good sir, what are you?
Edgar. A most poor man, made tame to fortune's
    blows,
Who, by the art of known and feeling sorrows,
Am pregnant to good pity. Give me your hand;   223
I'll lead you to some biding.   224
Gloucester   Hearty thanks.
The bounty and the benison of heaven
To boot, and boot.   226

               Enter OSWALD.

Oswald.   A proclaimed prize! Most happy;
That eyeless head of thine was first framed flesh
To raise my fortunes. Thou old unhappy traitor,
Briefly thyself remember. The sword is out   229
That must destroy thee.
Gloucester.   Now let thy friendly hand
Put strength enough to't.   [EDGAR *interposes.*
Oswald.   Wherefore, bold peasant,

192. "natural fool": born dupe, laughing-stock.

195. "seconds": supporters.

196. "salt": i.e., salt tears.

199. "smug": self-satisfied.

202. "there's life in't": i.e., all is not lost.

203. "Sa . . . sa": hunting cry used to excite the hounds.

207. "twain": i.e., Goneril and Regan.

210. "vulgar": i.e., known by everyone.

213. "main descry": the sight of the main body.

223. "pregnant to": able to feel.

224. "biding": place where you may bide.

226. "To boot": in addition.
"and boot": and may it help you.
"happy": lucky.

229. "thyself remember": i.e., in your prayers.

KING LEAR

ACT IV SCENE VI

dress, language and behavior. Oswald's diction — "Hence,/Lest that th' infection of his fortune take/Like hold on thee"—is answered by Edgar's blunt, honest, rural dialect (see glossary)— "Keep out, che vore ye, or Ise try whether your costard or my ballow be the harder."

Oswald's death is followed by the opening of Goneril's letter, containing the evidence of the plot on her husband's life, and the terse direction: "time and place will be fruitfully offered." Shakespeare leads us to the anticipation of two further developments: the plot on Albany's life and the rivalry between Regan and Goneril, and the expectation of the coming conflict, suggested here by the "beaten drum" which closes the scene.

Dar'st thou support a published traitor? Hence,
Lest that th' infection of his fortune take
Like hold on thee. Let go his arm.

Edgar. Chill not let go, zir, without vurther 'casion 235
Oswald. Let go, slave, or thou diest.
Edgar. Good gentleman, go your gait, and let poor 237
voke pass. An chud ha' bin zwaggered out of my life, 238
'twould not ha' bin zo long as 'tis by a vortnight.
Nay, come not near th' old man. Keep out, che vore 240
ye, or Ise try whether your costard or my ballow be 241
the harder. Chill be plain with you.

Oswald. Out, dunghill!   [*They fight.*

Edgar. Chill pick your teeth, zir. Come. No matter 244
vor your foins.   [OSWALD *falls.* 245

Oswald. Slave, thou hast slain me. Villain, take my
          purse.
If ever thou wilt thrive, bury my body,
And give the letters which thou find'st about me   248
To Edmund Earl of Gloucester. Seek him out
Upon the English party. O, untimely death!
Death!   [*He dies.*

Edgar. I know thee well. A serviceable villain,   252
As duteous to the vices of thy mistress
As badness would desire.

Gloucester.   What, is he dead?

Edgar. Sit you down, father; rest you.
Let's see these pockets; the letters that he speaks of
May be my friends. He's dead; I am only sorry
He had no other deathsman. Let us see.   258
Leave, gentle wax; and, manners, blame us not   259
To know our enemies' minds. We rip their hearts;
Their papers is more lawful.   [*Reads the letter.*
'Let our reciprocal vows be remembered. You have
many opportunities to cut him off. If your will want 263
not, time and place will be fruitfully offered. There
is nothing done, if he return the conqueror. Then
am I the prisoner, and his bed my gaol; from the
loathed warmth wherof deliver me, and supply the
place for your labour.
     'Your (wife, so I would say) affectionate servant,
                                         'GONERIL.'

O indistinguished space of woman's will —   271
A plot upon her virtuous husband's life,
And the exchange my brother! Here in the sands 273
Thee I'll rake up, the post unsanctified   274
Of murderous lechers; and in the mature time   275
With this ungracious paper strike the sight
Of the death-practiced Duke. For him 'tis well   277
That of thy death and business I can tell.   278

Gloucester. The King is mad. How stiff is my vile 279
     sense,
That I stand up, and have ingenious feeling   280
Of my huge sorrows! Better I were distract;   281
So should my thoughts be severed from my griefs,
And woes by wrong imaginations lose   283
The knowledge of themselves.   [*Drum afar off.*

Edgar.   Give me your hand.
Far off methinks I hear the beaten drum.
Come, father, I'll bestow you with a friend.
                                        [*Exeunt.*

235. "Chill": I'll. Edgar here and in what follows uses the rustic dialect of the southwest of England, the form in which all rustic characters spoke on the Elizabethan stage.

237. "gait": way.

238. "voke": folk.
"An chud": and if I could.
"zwaggered": frightened (by a swagger).

240-1. "che vore ye": I warn you.

241. "costard": head.
"ballow": cudgel.

244. "pick": knock out.

245. "foins": thrusts.

248. "letters": the letter; usually singular in Shakespeare.

252. "serviceable": usable.

258. "deathsman": executioner.

259. "wax": i.e., which sealed the letter.

263. "him": Albany.
"want not": is not lacking (in courage).

271. "indistinguished": unbounded.

273. "exchange": i.e., for Albany.

274. "rake up": i.e., rake under, hide.
"post": message.

275. "mature time": when the time is ripe.

277. "death-practiced": whose death has been plotted.

278. "thy": he indicates Oswald's body.

279. "stiff": unfeeling.

280. "ingenious feeling": consciousness.

281. "distract": mad.

283. "wrong imaginations": delusions.

KING LEAR

ACT IV SCENE VII

This is the 'reconciliation scene (as it is generally called) in which Lear is reunited with Cordelia. The sleep referred to (13) is more than simply physical rest. In Shakespeare's plays sleep usually has symbolic value. It represents peace and well-being, just as lack of sleep represents unrest and insecurity of some kind: thus Julius Caesar, about to enter into the evil of conspiracy, cannot sleep; nor can Macbeth, who, plagued with guilt, is said to "need the season of all natures, sleep." Earlier Lear has been denied "the rest" that might have "balmed the broken sinews." It is therefore a way of indicating a change for the better in Lear's state to announce that he has slept, just as the change from "weeds" to "fresh garments" suggests a rehabilitation of spirit. The music that plays (25) is also important; music in Shakespeare is more than a background effect. It is usually used in connection with peace and serenity. Here, as a symbolic sound, it is the opposite of the cacophony of the storm, which has been the other prominent sound in the play. As we have seen, storm signifies upset and disorder (in JULIUS CAESAR and MACBETH as well as KING LEAR), and music the restoration of order. Here it is associated with the recovery of Lear's "untuned and jarring senses."

Scene seven.

(THE FRENCH CAMP.)

Enter CORDELIA, KENT, Doctor, *and* Gentleman.

Cordelia. O thou good Kent, how shall I live and
    work
To match thy goodness? My life will be too short
And every measure fail me.
    Kent. To be acknowledged, madam, is o'erpaid.
All my reports go with the modest truth;   5
Nor more nor clipped, but so.
    Cordelia.   Be better suited.   6
These weeds are memories of those worser hours.   7
I prithee put them off.
    Kent.   Pardon, dear madam.
Yet to be known shortens my made intent.   9
My boon I make it that you know me not   10
Till time and I think meet.
    Cordelia. Then be't so, my good lord. [*to the Doctor*] How does the King?
    Doctor. Madam, sleeps still.
    Cordelia. O you kind gods,
Cure this great breach in his abused nature!
Th' untuned and jarring senses, O, wind up   16
Of this child-changed father!   17
    Doctor.   So please your Majesty
That we may wake the King? He hath slept long.
    Cordelia. Be governed by your knowledge, and
    proceed
I' th' sway of your own will. Is he arrayed?   20
    Enter LEAR *in a chair carried by* Servants.
    Gentleman. Ay, madam. In the heaviness of sleep
We put fresh garments on him.
    Doctor. Be by, good madam, when we do awake him.
I doubt not of his temperance.   24
    Cordelia.   Very well.   [*Music.*
    Doctor. Please you draw near. Louder the music
    there.
    Cordelia. O my dear father, restoration hang   26
Thy medicine on my lips, and let this kiss
Repair those violent harms that my two sisters
Have in thy reverence made.   29
    Kent.   Kind and dear princess.
    Cordelia. Had you not been their father, these white   30
    flakes
Did challenge pity of them. Was this a face
To be opposed again the jarring winds?
To stand against the deep dread-bolted thunder?   33
In the most terrible and nimble stroke
Of quick cross lightning to watch, poor perdu,   35
With this thin helm? Mine enemy's dog,   36
Though he had bit me, should have stood that night
Against my fire; and wast thou fain, poor father,   38
To hovel thee with swine and rogues forlorn
In short and musty straw? Alack, alack,
'Tis wonder that thy life and wits at once

---

5. "All my . . . so": i.e., what I report is neither more nor less than the truth.

6. "suited": dressed.

7. "weeds": clothes.

9. "made intent": plan.

10. "boon": favor.
"know me not": i.e., I remain disguised.

16. "wind up": tune.

17. "child-changed": i) changed to a child, and ii) changed by his children.

20. "I' th' sway": in obedience to.

24. "temperance": sanity, balance.

26. "restoration": the power of restoring health.

29. "reverence": aged and revered person.

30. "white flakes": i.e., hair and beard.

33. "deep dread-bolted": deep-voiced and bringing dreaded bolts.

35. "perdu": lost one.

36. "helm": helmet of hair.

38. "fain": glad.

74

KING LEAR

ACT IV SCENE VII

Lear's awakening is, in some ways, like Gloucester's recovery from his 'suicide.' Both have undergone their purgatorial trials. Both have, in a sense, 'died.' Gloucester's new life is a "miracle." Lear thinks that he wakes in a world beyond the grave; Cordelia appears to him as a "spirit." She will lead him now, just as Gloucester's wronged child leads him after his imagined death.

Notice the contrast between Lear's speech here and his earlier language. Compare 59-70 with, for example, the "Blow winds and crack your cheeks" passage at III,ii,1. There we feel Lear's overpowering fury; here the language is simple and childlike ("Pray, do not mock me . . ."). Lear's "great rage" has burned out, and given place to a new simplicity, and humility, which in turn gives the language a clarity and directness entirely different from the twisted ravings on the heath: "I am a very foolish, fond old man . . . And, to deal plainly,/I fear I am not in my perfect mind."

The scene is also meant to recall I,i, and Lear's banishment of Cordelia. There he demanded evidence of her love, here he recognizes his own guilt. Cordelia, he says, has "some cause" to deny him her love. Cordelia's answer— "No cause, no cause"—suggests again (as she suggested in I,i) that love is not a material, measurable thing. Lear need not "reason the need" of love here as Goneril and Ragan have done (II,-iv,261), since it is above need or exchange, or even rational assessment.

Had not concluded all. — He wakes. Speak to him. 42
Doctor. Madam, do you; 'tis fittest.
Cordelia. How does my royal lord? How fares your Majesty?
Lear. You do me wrong to take me out o' th' grave.
Thou art a soul in bliss; but I am bound
Upon a wheel of fire, that mine own tears 47
Do scald like molten lead.
Cordelia.   Sir, do you know me?
Lear. You are a spirit, I know. Where did you die?
Cordelia. Still, still, far wide! 50
Doctor. He's scarce awake. Let him alone awhile.
Lear. Where have I been? Where am I? Fair daylight?
I am mightily abused. I should e'en die with pity 53
To see another thus. I know not what to say.
I will not swear these are my hands. Let's see —
I feel this pin prick. Would I were assured
Of my condition.
Cordelia.   O look upon me, sir,
And hold your hand in benediction o'er me.
You must not kneel.
Lear.   Pray, do not mock me.
I am a very foolish fond old man,
Fourscore and upward, not an hour more nor less;
And, to deal plainly,
I fear I am not in my perfect mind.
Methinks I should know you, and know this man;
Yet I am doubtful, for I am mainly ignorant
What place this is; and all the skill I have
Remembers not these garments; nor I know not
Where I did lodge last night. Do not laugh at me;
For, as I am a man, I think this lady
To be my child Cordelia.
Cordelia.   And so I am! I am!
Lear. Be your tears wet? Yes, faith. I pray weep not.
If you have poison for me, I will drink it.
I know you do not love me; for your sisters
Have, as I do remember, done me wrong.
You have some cause, they have not.
Cordelia.   No cause, no cause.
Lear. Am I in France?
Kent.   In your own kingdom, sir.
Lear. Do not abuse me.
Doctor. Be comforted, good madam. The great 78
rage
You see is killed in him; and yet it is danger
To make him even o'er the time he has lost. 80
Desire him to go in. Trouble him no more
Till further settling. 82
Cordelia. Will't please your Highness walk?
Lear.   You must bear with me.
Pray you now, forget and forgive. I am old and foolish.

            [*Exeunt all but* KENT *and* Gentleman.

Gentleman. Holds it true, sir, that the Duke of Cornwall was so slain?
Kent. Most certain, sir.
Gentleman. Who is conductor of his people?

42. "concluded": ended completely.

47. "wheel of fire": "an implement combining the tortures of breaking and burning, figuring in medieval visions of hell" (Harbage).

50. "wide": of the mark.

53. "abused": misled, confused.

78. "rage": frenzy, madness.

80. "make . . . o'er": take him back over.

82. "settling": calming.

Kent. As 'tis said, the bastard son of Gloucester.

Gentleman. They say Edgar, his banished son, is with the Earl of Kent in Germany.

Kent. Report is changeable. 'Tis time to look about; the powers of the kingdom approach apace.

Gentleman. The arbitrement is like to be bloody. 94 Fare you well, sir.   [*Exit.*

Kent. My point and period will be throughly 96 wrought,

Or well or ill, as this day's battle's fought.   [*Exit.*

94. "arbitrement": decision.

96. "My point . . . wrought": my future will be finally decided.

KING LEAR

ACT V SCENE 1

The discussion between Edmund and Regan (5-16) further emphasizes the dissension in the evil camp, with the conflict here directly related to the sexual desires of the sisters. To Regan's question at 9 Edmund gives a deliberately mock-chivalric answer — "In honoured love" — with cynical emphasis on the "honoured." Regan brushes this evasion aside, to get at what is, for her, the important thing, the truth about their physical relation (10-11). Both Regan and Goneril ought to be acted on the stage with a heavy suggestion of Lear's "fitchew and soiled horse." Edmund remains coolly unentangled, thus giving an added irony to the sisters' efforts at seduction.

The landing of a foreign army on English shores gives Shakespeare some difficulty, as we saw earlier at IV,iii. Here, at 24-27, "it may account for some obscurity of language, though corruption of the text is not improbable. Albany is in the position of commanding where he has much sympathy with the other side, while the dramatist has to show before an audience that had not forgotten either the Spanish Armada or the traditional enmity with France, an invader landed to vindicate the right of an abused king. The 'others' of 26 may include Edgar" (Clarendon edition).

The conflict continues at 34-37. Regan insists that Goneril leave the stage with her, rather than with Edmund; the mutual hatred will be heavily underlined in the stage action. In the more general terms of the plot, there is a balance between the disunion here, and the new union between Lear and Cordelia. Those who have been divided are united, and those who have been united are divided.

ACT FIVE, scene one.

(THE BRITISH CAMP NEAR DOVER.)
Enter, with Drum and Colours, EDMUND, REGAN,
Gentleman *and Soldiers.*   s.d.

Edmund. Know of the Duke if his last purpose hold,   1
Or whether since he is advised by aught
To change the course. He's full of alteration
And self-reproving. Bring his constant pleasure.   4
                    [*Exit an* Officer.

Regan. Our sister's man is certainly miscarried.
Edmund. 'Tis to be doubted, madam.   6
Regan.   Now, sweet lord,
You know the goodness I intend upon you.
Tell me, but truly — but then speak the truth —
Do you not love my sister?
Edmund.   In honoured love.   9
Regan. But have you never found my brother's
    way
To the forfended place?   11
Edmund.   That thought abuses you.
Regan. I am doubtful that you have been conjunct   12
And bosomed with her, as far as we call hers.
Edmund. No, by mine honour, madam.
Regan. I never shall endure her. Dear my lord,
Be not familiar with her.
Edmund.   Fear me not.
She and the Duke her husband!

Enter, with Drum and Colours, ALBANY,
GONERIL, Soldiers.

Goneril. [*aside*] I had rather lose the battle than
    that sister
Should loosen him and me.   19
Albany. Our very loving sister, well bemet.
Sir, this I heard: the King is come to his daughter
With others whom the rigour of our state   22
Forced to cry out. Where I could not be honest,
I never yet was valiant. For this business,
It touches us as France invades our land,
Not bolds the King with others, whom I fear   26
Most just and heavy causes make oppose.
Edmund. Sir, you speak nobly.
Regan.   Why is this reasoned?   28
Goneril. Combine together 'gainst the enemy;
For these domestic and particular broils   30
Are not the question here.
Albany.   Let's then determine
With th' ancient of war on our proceeding.   32
Edmund. I shall attend you presently at your tent.   33
Regan. Sister, you'll go with us?
Goneril. No.
Regan. 'Tis most convenient. Pray go with us.   36
Goneril. O ho, I know the riddle. — I will go.
                [*Exeunt both the Armies.*

Stage Direction "Drum and Colours": the army is represented on the stage by a drummer, a standard bearer, and several soldiers.

1. "Know": find out.
"last purpose": most recent intention.

4. "constant pleasure": his continuing intention.

6. "doubted": suspected, feared.

9. "honoured": honorable.

11. "forfended": forbidden.

12-3. "I am . . . hers": i.e., I suspect you have been intimate with her in both mind and body.

19. "loosen": seperate.

22. "state": rule.

26-7. "Not bolds . . . oppose": i.e., not that he supports the king and those who have real grievances against us.

28. "reasoned": argued in this way.

30. "particular broils": private feuds.

32. "ancient of war": veteran officers.

33. "presently": at once.

36. "convenient": in order.
"with us": i.e., with Regan and her army rather than with Edmund and his.

KING LEAR

ACT V SCENE I

Edmund's soliloquy at the scene's end is a set-piece of Machiavellian reasoning. He introduces the sisters with the image of the "adder," and the association prevents us from imagining anything like love in this sexual triangle. Edmund outlines his difficulty as though it were a textbook problem to be solved: "Which of them shall I take?/Both? One? Or neither?" For him the matter is one of tactics, divorced from anything like loyalty, or affection, or even desire.

ACT V SCENE II

Shakespearean battle scenes are usually more extended than this one, but then Shakespearean heroes are also soldiers, like Antony and Macbeth. Here Lear is not involved in the battle, only in its outcome. Consequently this scene is compressed, and the final scene expanded.

We see Gloucester for the last time, with Edgar again fulfilling his guiding, illuminating role. The famous line "Ripeness is all" has

Enter EDGAR.

Edgar. [*to Albany*] If e'er your Grace had speech with man so poor,
Hear me one word.
  Albany.   [*to those departing*] I'll overtake you. [*to Edgar*] Speak.
  Edgar. Before you fight the battle, ope this letter.
If you have victory, let the trumpet sound   41
For him that brought it. Wretched thou I seem,
I can produce a champion that will prove
What is avouched there. If you miscarry,   44
Your business of the world hath so an end,   45
And machination ceases. Fortune love you.   46
  Albany. Stay till I have read the letter.
  Edgar.   I was forbid it.
When time shall serve, let but the herald cry,
And I'll appear again.
  Albany. Why, fare thee well. I will o'erlook thy   50
    paper.   [*Exit* EDGAR.

Enter EDMUND.

Edmund. The enemy's in view; draw up your powers.
Here is the guess of their true strength and forces
By diligent discovery; but your haste   53
Is now urged on you.
  Albany.   We will greet the time.   [*Exit.*   54
  Edmund. To both these sisters have I sworn my love;
Each jealous of the other, as the stung   56
Are of the adder. Which of them shall I take?
Both? One? Or neither? Neither can be enjoyed,
If both remain alive. To take the widow
Exasperates, makes mad her sister Goneril;
And hardly shall I carry out my side,   61
Her husband being alive. Now then, we'll use
His countenance for the battle, which being done,   63
Let her who would be rid of him devise
His speedy taking off. As for the mercy
Which he intends to Lear and to Cordelia —
The battle done, and they within our power,
Shall never see his pardon; for my state
Stands on me to defend, not to debate.   [*Exit.*

Scene two.

(A FIELD BETWEEN THE TWO CAMPS.)

Alarum within. Enter, with Drum and Colours, LEAR
held by the hand by CORDELIA; *and* Soldiers
of France, over the stage and exeunt.
Enter EDGAR *and* GLOUCESTER.

Edgar. Here, father, take the shadow of this tree
For your good host. Pray that the right may thrive.
If ever I return to you again,
I'll bring you comfort.
  Gloucester.   Grace go with you, sir.
                     [*Exit* EDGAR.

41. "sound": i.e., sound a summons.

44. "avouched": set forth as a challenge or accusation.

45. "business . . . world": worldly concerns, life.

46. "machination": plotting.

50. "o'erlook": look at.

53. "discovery": spying.

54. "greet": i.e., be ready.

56. "jealous": wary, suspicious.

61. "carry out my side": i.e., do what I plan to do.

63. "countenance": authority, prestige.

KING LEAR

ACT V SCENE II

been much discussed. Briefly, we may take it in connection with Gloucester's attempted suicide at IV,vi,41. Edgar is again urging Gloucester to "endure." Yet the word "ripeness" has the larger sense of fulfilment, as of a plant or flower achieving its destined form. Edgar seems to be saying that man's task is to fulfil, or complete his destiny, no matter how painful that may prove.

ACT V SCENE III

In this, the final scene, Shakespeare brings the double-plot to its conclusion, and events are necessarily crowded together. We may consider the scene here as falling into three parts: i) Lear and Cordelia imprisoned, ii) Edgar's defeat of Edmund and the deaths of Regan and Goneril, and iii) Lear's death.

i) Cordelia's forces have been defeated, and the downfall of Lear's party is complete. Yet, paradoxically, this turn of events produces something like an ecstacy of joy and release in the old king. Cordelia asks "Shall we not see these daughters and these sisters?", but to Lear, since his reawakening, the world of Goneril and Regan, of his suffering and madness, seems remote. His fourfold "No!" dismisses them, and after the oblique reference at 24 he never speaks of them again. Instead Lear welcomes the notion of prison, in one of Shakespeare's most rich and moving speeches. It is impossible to reduce lines 8 to 19 to prose thought—their effect lies in the reverberations of the verbal imagery—but several points ought to be made about the speech as representing Lear's new state of mind.

Lear, then, welcomes the notion of prison. The word suggests "cage" to him, but this is not a cage for prisoners, but for birds who will "sing alone." The "we two alone" comes, at this point in the play, with a sense of intense relief. One feels that Lear's ordeals have been such that imprisonment can be seen as a release, and not an incarceration. It is also noteworthy that, after the flow of animal imagery in the play which has suggested vicious and predatory behavior, we have here the image of two singing birds: nature is at last seen, for a brief moment, as harmonious instead of self-destructive. In lines 10-11 the ceremonial rituals of "blessing" and

Alarum and retreat within. Enter EDGAR.   s.d.

Edgar. Away, old man! Give me thy hand. Away!
King Lear hath lost, he and his daughter ta'en.
Give me thy hand. Come on.
Gloucester. No further, sir. A man may rot even
  here.
Edgar. What, in ill thoughts again? Men must
  endure
Their going hence, even as their coming hither;
Ripeness is all. Come on.   11
Gloucester.   And that's true too.   [*Exeunt.*

Scene three.

(THE BRITISH CAMP.)

Enter, in conquest, with Drum and Colours, EDMUND;
LEAR *and* CORDELIA *as prisoners;* Soldiers, Captain.

Edmund. Some officers take them away. Good
  guard
Until their greater pleasures first be known   2
That are to censure them.
Cordelia.   We are not the first
Who with best meaning have incurred the worst.
For thee, oppressed king, I am cast down;
Myself could else outfrown false Fortune's frown.
Shall we not see these daughters and these sisters?
Lear. No, no, no, no! Come, let's away to prison.
We two alone will sing like birds i' th' cage.
When thou dost ask me blessing, I'll kneel down
And ask of thee forgiveness. So we'll live,
And pray, and sing, and tell old tales, and laugh
At gilded butterflies, and hear poor rogues   13
Talk of court news; and we'll talk with them too —
Who loses and who wins; who's in, who's out —
And take upon 's the mystery of things   16
As if we were God's spies; and we'll wear out,   17
In a walled prison, packs and sects of great ones   18
That ebb and flow by th' moon.
Edmund.   Take them away.
Lear. Upon such sacrifices, my Cordelia,   20
The gods themselves throw incense. Have I caught
  thee?
He that parts us shall bring a brand from heaven   22
And fire us hence like foxes. Wipe thine eyes.
The goodyears shall devour them, flesh and fell,   24
Ere they shall make us weep! We'll see 'em starved
  first.
Come.   [*Exeunt* LEAR *and* CORDELIA, *guarded.*
Edmund.   Come hither, captain; hark.
Take thou this note. [*Gives a paper.*] Go follow
  them to prison.
One step I have advanced thee. If thou dost   28
As this instructs thee, thou dost make thy way
To noble fortunes. Know thou this, that men
Are as the time is. To be tender-minded   31
Does not become a sword. Thy great employment

11. "Ripeness": to grow to fruition and maturity (as fruit) and, by implication, to die.

2. "greater pleasures": the will of those in command.

13. "gilded butterflies": there are probably two senses of the phrase present here, i) the things that children laugh at in their innocence, and ii) the fashionable courtiers, who can no longer have any importance for Lear and Cordelia.

16. "And take . . . spies": i.e., see the truth, or penetrate the 'mystery' of existence from the exalted position of God.

17. "wear out": outlast.

18. "packs and sects": groups, factions.

20. "sacrifices": i.e., as we ourselves are about to make.

22-3. "He that . . . foxes": the reference here is to the practice of forcing foxes from their lair by fire; to do this to Lear and Cordelia will require fire 'from heaven.'

24. "goodyears": the word is usually taken to refer to the forces of evil, in accordance with the folk tradition of calling evil spirits by innocent names, e.g. 'little people' for 'goblins.'

28. "advanced": promoted.

31. "as the time is": i.e., without scruple in war.

KING LEAR

ACT V SCENE III

"forgiveness" are related to the "bond" (Cordelia, I,i,94) and the "holy cords" (Kent, II,ii,78) that hold people together in a spiritual communion transcending the amoral, competitive society that "preys upon itself." In lines 11-19 Lear creates a world of fantasy in which he and Cordelia can dwell and which is, for Lear, far more real than the world around him. Instead of the destructive struggle of the court it has prayer, and song, and fable; in it the schemers and intriguers of the court world become the "gilded butterflies" and "pacts and sects of great ones" who are not finally great at all, but "ebb and flow by the moon." Some critics have considered this great speech as exhibiting something that might be called 'escapism,' but we ought not to take this word in its contemporary sense of 'evasion;' we must recall what it is Lear is 'escaping.' The vision here comes after visions of a very different sort: "There's hell, there's darkness, there is the sulphurous pit! Burning, scalding, stench, consumption . . ." Lear has been translated from a world of hatred and madness to Cordelia's love and the harmony of the singing birds.

Immediately after this vision comes its antithesis. From Lear's fantasy of happiness we are returned (and it is a deliberately rapid and violent transition) to the "pacts and sects of great ones," the world of the court and of intrigue and betrayal. Edmund takes the Captain aside and orders him to kill Lear and Cordelia, knowing that Albany will save them. Lear may feel himself safe from the "poor rogues" dependent upon the "ebb and flow" of power. Here, in the Captain, we have one of them, the hired assassin ("Thou dost make thy way/To noble fortunes"), who chooses this task rather than to "draw a cart, or eat dried oats." It is a special irony that after all Lear has been through the final blow—the hanging of Cordelia—should be delivered by such a man. Shakespeare makes a special point of his total lack of humanity in the line "If it be man's work, I'll do it." We think of Macbeth, also contemplating murder, but with the addition of a moral conscience: "I dare do all that may become a man/Who dares do more is none."

ii) In the dialogue between Albany and Edmund (40-60) we see another of Edmund's assumed roles, that of the 'good soldier.' Edmund's desire is total rule, and anyone who stands between him and the throne must die. In order to effect the deaths of Lear and Cordelia he must stall for time and

Will not bear question. Either say thou'lt do't, 33
Or thrive by other means.
    Captain.   I'll do't, my lord.
    Edmund. About it; and write happy when th' hast 35
done.
Mark, I say instantly, and carry it so
As I have set it down.
    Captain. I cannot draw a cart, nor eat dried oats —
If it be man's work, I'll do't.   [*Exit.*
    Flourish. Enter ALBANY, GONERIL, REGAN, Soldiers.
    Albany. Sir, you have showed to-day your valiant
        strain,
And fortune led you well. You have the captives
Who were the opposites of this day's strife.
I do require them of you, so to use them
As we shall find their merits and our safety
May equally determine.
    Edmund.   Sir, I thought it fit
To send the old and miserable King
To some retention and appointed guard; 47
Whose age had charms in it, whose title more,
To pluck the common bosom on his side
And turn our impressed lances in our eyes 50
Which do command them. With him I sent the
        Queen,
My reason all the same; and they are ready
To-morrow, or at further space, t' appear
Where you shall hold your session. At this time
We sweat and bleed, the friend hath lost his friend,
And the best quarrels, in the heat, are cursed 56
By those that feel their sharpness.
The question of Cordelia and her father
Requires a fitter place.
    Albany.   Sir, by your patience,
I hold you but a subject of this war, 60
Not as a brother.
    Regan.   That's as we list to grace him. 61
Methinks our pleasure might have been demanded
Ere you had spoke so far. He led our powers,
Bore the commission of my place and person,
The which immediacy may well stand up 65
And call itself your brother.
    Goneril.   Not so hot!
In his own grace he doth exalt himself
More than in your addition. 68
    Regan.   In my rights
By me invested, he compeers the best. 69
    Albany. That were the most if he should husband 70
    you.
    Regan. Jesters do oft prove prophets.
    Goneril.   Holla, holla!
That eye that told you so looked but asquint. 72
    Regan. Lady, I am not well; else I should answer
From a full-flowing stomach. General, 74
Take thou my soldiers, prisoners, patrimony;
Dispose of them, of me; the walls is thine 76
Witness the world that I create thee here
My lord and master.
    Goneril.   Mean you to enjoy him?

33. "bear question": admit debate or examination.

35. "write": i.e., consider yourself.

47. "retention": imprisonment.

50. "impressed . . . eyes": i.e., cause our conscripted forces to turn against us.

56. "best quarrels": best causes.

60. "subject": one of inferior rank.

61. "list to grace": choose to honor.

65. "immediacy": i.e., his present position as a commander.

68. "your addition": your awarded honors.

69. "compeers": equals.

70. "most . . . you": i.e., that would only be if he were your husband.

72. "asquint": crookedly, falsely.

74. "stomach": capacity for anger.

76. "the walls is thine": i.e., you have conquered my body (walls of my castle).

80

KING LEAR

ACT V SCENE III

he does so, adopting the mask of the humane commander who sees to his troops: "We sweat and bleed, the friend hath lost his friend . . . The question of Cordelia and her father/Requires a fitter place." Albany's rebuke ("I hold you but a subject of this war") introduces the strife which occupies the middle portion of the scene and ends in the deaths of all of the evil party. Regan disputes Albany's suppression of Edmund and in the middle of her defence of him Goneril's poison strikes her. It is eminently fitting that Regan should express her love for Edmund just as the poison — a direct consequence of that love — begins to work; on the stage the actress can give weight to this piece of irony.

The summoning of Edgar takes a special place in the scene. It is done with elaborate ceremony, the charge being read, the trumpet sounded three times, and Edgar responding to it. This formality is deliberate. The world of Lear and his court at the beginning of the play had been a world of law and order, and the ceremony that

Albany. The let-alone lies not in your good will. 79
Edmund. Nor in thine, lord.
Albany. Half-blooded fellow, yes. 80
Regan. [*to Edmund*] Let the drum strike, and 81
  prove my title thine.
Albany. Stay yet; hear reason. Edmund, I arrest
  thee
On capital treason; and, in thy attaint, 83
This gilded serpent. [*Points to Goneril.*] For your
  claim, fair sister.
I bar it in the interest of my wife.
'Tis she is subcontracted to this lord,
And I, her husband, contradict your banes, 87
If you will marry, make your loves to me;
My lady is bespoke.
Goneril. An interlude! 89
Albany. Thou art armed, Gloucester. Let the trumpet sound.
If none appear to prove upon thy person
Thy heinous, manifest, and many treasons,
There is my pledge. [*Throws down a glove.*] I'll 93
  make it on thy heart,
Ere I taste bread, thou art in nothing less 94
Than I have here proclaimed thee.
Regan. Sick, O, sick!
Goneril. [*aside*] If not, I'll ne'er trust medicine. 96
Edmund. There's my exchange. [*Throws down a
  glove.*] What in the world he is
That names me traitor, villain-like he lies.
Call by the trumpet. He that dares approach,
On him, on you, who not? I will maintain
My truth and honour firmly.
Albany. A herald, ho!
Edmund. A herald, ho, a herald!
Albany. Trust to thy single virtue; for thy soldiers,
All levied in my name, have in my name
Took their discharge.
Regan. My sickness grows upon me.
Albany. She is not well. Convey her to my tent.
  [*Exit* REGAN, *attended.*

Enter a Herald.

Come hither, herald. Let the trumpet sound,
And read out this.
Captain. Sound, trumpet! [*A trumpet sounds.*
Herald. [*reads*] 'If any man of quality or degree 110
within the lists of the army will maintain upon Edmund, supposed Earl of Gloucester, that he is a manifold traitor, let him appear by the third sound of the trumpet. He is bold in his defence.'
Edmund. Sound! [*First trumpet.*
Herald. Again! [*Second trumpet.*
Again! [*Third trumpet.*
  [*Trumpet answers within.*
Enter EDGAR, *armed, at the third sound, a Trumpet* s.d.
  before him.
Albany. Ask him his purposes, why he appears
Upon this call o' th' trumpet.
Herald. What are you?
Your name, your quality, and why you answer
This present summons?

79. "let-alone": the permitting or forbidding.
80. "Half-blooded": by birth only half noble.
81. "Let . . . thine": i.e., fight and win my title for yourself.

83. "in thy attaint": as a confederate.

87. "contradict your banes": forbid the banns to your marriage. In standing between Edmund and Regan in the interests of his wife who is 'subcontracted' to Edmund, Albany speaks with savage irony.
89. "interlude": originally a dramatic farce.

93. "make": prove.

94. "nothing less": in nothing less guilty.

96. "medicine": ironic for poison.

110 "degree": rank.

Stage Direction "Trumpet before him": preceded by a trumpeter.

KING LEAR

ACT V SCENE III

derives from order. Lear, in his blindness, opened the way for that world's destruction. Under the usurpers the machinations of power and 'policy' were carried out by deceit and secrecy — "threading dark-eyed night," as Regan put it. Now Edgar, come to restore the right, does it with the ceremony and legality of the stable society. The world which has been ruled by Edmund's "Nature" will now be returned to order, exemplified in the careful procedure of Edgar's challenge to Edmund. Edgar comes as an anonymous champion; though he is "noble," his name has been "lost." In these lines he refers to his disguises, but also to the fact that right and truth have lost their "name," and have been obliged to go disguised in the world of Edmund, Goneril and Regan (see commentary at I,iv and II,iii on disguise). When good was most oppressed, Edgar assumed "the basest and most poorest shape;" now, with the evil-doers defeated he can appear, as Albany says, with a "gait" of "royal nobleness."

Edgar.   Know my name is lost,
By treason's tooth bare-gnawn and canker-bit; 122
Yet am I noble as the adversary
I come to cope.
   Albany.   Which is that adversary?
   Edgar. What's he that speaks for Edmund Earl of
     Gloucester?
   Edmund. Himself. What say'st thou to him?
   Edgar.   Draw thy sword.
That, if my speech offend a noble heart,
Thy arm may do thee justice. Here is mine.
Behold it is my privilege,
The privilege of mine honours,   130
My oath, and my profession. I protest —
Maugre thy strength, place, youth, and eminence, 132
Despite thy victor sword and fire-new fortune,   133
Thy valour and thy heart — thou art a traitor,
False to thy gods, thy brother, and thy father,
Conspirant 'gainst this high illustrious prince,
And from th' extremest upward of thy head
To the descent and dust below thy foot
A most toad-spotted traitor. Say thou 'no,'   139
This sword, this arm, and my best spirits are
     bent
To prove upon thy heart, whereto I speak,
Thou liest.
   Edmund.   In wisdom I should ask thy name, 142
But since thy outside looks so fair and warlike,
And that thy tongue some say of breeding breathes, 144
What safe and nicely I might well delay
By rule of knighthood I disdain and spurn.
Back do I toss these treasons to thy head,
With the hell-hated lie o'erwhelm thy heart,   148
Which — for they yet glance by and scarcely
     bruise —
This sword of mine shall give them instant way   150
Where they shall rest for ever. Trumpets, speak!
           [*Alarums. Fight. Edmund falls.*
   Albany. Save him, save him.   152
   Goneril.   This is practice, Gloucester.
By th' law of war thou wast not bound to answer
An unknown opposite. Thou art not vanquished,
But cozened and beguiled.   155
   Albany.   Shut your mouth, dame,
Or with this paper shall I stop it. — Hold, sir. —
[*To Goneril*] Thou worse than any name, read thine
     own evil.
No tearing, lady! I perceive you know it.
   Goneril. Say if I do — the laws are mine, not thine. 159
Who can arraign me for't?
   Albany.   Most monstrous! O,
Know'st thou this paper?
   Goneril.   Ask me not what I know. [*Exit.*
   Albany. Go after her. She's desperate; govern 162
     her.
               [*Exit an* Officer.
   Edmund. What you have charged me with, that
     have I done,
And more, much more. The time will bring it out.
'Tis past, and so am I. — But what art thou

122. "canker-bit": eaten as by a canker on a plant.

130-1. "honours, oath, profession": i.e., as a knight.

132. "Maugre": despite.

133. "fire-new": newly minted.

139. "toad-spotted": it was believed that the toad exuded venom through its spots.

142. "wisdom": prudence.

144. "say": suggestion.

148. "hell-hated": hated as hell is.

150. "instant way": i.e., direct passage into your heart.

152. "Save him": i.e., in order to obtain the confession at l.163. "practice": trickery.

155. "cozened": cheated.

159. "laws are mine": i.e., as ruler.

162. "govern": restrain.

KING LEAR

ACT V SCENE III

Edgar recounts his travels with his father, how he "led him, begged for him, saved him from despair," and finally revealed himself to him. We have seen how the stages in Gloucester's progress have paralleled those in Lear's. Gloucester's death takes a form—"'Twixt two extremes of passion, joy and grief"—which is an anticipation of Lear's. Kent is also included in this account, and his death is anticipated: "the strings of life/Began to crack." We shall see Kent again, but only when he comes to bid Lear "aye good night."

In contrast to Gloucester's death (whose heart "burst smilingly") are the deaths of Goneril and Regan, announced by someone "with a bloody knife," which "smokes." Now Edmund's suave and cynical response to Goneril —"Yours in the ranks of death" —is given dramatic reality. Goneril's murder of Regan, and her self-slaughter, inevitably bring to mind Albany's words to her at IV,ii,32. A "nature" that "contemns its origin," as she has done in her treatment of her father, will destroy itself. Albany had put the idea in the metaphor of a growing tree "that herself will sliver and disbranch/From her material sap, perforce must wither/And come to deadly use." The destruction of the self is simply an extension of the destruction of the "origin."

Edmund's role in the final scene has caused much comment. On the one hand it has been maintained that the line "Yet Edmund was beloved" is a pathetic admission of the need for love beneath the hard, Machiavellian exterior, and that Edmund now undergoes a change of heart that leads to the attempt to save Lear and Cordelia. Perhaps it is more plausible to say (while recognizing the pathos of Edmund's sudden recognition of "love") that his decision to save the prisoners he had ordered executed is a device on Shakespeare's part to sustain the dramatic tension of the final scene. The possibility of Cordelia's reprieve, followed by the fact of her death, is another example of the arbitrary and malignant fate that surrounds the central characters. This is best discussed in connection with the ending of the play.

That hast this fortune on me? If thou'rt noble,
I do forgive thee.   166

Edgar.   Let's exchange charity.   167
I am no less in blood than thou art, Edmund;
If more, the more th' hast wronged me.
My name is Edgar and thy father's son.
The gods are just, and of our pleasant vices
Make instruments to plague us.
The dark and vicious place where thee he got   173
Cost him his eyes.

Edmund.   Th' hast spoken right; 'tis true.
The wheel is come full circle; I am here.   175

Albany. Methought thy very gait did prophesy   176
A royal nobleness. I must embrace thee.
Let sorrow split my heart if ever I
Did hate thee, or thy father.

Edgar.   Worthy prince, I know't.

Albany. Where have you hid yourself?
How have you known the miseries of your father?

Edgar. By nursing them, my lord. List a brief tale;
And when 'tis told, O that my heart would burst!
The bloody proclamation to escape
That followed me so near (O, our lives' sweetness!   185
That we the pain of death would hourly die
Rather than die at once) taught me to shift
Into a madman's rags, t' assume a semblance
That very dogs disdained; and in this habit   189
Met I my father with his bleeding rings,   190
Their precious stones new lost; became his guide,
Led him, begged for him, saved him from despair;
Never — O fault! — revealed myself unto him
Until some half hour past, when I was armed,
Not sure, though hoping of this good success,
I asked his blessing, and from first to last
Told him our pilgrimage. But his flawed heart —   197
Alack, too weak the conflict to support —
'Twixt two extremes of passion, joy and grief,
Burst smilingly.

Edmund.   This speech of yours hath moved me,
And shall perchance do good; but speak you on —
You look as you had something more to say.

Albany. If there be more, more woeful, hold it in,
For I am almost ready to dissolve,   204
Hearing of this.

Edgar.   This would have seemed a period   205
To such as love not sorrow; but another,   206
To amplify too much, would make much more,
And top extremity.
Whilst I was big in clamour, came there in a man,   209
Who, having seen me in my worst estate,   210
Shunned my abhorred society; but then, finding
Who 'twas that so endured, with his strong arms
Has fastened on my neck, and bellowed out
As he'd burst heaven, threw him on my father,
Told the most piteous tale of Lear and him
That ever ear received; which in recounting
His grief grew puissant, and the strings of life   217
Began to crack. Twice then the trumpets sounded,
And there I left him tranced.   219

166. "fortune on": victory over.

167. "charity": forgiveness.

173. "got": begot.

175. "the wheel": the wheel of Fortune. "here": i) on the ground, mortally wounded and ii) at the lowest point on the wheel.

176. "prophesy": promise, indicate.

185-7. "our lives' . . . at once": i.e., life is so sweet that we prefer to suffer the fear of death hourly, rather than die.

189. "habit": dress.

190. "rings": eye-sockets.

197. "flawed": cracked.

204. "dissolve": into tears.

205. "period": limit, end.

206-8. "but another . . . extremity": i.e., yet another sorrow, described in full, would exceed the limit.

209. "big in clamour": fiercely lamenting.

210. "estate": state.

217. "puissant": powerful.

219. "tranced": in a trance, insensible.

83

KING LEAR

ACT V SCENE III

(iii) The delay in executing Lear and Cordelia has the effect of suggesting that they may be saved, and their deaths are consequently all the more crushing in their tragic impact. The great eighteenth century critic Samuel Johnson confessed he found the last scene too painful to re-read. For a long time an altered version of the play was popular, in which Lear survives to preside over the approaching nuptials of Cordelia and Edgar, in a happy sunset glow worthy of Hollywood. Of course such a conclusion falsifies Shakespeare's play completely; but Shakespeare's own ending has raised many questions. On the one hand it seems to suggest final and total pessimism as being the only possible response to human suffering. On the other hand many critics have said that both Gloucester and Lear only after they have achieved new insight, that their sufferings are ennobling, and reflect the heroism and dignity of mankind in general. It is a measure of the greatness and many-sidedness of the play that there can be this difference of critical opinion on its final meaning. We must bear in mind that no play by Shakespeare can be reduced to a simple, straightforward 'meaning,' since it is a re-creation of life, not a lecture or philosophical argument. It may be instructive to look at some of the critical attempts to come to terms with the final effect of KING LEAR.

The poet Swinburne quotes Gloucester's "As flies to wanton boys are we to the gods;/They kill us for their sport" and goes on to write that "The words just cited are not casual or episodical; they strike the keynote of the whole poem, lay the keystone of the whole arch of thought. [But see commentary at IV, i.] There is no contest of conflicting forces, no judgment so much as by casting of lots: far less is there any light of heavenly harmony or of heavenly wisdom, of Apollo or Athene from above. We have heard much and often from the theologians of the light of revelation: and some such thing indeed we find in Aeschylus; but the darkness of revelation is here."

A more recent critic, D. G. James, agrees that KING LEAR seems to exhibit, especially at its end, an unrelieved pessimism. He considers the examples of Edgar, who does not reveal himself to his father in the latter's hour of need [but see commentary at IV,vi], of Kent who "could and would have brought comfort and companionship" to Lear if he had chosen to disclose his real identity to the King, and of Edmund who, although "changed," delays too long to save Cordelia. ". . . all three examples I have given show Shake-

Albany.   But who was this?

Edgar. Kent, sir, the banished Kent; who in disguise

Followed his enemy king and did him service   221
Improper for a slave.

       Enter a Gentleman *with a bloody knife.*

Gentleman. Help, help! O, help!

Edgar.   What kind of help?

Albany.   Speak, man.

Edgar. What means this bloody knife?

Gentleman.   'Tis hot, it smokes.
It came even from the heart of—O, she's dead.

Albany. Who dead? Speak, man.

Gentleman. Your lady, sir, your lady; and her sister
By her is poisoned; she confesses it.

Edmund. I was contracted to them both. All three
Now marry in an instant.   230

Edgar.   Here comes Kent.

        Enter KENT.

Albany. Produce the bodies, be they alive or dead.
              [*Exit* Gentleman.

This judgment of the heavens, that makes us tremble,
Touches us not with pity. — O, is this he?
The time will not allow the compliment
Which very manners urges.   235

Kent.   I am come
To bid my king and master aye good night.   236
Is he not here?

Albany.   Great thing of us forgot!
Speak, Edmund, where's the King? and where's Cordelia?

      [GONERIL's *and* REGAN's *bodies brought out.*

Seest thou this object, Kent?   239

Kent. Alack, why thus?

Edmund.   Yet Edmund was beloved.
The one the other poisoned for my sake,
And after slew herself.

Albany. Even so. Cover their faces.

Edmund. I pant for life. Some good I mean to do, 244
Despite of mine own nature. Quickly send —
Be brief in it — to the castle, for my writ   246
Is on the life of Lear and on Cordelia.
Nay, send in time.

Albany.   Run, run, O, run!

Edgar. To who, my Lord? Who has the office? Send 249
Thy token of reprieve.

Edmund. Well thought on. Take my sword;
Give it the captain.

Edgar.   Haste thee for thy life.
              [*Exit* Officer.

Edmund. He hath commission from thy wife and me
To hang Cordelia in the prison and
To lay the blame upon her own despair
That she fordid herself.   256

Albany. The gods defend her! Bear him hence awhile.

       [EDMUND *is borne off.*

221. "enemy": hostile, i.e., in having banished Kent.

230. "marry": come together in death.

235. "very manners": proper formality.

236. "aye good night": good night forever.

239. "object": sight.

244. "pant for life": struggle to breathe a little longer.

246. "writ": order for execution.

249. "office": i.e., job of execution.

256. "fordid": destroyed.

KING LEAR

ACT V SCENE III

speare removing virtue away from efficacy and power over the course of events. Lear must go on suffering uncomforted by the knowledge of Kent's presence, and Gloucester by the knowledge of Edgar's; and when Edmund at last repents, he is checked from influencing the course of the plot. On the one side, therefore, is surpassing good, and on the other extreme evil; but the scales are hopelessly weighted on one side; against the wickedness of Cornwall, Goneril, and Regan, what beneficence human nature is shown to possess is not allowed to issue in action; it is kept as far as may be in silence and suffering ... For the truth is, or so it seems to me, that in this play Shakespeare is little enough concerned with strict dramatic plot or with character in the ordinary sense. He is, above all, concerned to exhibit certain moral ideas or states, imaginatively apprehended indeed, yet still ideas of evil and good. To evil he gives the initiative, the force, the driving power of the plot. Over against it he sets good; but he forbids it, so far as he may, to interfere with and control the action and consequences of evil; it is made silent and patient; it is suffering love; it has little influence upon the executive ordering of the world; it merely IS and suffers; it is not what it does but what it is, as it is shown in a Cordelia and an Edgar, that we contemplate. Evil drives on, dynamic and masterful, but to its own destruction; good is still, patient, and enduring, but is also destroyed; no limit, not even that of death, is put to what it must endure."

Over against this feeling that the play's final statement is one of complete disenchantment, we may set the view of A. C. Bradley, who best represents those who have seen in KING LEAR an exaltation of man in the midst of his suffering. For Bradley "there is nothing more noble and beautiful in literature than Shakespeare's exposition of the effect of suffering in reviving the greatness and eliciting the sweetness of Lear's nature. The occasional recurrence, during his madness, of autocratic impatience or of desire for revenge serves only to heighten this effect, and the moments when his insanity becomes merely infinitely piteous do not weaken it. The old King who in pleading with his daughters feels so intensely his own humiliation and their horrible ingratitude, and yet, at fourscore and upward, constrains himself to practise a self-control and patience so many years disused; who out of old affection for his Fool, and in repentance for his injustice to the Fool's beloved mistress, tolerates incessant and cutting reminders of his

Enter LEAR, *with* CORDELIA *in his arms, Gentleman, and others following.*

Lear. Howl, howl, howl! O, you are men of stones.
Had I your tongues and eyes. I'd use them so
That heaven's vault should crack. She's gone for
    ever.
I know when one is dead, and when one lives.
She's dead as earth. Lend me a looking glass.
If that her breath will mist or stain the stone,   263
Why then she lives.
Kent.   Is this the promised end?   264
Edgar. Or image of that horror?
Albany.   Fall and cease.   265
Lear. This feather stirs; she lives! If it be so,
It is a chance which does redeem all sorrows
That ever I have felt.
Kent.   O my good master.
Lear. Prithee away.
Edgar.   'Tis noble Kent, your friend.
Lear. A plague upon you murderers, traitors all;
I might have saved her; now she's gone for ever.
Cordelia, Cordelia, stay a little. Ha,
What is't thou say'st? Her voice was ever soft,
Gentle, and low — an excellent thing in woman.
I killed the slave that was a-hanging thee.
Gentleman. 'Tis true, my lords, he did.
Lear.   Did I not, fellow?
I have seen the day, with my good biting falchion   277
I would have made them skip. I am old now,
And these same crosses spoil me. Who are you?   279
Mine eyes are not o' th' best. I'll tell you straight.   280
Kent. If fortune brag of two she loved and hated,   281
One of them we behold.
Lear. This is a dull sight. Are you not Kent?   283
Kent.   The same:
Your servant Kent; where is your servant Caius?   284
Lear. He's a good fellow, I can tell you that.
He'll strike, and quickly too. He's dead and rotten.
Kent. No, my good lord; I am the very man.
Lear. I'll see that straight.   288
Kent. That from your first of difference and decay   289
Have followed your sad steps.
Lear.   You are welcome hither.
Kent. Nor no man else. All's cheerless, dark, and   291
    deadly.
Your eldest daughters have fordone themselves,
And desperately are dead.
Lear.   Ay, so I think.
Albany. He knows not what he says; and vain
    is it
That we present us to him.
Edgar.   Very bootless.   295

Enter a Messenger.

Messenger. Edmund is dead, my lord.
Albany.   That's but a trifle here.
Your lords and noble friends, know our intent.
What comfort to this great decay may come   298
Shall be applied. For us, we will resign,
During the life of this old Majesty,

263. "stone": glass.

264. "promised end": the predicted end of the world.

265. "Fall and cease": i.e., let Heaven strike once, and for all.

277. "falchion": short sword.

279. "crosses": adversities.

280. "straight": in a moment.

281. "two": i.e., two hypothetical individuals, one of whom Fortune hates, and one whom she loves; Lear is the first.

283. "dull sight": i.e., Lear's sight is unclear; at this point Lear is weeping, and he neither sees nor understands properly.

284. "Caius": Kent's name while in disguise.

288. "see that straight": understand that in a moment.

289. "difference and decay": change and decline.

291. "Nor no man else": i.e., no, nor is anyone welcome to such a scene.

295. "bootless": useless.

298. "this great decay": i.e., Lear's downfall, and the catastrophe in general.

KING LEAR

ACT V SCENE III

own folly and wrong; in whom the rage of the storm awakes a power and a poetic grandeur surpassing even that of Othello's anguish; who comes in his affliction to think of others first, and to seek, in tender solicitude for his poor boy, the shelter he scorns for his own bare head; who learns to feel and to pray for the miserable and houseless poor, to discern the falseness of flattery and the brutality of authority, and to pierce below the differences of rank and raiment to the common humanity beneath; whose sight is so purged by scalding tears that it sees at last how power and place and all things in the world are vanity except love; who tastes in his last hours the extremes both of love's rapture and of its agony, but could never, if he lived on or lived again, care a jot for aught beside —there is no figure, surely, in the world of poetry at once so grand, so pathetic, and so beautiful as his. Well, but Lear owes the whole of this to those sufferings which made us doubt whether life were not simply evil, and men like the flies which wanton boys torture for their sport. Should we not be at least as near the truth if we called this poem THE REDEMPTION OF KING LEAR, and declared that the business of 'the gods' with him was neither to torment him, nor to teach him a 'noble anger,' but to lead him to attain through apparently hopeless failure the very end and aim of life? One can believe that Shakespeare had been tempted at times to feel misanthropy and despair, but it is quite impossible that he can have been mastered by such feelings at the time when he produced this conception." Bradley goes on to describe a feeling of redemption, or justification, which occurs at the end of all Shakespeare's great tragedies. "I believe we shall find that it is a feeling not confined to KING LEAR, but present at the close of other tragedies; and that the reason why it has an exceptional tone or force at the close of KING LEAR lies in that very peculiarity of the close which also—at least for the moment—excites bewilderment, dismay, or protest. The feeling that I mean is the impression that the heroic being, though in one sense and outwardly he has failed, is yet in another sense superior to the world in which he appears; is, in some way which we do not seek to define, untouched by the doom that overtakes him; and is rather set free from life than deprived of it."

To him our absolute power; [*to Edgar and Kent*]
    you to your rights,
With boot and such addition as your honours   302
Have more than merited. All friends shall taste
The wages of their virtue, and all foes
The cup of their deservings. — O, see, see!

  Lear. And my poor fool is hanged: no, no, no life? 306
Why should a dog, a horse, a rat, have life,
And thou no breath at all? Thou'lt come no more,
Never, never, never, never, never.
Pray you undo this button. Thank you, sir.
Do you see this? Look on her! Look her lips,
Look there, look there —   [*He dies.*

  Edgar.   He faints. My lord, my lord —
  Kent. Break, heart, I prithee break!
  Edgar.   Look up, my lord.
  Kent. Vex not his ghost. O, let him pass! He hates
    him
That would upon the rack of this tough world   315
Stretch him out longer.
  Edgar.   He is gone indeed.
  Kent. The wonder is, he hath endured so long.
He but usurped his life.   318

  Albany. Bear them from hence. Our present
    business
Is general woe. [*to Kent and Edgar*] Friends of my
    soul, you twain
Rule in this realm, and the gored state sustain.   321

  Kent. I have a journey, sir, shortly to go.
My master calls me; I must not say no.

  Edgar. The weight of this sad time we must obey, 324
Speak what we feel, not what we ought to say.
The oldest have borne most; we that are young
Shall never see so much, nor live so long.
             [*Exeunt with a dead march.*

302. "With boot": i.e., with whatever else you deserve.

306. "fool": most commentators take this to be Cordelia rather than the Fool; 'fool' was a term of endearment for the Elizabethans, usually having the sense of 'simple and beloved.' For the possible confusion in Lear's mind between Cordelia and the Fool see commentary.

315. "rack": instrument of torture.

318. "usurped": i.e., at the end he barely, or unnaturally maintained life.

321. "gored": maimed, injured.

324. "obey": accept.

Bibliography

EDITIONS

A New Variorum Edition of Shakespeare, ed. Horace H. Furness. New York: J. B. Lippincott, 1871——. (Reprints by The American Scholar and Dover Publications.) Each play is dealt with in a separate volume of monumental scholarship.

The Yale Shakespeare, ed. Helge Kökeritz and Charles T. Prouty. New Haven: Yale University Press, 1955——. A multi-volume edition founded on modern scholarship.

COMMENTARY AND CRITICISM

Bentley, G. E. *Shakespeare and His Theatre.* Lincoln: University of Nebraska Press, 1964 (paperback). Illuminating discussion of the actual conditions under which, and for which, Shakespeare wrote.

Bradley, A. C. *Shakespearean Tragedy: Lectures on Hamlet, Othello, King Lear, Macbeth.* New York: Macmillan, 1904. (Paperback ed.; New York: Meridian Books, 1955.) A classic examination of the great tragedies.

Chambers, Edmund K. *William Shakespeare: A Study of Facts and Problems,* 2 vols. Oxford: Clarendon Press, 1930. Indispensable source for bibliographical and historical information.

Chute, Marchette. *Shakespeare of London.* New York: E. P. Dutton, 1949. A vivid account of Shakespeare's career in the dynamic Elizabethan metropolis.

Granville-Barker, Harley. *Prefaces to Shakespeare.* London: Sidgwick & Jackson, 1927-47. (2 vols.; Princeton: Princeton University Press, 1947.) Stimulating studies of ten plays by a scholarly man of the theater.

Harbage, Alfred. *Shakespeare's Audience.* New York: Columbia University Press, 1941. Revealing approach to Shakespeare as a practical man of the theater.

Knight, Wilson. *The Wheel of Fire.* London: Oxford University Press, 1930. Stresses the power of intuition to capture the total poetic experience of Shakespeare's work.

Spurgeon, Caroline. *Shakespeare's Imagery and What It Tells Us.* Cambridge: Cambridge University Press, 1935. A psychological study of the playwright's imagery as a means to understanding the man himself.

87